Doing Time

An Introduction to the Sociology of Imprisonment

Roger Matthews
Professor of Sociology
Middlesex University
Enfield
Middlesex

First published in Great Britain 1999 by
MACMILLAN PRESS LTD
Houndmills, Basingstoke, Hampshire RG21 6XS and London
Companies and representatives throughout the world

A catalogue record for this book is available from the British Library.

ISBN 0–333–75230–9 hardcover
ISBN 0–333–75231–7 paperback

 First published in the United States of America 1999 by
ST. MARTIN'S PRESS, INC.,
Scholarly and Reference Division,
175 Fifth Avenue, New York, N.Y. 10010

ISBN 0–312–22239–4

Library of Congress Cataloging-in-Publication Data
Matthews, Roger, 1948–
Doing time : an introduction to the sociology of imprisonment /
Roger Matthews.
p.   cm.
Includes bibliographical references and index.
ISBN 0–312–22239–4 (cloth)
1. Imprisonment.   2. Prisoners.   I. Title.
HV8705.M386   1999
365—dc21   99–18648
                                                              CIP

This book is printed on paper suitable for recycling and made from fully managed and sustained forest sources.

10   9   8   7   6   5   4   3   2
08   07   06   05   04   03   02   01   00

Printed and bound in Great Britain by
Antony Rowe Ltd, Chippenham, Wiltshire

Contents

List of Tables and Figures

Tables

Figures

Note: Figures 2.1, 2.2, 2.3 and 2.4 are taken from John Ditchfield (1990) *Control in Prison: A Review of the Literature* (London: HMSO).

Preface

This is both a modest and an ambitious book. It is modest in the sense that its fundamental aim is to provide a general introduction to some of the main issues and debates relating to the process of imprisonment. There is, of course, no shortage of books on the subject of imprisonment but the majority of these are specialist texts which tackle specific issues in some depth and often assume a considerable degree of familiarity with the relevant literature. On the other hand, there have emerged in recent years a number of useful introductory books and articles that aim to provide basic information and to describe the operation of the penal system. This book aims to serve as a bridge between these basic and specialist texts and to present some relevant empirical material within a broad sociological framework. In essence, the book is largely expositional and aims to provide an introduction to some of the classic themes and debates in penology for students, researchers, practitioners and policy-makers.

Thus, for the most part I have tried to summarise the relevant material in a reasonably objective and impersonal way by simply reviewing the literature and laying out different positions and options. It was, however, in the course of selecting material and trying to locate it within a conceptual framework that the book took on a more ambitious character. A number of theoretical and methodological issues arose which could not be avoided and had in some way to be tackled. As a result the book takes on a positional and even polemical character in certain places. Summarising the literature in an even-handed and impersonal way proved to be a strenuous exercise in self-discipline, since it involves engaging with material of different quality and orientation, some of which I personally have long-standing disagreements. However, it is one of the unfortunate truths of academic life that we are stimulated and motivated at least as much by writings with which we disagree or which we feel are inadequate as those we agree with and revere.

The critical and discerning reader will soon discover that behind the thin veneer of objectivity and indifference there is a whole series of ongoing themes, sub-texts, and assumptions which guide the text. At certain points the text becomes overtly critical and demonstrably takes issue with certain writers and lines of argument. I make no excuse for this, since many of the issues which are addressed are hotly contested. They involve real people, real problems and real suffering. It is the recognition of the importance of these issues, together with the awareness that these debates have practical implications, that draws many of us into this subject area in the first place.

Probably the most ambitious aspect of the book is the attempt to reconnect the study of imprisonment with an examination of crime, the state and the changing relations of production. It is an implicit argument of the book that examining imprisonment without reference to these related processes not only limits our understanding of the significance of imprisonment in modern society but is also detrimetal to our appreciation of the possibilities of penal reform.

ROGER MATTHEWS

Acknowledgements

Many people have contributed in different ways to the production of this book. Students and colleagues at Middlesex University have played a major part in helping to develop ideas, have provided useful information and have often made constructive suggestions on the appropriate focus of the book.

I am indebted to Pat Carlen, Francis Cullen, and Peter Francis for their comments on the first draft. Thanks also go to Catrina Woolner and Catherine Benson for their typing and help in gathering data as well as to Malcolm Read for his assistance in producing the graphs and figures.

ROGER MATTHEWS

1 The Emergence of the Modern Prison

INTRODUCTION

The seventeenth century marked a watershed in the history of punishment across northern Europe. During this period thousands of the poor, the destitute, the vagrant, the insane and the deviant found themselves segregated and confined in special institutions designed to remove them either temporarily or permanently from mainstream society. This period has been described as 'The Great Confinement' (Foucault, 1971). It marked an era in which the main forms of punishment began to shift from public executions, whippings and floggings, as well as the widespread use of forms of public shaming in the pillory or the stocks, to one in which institutions such as bridewells, workhouses, asylums and jails became the preferred response to the management of 'problem populations'.

These developments, until relatively recently, have been poorly documented. Until the 1970s the few available books on the history of imprisonment tended to present the prison as a naturally evolving institution which developed out of the local jails that were widely used in the medieval period. Although these historical accounts provide useful descriptions of the administrative and institutional changes that have occurred, they tend to ignore the specific historical characteristics of the modern prison, and to overlook the wider social context in which it emerged. These 'administrative' or 'traditional' histories lack an analysis of 'passion, power and conflict' (Howe, 1994), and are generally 'long on facts and short on interpretation' (Rothman, 1971). In particular, they fail to examine the differences between medieval jails and fortresses – which were primarily places where prisoners were held while awaiting trial, execution or deportation – and the modern prison – in which the deprivation of liberty itself for a specified period of time becomes the dominant mode of punishment.

The new histories of incarceration that emerged in the 1970s and 1980s were also generally critical of the earlier Whig histories, which attempted to explain the shift from one type of punishment to another as a product of humanism, involving a shift from barbarism to

1

civilisation. Such explanations, it was argued, failed to recognise that the new forms of incarceration were, by and large, directed at significantly different populations, and that it was not so much a case of less punishment or more benign punishment, but a different *form* of punishment. The crucial question for the new 'revisionist' histories was: 'Why Prison?' That is, why it was this particular form of confinement rather than any other type of punishment that came to dominate in the seventeenth and eighteenth centuries. There was also a related question of how this change in the form of punishment was connected to changing social and economic conditions.

THE SPECTACLE OF SUFFERING

In the introduction to *Discipline and Punish*, Michel Foucault (1977) provides a vivid and gruesome description of the processes by which Robert François Damiens was hanged, drawn and quartered in Paris in 1757 for attempting to take the life of King Louis XV. As a consequence of Damien's unusual strength and because the horses were not accustomed to drawing, his execution was a long and painful spectacle, involving the severing of his legs at the joints and 'the same was done to the arms, the shoulders, the arm pits and the four limbs; the flesh had to be cut almost to the bone, the horses pulling hard carried off the right arm first and the other afterwards' (Foucault, 1977: 5).

Spectacles of this kind, involving offenders being hanged, drawn and quartered, were relatively rare events in the eighteenth century. Foucault, however, uses this particular case to exemplify how, despite the gruesome nature of these public executions, they were an accepted form of punishment; and how this particular sanction, involving the infliction of severe physical pain and ultimately death, formed an essential part of the formal response to particular types of transgression in this period. The spectacle of suffering was intended to put the crowd in mind of the vastly greater terrors of hell. Culprits were expected to show repentance and to confess their crimes before the assembled crowd. Public confessions were often the route to a quick and relatively painless death.

In England, death by hanging was widely practised throughout the seventeenth and eighteenth centuries. There were eight hanging days in every year. In London, hangings were carried out at Tyburn (now Marble Arch) until 1783, after which time they were conducted at Newgate prison. These events were well attended by local populations and attracted, among others, the vagabond population of London, who were often referred to as the 'London Mob':

On the morning of a hanging day the bells of the churches of London were rung buffeted. The cries of hawkers selling ballads and 'Last Dying Speeches' filled the streets. The last preparations for death in the chapel at Newgate were open to those able to pay the gaoler his fee. The malefactor's chains were struck off in the press yard in front of friends and relations, the curious, the gaping and onlookers at the prison gate. The route of the hanging procession crossed the busiest axis of the town at Smithfield, passed through one of the most heavily populated districts in St. Giles's and St. Andrews, Holborn and followed the most-trafficked road, Tyburn Road, to the gallows. There the assembled people on foot, upon horseback, in coaches, crowding nearby houses, filling the adjoining roads, climbing ladders, sitting on the wall enclosing Hyde Park and standing on its contiguous cow pastures, gathered to witness the hanging. (Linebaugh, 1977: 67)

Public support for hangings, however, began to wane in the eighteenth century, and the 'hanging match', as it was called, increasingly became a focus of disturbances, brawls and riots. As the century progressed, these public executions rested less on spontaneous public support and more on the force of arms. On a number of occasions, individuals were plucked from the jaws of death by members of the crowd. Hangmen were jeered and attacked, and increasingly public hangings became uncertain, precarious events, particularly in cases in which those to be hanged were seen as the victims of injustice or were popular characters. One point of concern was the snatching of bodies by the surgeons, who paid high prices for fresh corpses on which to practise their medical skills (Linebaugh, 1977).

But the fading support for public executions went much deeper than the activities of the surgeons or the saving of particular souls from the scaffold. Among the social elite, public executions were viewed with increased scepticism, and hangings were seen as being more likely to undermine public order than to reinforce social norms. In short, towards the end of the eighteenth century public forms of punishment lost their legitimacy in England as well as other parts of Europe (Spierenburg, 1984).

Influential writers and social commentators, including Daniel Defoe (1728), Bernard de Mandeville (1725) and Henry Fielding (1751), advocated the removal of hangings from public view. Alongside those calling for the cessation of public hangings were those who advocated the use of imprisonment, particularly in the form of solitary confinement, as a more effective and more appropriate form of punishment.

A JUST MEASURE OF PAIN

Throughout Europe in the seventeenth and eighteenth century there were major changes taking place in the nature of social and economic relations. The old feudal order was breaking down, and the predominantly agricultural economy was gradually being replaced by new forms of production and government. During this period, there was an increasing concern with vagrants, rogues and beggars, and particularly with the increased levels of theft, which was seen by some commentators to be a consequence of the instigation of absolute private property and the growing number of goods that had become available (Marx and Engels, 1975).

Bound up with these changes was the introduction of new penal codes. Old laws appeared crude and ineffective and pressure for reform came from both inside and outside the legal profession. The traditional forms of legality were seen to lead to injustices and as being unable to provide adequate protection for the new forms of property (Thompson, 1975). These changes were accompanied by the emergence of the nation-state, which claimed monopoly of the use of coercive force. These developments had two important consequences. First, the right to punish shifted from the vengeance of the sovereign to the defence of society. Second, these new penal codes were characterised by the separation of illegality from the protection of rights and the protection of private property. The aim was to introduce a new penal code in which there would be a clearer codification of penalties and which would lay down new principals for administering punishment. In contrast to the variable and personalised system of penalties which was prevalent prior to the eighteenth century, the new penal system was charged with the task of administering the criminal law in a more rigorous, certain and efficient manner.

A key figure in this process was Cesare Beccaria, whose book *An Essay on Crimes and Punishment* (1764) was translated into a number of European languages and whose writings deeply influenced the formulation of new penal codes and strategies across Europe.

Central to Beccaria's approach is the assumption that crime is a rational activity in which individuals assess the benefits and consequences of their action and that the pains of punishment should be just enough to outweigh the potential advantages of engaging in crime. In this way he sought to maximise the deterrent effects of punishment, while minimising cost and effort. Punishment, he maintained, should be certain and firm, without being unnecessarily brutal or prolonged. In outlining this 'classicist' approach Beccaria emphasised that punishment should be applied equally and should be linked to the seriousness of the offence (Roshier, 1989). The major focus should be on the proportionality of punishment, which in turn requires a precise calibration of offences on a scale of seriousness. Among many reformers the objective was to develop a system which was able to dispense punishment equally to all those engaged in illegalities and thereby to provide a just measure of pain.

Crime, in the new order, came to be seen as a transgression not against the sovereign but against society. The offender, having broken the 'social contract', is not to be brutalised or ridiculed, but rather should be allowed to repay society in a way which would regenerate respect for property, liberty and the freedom of others. As formally free and equal citizens, the perpetrators of crimes require a form of punishment which treats them equally, and which deprives them of the one thing they have in common: individual liberty. From this perspective the emphasis is upon the act, and not the motivation or background of the offender. The aim was to promote formal equality, which meant that all offenders should be treated the same, irrespective of personal or social circumstances. Consequently, the rich and the poor, young and old, males and females should receive equal punishment, whatever their substantive differences.

The roots of the prison system lay in mercantilism, and its promotion and elaboration was the task of the Enlightenment. The dual aspiration of Enlightenment thinkers was that prison could perform the function of reforming the individual offender, while simultaneously improving society. It could make the idle poor industrious and thereby turn a social deficit into something productive. Through the application of scientific and rational principles, it should aim to produce useful obedient subjects. These modernising influences found expression in the prison (Morrison, 1996). Imprisonment provided a form of punishment which could be based on precise calculations of time. By removing people from the contaminating influences of the community, the prison promised to provide an environment in which

the prisoner could be reformed. At the same time, the deprivation of
liberty would serve as a continuous reminder to others of the consequences of non-conformity. Through the combination of these different forces, imprisonment became widely seen as an obvious and
almost irresistible option.

JAILS, WORKHOUSES AND HOUSES OF CORRECTION

The modern prison did not emerge at the end of the eighteenth
century fully formed and functioning. In fact, it was the combination
of a number of institutions which had been used for holding captives.
The modern prison grew on one side out of the local jails which had
been used as places of detention, and on the other from the houses of
correction which had emerged from the old bridewells. Thus the term
'prison' is often used generically to cover a number of different
institutions (McConville, 1995).

In order to distinguish between previous forms of confinement and
the modern prison which arose at the end of the eighteenth century,
and which appeared fully formed in England and Wales during the
1840s with the opening of Pentonville, it is necessary to examine
briefly the development of the various forms of confinement that were
in use between the beginning of the seventeenth century and the end
of the eighteenth century.

From as early as 1556, bridewells were established in England in
order to suppress idleness and vagrancy, in light of the apparent
inefficacy of the traditional remedies for begging and moral offences.
By the law of James I passed in 1609 it became obligatory for all
English counties to provide bridewells, or 'houses of correction' as
they became widely known. The other major institution for dealing
with the poor was the workhouse, which was established throughout
England in the seventeenth and eighteenth century. Workhouses,
which operated as a form of surrogate 'household', were often family-
run enterprises, providing basic relief and employment for the poor,
vagrants and the destitute. They were originally established as institutions designed to deter the poor from making applications for public
relief. In the eighteenth century the aim of workhouses became more
focused on setting the poor to work. Children tended to predominate
among the inmates of workhouses and meagre wages were paid to
those who stayed there. There was some overlap between the workhouses and the bridewells, based upon the often arbitrary distinction

between the 'deserving' and 'undeserving' poor. Workhouses and bridewells can be seen as providing a complementary approach to the same problem. With the threat of the workhouse or the bridewell hanging over their heads, the local poor might be driven to work, while vagabonds from elsewhere might be scared away (Innes, 1987).

Since the fourteenth century local jails had been used for a number of purposes apart from holding those awaiting trial or transportation. They had been widely used to hold debtors until they were able to pay their debts. In the debtors prisons friends and the curious were generally admitted, and in prisons like the Fleet and the Marshalsea in London members of the family could be accommodated within the institution (Byrne, 1992). These establishments were privately run, and jailers could make a profit from the sale of ale and other goods, or through the provision of services. The experience of confinement was largely conditioned by the ability of prisoners to pay for the available goods and services. Disorder and neglect were the dominant features of the eighteenth-century prison, in which different categories of prisoners mingled together:

> On entering the jail one was confronted with the noise and smell of the place. It was seldom easy to distinguish those who belonged to the prison from those who did not. Only the presence of irons differentiated the felons from the visitors or the debtors from their families. The jail appeared to be a particular type of lodging house with a mixed clientele. Some of its inhabitants lived in ease while others suffered in squalor. There was little evidence of authority. Some prisoners gambled while others stood drinking at the prison tap. (McGowan, 1995: 79)

Squalor and corruption, which were both widespread in these eighteenth-century houses of correction, became a cause of concern among prison visitors. A number of prison reformers, including John Howard (1777) and Elizabeth Fry (1827), campaigned to rid the prison of these abuses. Howard, Fry and other evangelically-minded reformers wanted prisons to operate as healthy and efficient institutions. They were opposed to the indiscriminate mixing of inhabitants and placed great emphasis upon the benefits of solitude and isolation in order to remove individuals from the corrupting influence of other prisoners. Confinement, in the eyes of the reformers, should be coupled with a religious purpose. Prisoners, it was felt, should not be able to drink, gamble or spend their time in idleness. Thus, in contrast to the disordered and profligate nature of the eighteenth-century penal institution, penal reformers wanted to introduce the 'well-ordered prison', which would stand as a counterpoint to the disorder from which crime and other social problems sprang. In his survey of prisons in the 1770s, John Howard (1777) estimated that the prison population was just over 4000, of which over half of those imprisoned were debtors (59.7 per cent), while felons awaiting trial, execution or transportation made up approximately a quarter (24.3 per cent), and petty offenders made up the rest of the population.

The Prison Act of 1865 formally amalgamated the jail and the house of correction and the resulting institution became known as a prison. Local prisons remained in operation but only served as places of punishment for those sentenced for terms of up to two years. Thus, by the mid-nineteenth century, imprisonment had become more centralised and more firmly established as a disciplinary institution. Although confinement in its various forms had become the dominant form of punishment by the eighteenth century, other forms of punishment also prevailed: notably transportation.

TRANSPORTATION AND THE HULKS

From the early eighteenth century onward, transportation overseas was used for felons, and some 30 000 people were transported to the American colonies between 1718 and 1775. The reported rising tide of crime and overcrowding in prisons overcame the reservations which certain critics had concerning the effects of transportation and made it a relatively attractive option. However, the abrupt interruption of transportation in 1775 caused a crisis in the prison system. This was resolved in 1776 by the use of old vessels which became known as hulks. These were used as places of temporary confinement. Prisoners were set to work during the day clearing the Thames and other seaports, returning to the vessels at night to eat and sleep. This form of punishment was generally viewed with disfavour and there was widespread criticism of the conditions on these vessels.

After the curtailment of transportation to the American colonies following the American Revolution, the focus turned to Australia as an alternative destination. In 1787 the first fleet of 11 ships set sail for Botany Bay. In some of the early voyages the death rates on convict ships were as high as 25 per cent (Hirst, 1995; Hughes, 1987). By the

1840s transportation was abolished to New South Wales, and all transported convicts were sent to Van Diemen's Land (Tasmania). Charges of inefficiency, corruption and the decreased demand for labour made the task of finding work for convict gangs more difficult. These problems were compounded by the discovery of gold in New South Wales and Victoria, which made punishment in exile to these places appear an absurdity, while the rapid rise in prices during the gold rush made the whole process of transportation and exile more expensive to the British government. In 1852 transportation to Van Diemen's Land was abandoned. In place of transportation the government implemented the Australian 'ticket of leave' scheme, which was a precursor to parole.

LABOUR, DISCIPLINE AND PUNISHMENT

In their pioneering work *Punishment and Social Structure* (1968), which was first published in 1939, Georg Rusche and Otto Kirchheimer argued that the nature of punishment is determined by the form of productive relations in any period. There are two basic methodological principles which inform the text: 1) 'every system of production tends to discover punishments which correspond to its productive relationships'; and 2) 'punishments as such do not exist, only concrete systems of punishment and specific criminal practices exist'.

For them, the use of transportation, for example, was primarily motivated not so much by the humanitarian impulse to give convicts a fresh start in a new country as by the need to overcome the shortage of free labour in the colonies in a period in which there was a surplus of labour in England. Although decisions to adopt or abandon a particular mode of punishment may be couched in terms of humanism, these decisions, Rusche and Kirchheimer argue, are underpinned by material interests (Weiss, 1987). Therefore, they suggest that one should be careful in simply attributing penal change to the activities of reformers, as historians like David Rothman (1971) tend to do. Instead, there is a need to look behind the rhetoric of reformers and ask why it should be that in any particular period certain arguments should find an attentive audience. At the same time, the manner and speed with which prison reform takes place, Rusche and Kirchheimer argue, is not only a function of the weight of the arguments for change but is also dependent upon wider social conflicts and struggles between classes (Ignatieff, 1981). Rusche and Kirchheimer maintain that prisons are part of a disciplinary network for regulating the poor and for imposing discipline. For these reasons, they argue that conditions in prisons are governed by the principle of 'less eligibility', such that conditions in prisons must be no better than those experienced by the poorest sections of the working classes, otherwise members of the lowest social strata will not be deterred from committing crimes (Melossi and Pavarini, 1981).

But although Rusche and Kirchheimer (1968) recognise the role of the prisons in encouraging time and work discipline in industrial capitalism, their explanation of the emergence of the modern prison is tied more specifically to the system of productive relations. Their basic axiom that: 'Every system of production tends to discover punishments which *correspond* to its productive relationships' (emphasis added) clearly expresses their view that it was the changing form of production and associated changes in the organisation of labour which were the main determinants of the prison. A close reading of Rusche and Kirchheimer, however, makes it clear that the *correspondence* between the emergence of industrial capitalism and the prison is far more complex than the disciplining of 'free labour'. They were abundantly aware, as was Marx, that all systems of production are systems of 'social production', and that there is a complex dynamic relation between agency and structure. Along with Marx they would no doubt recognise that; 'people make the world but not under conditions of their own choosing'. It is also evident to Rusche and Kirchheimer that the formal equality which operates in the sphere of consumption and distribution in capitalist societies is an essential element in the development of a form of punishment which incorporates the principal of equivalence.

Also, like Pashukanis, Rusche and Kirchheimer recognised that the commodification of time was an essential component in the development of the modern prison:

> Deprivation of freedom for a period stipulated in the court sentence is the specific form in which modern, that is to say, bourgeois capitalist, criminal law embodies the principal of equivalent recompense. This form is unconsciously yet deeply linked with the conception of man in the abstract and abstract human labour measurable in time. (Pashukanis, 1978: 180–1)

Thus for Rusche and Kirchheimer the emergence of the modern prison was seen to be 'overdetermined', in that it was the product of a number of overlapping and mutually reinforcing determinations. But they were also aware that political movements too could influence the use of imprisonment. The development of Fascism throughout Europe in the 1930s, which affected both these authors personally, had a number of direct effects on the nature of law, the administration of sanctions and the direction of penal reform. In Germany new laws were passed or were interpreted within a racist framework, while judicial independence diminished and 'special courts' were introduced. There was a return to capital punishment and prison conditions deteriorated rapidly.

Although *Punishment and Social Structure* has been highly influential in changing the way in which the history of imprisonment has been conceived, it has been criticised by some commentators for being too economistic and reductionist, despite the fact that it offers a number of different levels of social and political analysis. Other commentators have criticised it for not being economistic enough (Garland, 1990; Howe, 1994; Melossi, 1978; Weiss, 1987; Zimring and Hawkins, 1991). Strangely, a number of critics who accuse Rusche and Kirchheimer of reductionism themselves engage in reductionist analysis, usually in the form of sociological or political reductionism, or alternatively offer an unmitigated eclecticism with no identifiable determinants or causal process. In fact, the majority of critics demonstrate a consistent failure to address what has been called 'the problem of determinations', which raises the question of the relationship between the economic, political, social and cultural 'levels' and the (relative) autonomy of each (Barrett, 1991). Needless to say, as members of the renowned Frankfurt School, Rusche and Kirchheimer would have been only too aware of the problems of reductionism and economism, since these issues were central to the work of the School in the 1930s (Jay, 1973).

The two key terms in Rusche and Kirchheimer's analysis which have been the basis of much discussion and confusion are 'determines' and 'corresponds'. The term 'determines' may be used in a hard or a soft form (Williams, 1980). In the soft form it means 'setting limits on' or 'exerting pressure'. It is in this way that it is used by Rusche and Kirchheimer. The term 'corresponds' expresses the ways in which these pressures are exerted in different social formations, recognising that there may be variations in the 'fit' between the dominant forms of social production and the forms of state, law and systems of punishment. At the same time, as Rusche and Kirchheimer themselves note, to say that a form of punishment 'corresponds' to the system of productive relations is itself a tautology. However, they use the term 'correspond' to signify that there is a definite relationship which is of a causal rather than contingent nature.

One writer who clearly recognises the significance of Rusche and Kirchheimer's work is Michel Foucault. Although Foucault (1977) addresses a different problematic from that covered by Rusche and Kirchheimer, he recognises the need to analyse 'concrete systems of punishment', and acknowledges that the writings of Rusche and Kirchheimer 'provide a number of essential reference points' (ibid.: 24). In fact, it is arguably the case that Foucault's account of *The Birth of the Prison* is underpinned by the same type of materialist analysis as is presented by Rusche and Kirchheimer (see Smart, 1983). Like Rusche and Kirchheimer, Foucault emphasises that the role of the emerging forms of punishment in the eighteenth and nineteenth centuries was not necessarily more humanitarian than previous forms of public torture and humiliation. Indeed, the aim was not to punish less, but to punish better. Punishment was required to be more universal and to penetrate more deeply into the social body if it was to create a docile and responsive workforce.

The new forms of disciplinary punishment which were developed in the prison were not simply repressive, but were also designed to be positive and productive. In Foucault's account, prisons produced new techniques for controlling individuals through systems of surveillance, classification and examination. The forms of discipline implemented in the prison were the embodiment of new modalities of power. Whereas sovereign power, which had been dominant in the Middle Ages, promoted public forms of punishment aimed at the body, the emerging forms of juridical power in the eighteenth century were aimed primarily at the soul. These new power relations found expression in a number of different institutions, often involving similar techniques for managing individuals and groups. Is it any wonder, Foucault asks, that prisons resemble factories, schools, barracks, hospitals, which all in turn resemble prisons?

Foucault is particularly interested in the ways in which power is crystallised in institutions such as the prison, and in how such institutions, once established, generate their own knowledges, discourses, practices and effects. He outlines the ways in which the prison created a new institutional space in which offenders could be studied and analysed. It was within this space that the 'delinquent' was born and accredited with a biography and a personality which was held to exist outside and beyond the commission of a specific act. Thus it was not, Foucault maintains, the scientific study of crime that created the possibility of the prison. On the contrary, it was the invention of the prison that created the possibility for the scientific study of crime. The enduring legacy of the prison, whatever its failures and limitations as a site of reform or deterrence, is that it gave birth to a new form of scientific knowledge – criminology.

It is through the analysis of power that Foucault aims to explode the self-evident character of the prison, and explain its apparent naturalness and how we have come almost unthinkingly to associate prison and punishment in contemporary society. The task of enquiry, Foucault maintains, is to explain the 'obvious', the taken-for-granted aspects, and to reveal the underlying processes and assumptions upon which the modern prison rests. His work has been highly influential in relation not only to how we think about imprisonment but also to more general contemporary debates on punishment, social control and power (Dreyfus and Rabinow, 1982; Garland, 1990; McNay, 1992).

Foucault's work, however, like that of many of his predecessors, has been criticised for not examining the application of discipline and punishment to women. The masculinist bias of many of the 'histories' of imprisonment, it has been argued, fails to consider the specific role of women's prisons. A consideration of 'herstory', it has been suggested, could potentially throw some new light on, or even force a rethinking of, the role and development of imprisonment.

WOMEN'S IMPRISONMENT

An examination of the development of the confinement and imprisonment of women raises a number of questions for historians. Even a cursory review of the subject reveals that there are major differences in the pace and processes of development of women's prisons. There are also noticeable differences in the organisation and functioning of women's prisons, and the types of offences for which women were incarcerated. More generally, the history of women's confinement raises issues about the relationship between the labour market and imprisonment, and also the value of 'social contract' theories, since women did not become fully enfranchised citizens until the twentieth century.

Women prisoners have been counted and discounted. However, women have a long history of confinement, as Sherrill Cohen points out:

> From the sixteenth century onwards more and more women were subject to some form of institutionalisation in poorhouses, bridewells and asylums. In earlier periods women had been confined to convents and Magdalene homes and consequently the ideology of the institutional segregation of women either as a form of punishment or as a sanctuary was well established by the seventeenth century. (Cohen, 1992, 17)

Women made up a considerable percentage of the population of bridewells. In fact, in London during the seventeenth and eighteenth centuries the number of women confined in bridewells was often greater than the number of men. Although bridewells were used mostly for vagabonds and thieves, they were also used for offences against public morals and disturbing the peace, with the result that prostitution and other forms of sexual immorality were favoured targets. By the beginning of the eighteenth century, women could be confined to bridewells for a range of moral offences, including 'bearing bastard children', 'lewdness', or 'failure to maintain their families':

> Surviving 'calenders' of commitments from the Westminster bridewell show men and women being committed at a rate of forty to fifty a month, women being committed as frequently as men. Most commitments seem to have arisen from street offences. Common grounds for commitment include 'idle and disorderly' or 'lewd, idle and disorderly' behaviour, 'nightwalking' and 'pilfering'. Some of the chattier entries reveal to us people taken by the watch in the middle of the night from a suspected bawdy house; taken endeavouring to break open a goldsmiths' show glass; giving great abuse to Their Majesties' people; threatening to burn houses; keeping a disorderly house and disturbing the neighbours; pilfering linen from a poor washerwoman's room and pilfering a bunch of sausages. (Innes, 1987: 84–5)

In many bridewells work was irregular, menial and yielded little profit. The work available often involved such tasks as the crushing of hemp or flax, which were the preliminary stages in the manufacture of textiles.

The available bridewell records indicate that women were more productive in this work and this may be part of the reason why the 'Master' of the bridewells might have been more willing to refer women to these institutions. A further reason why women might have been welcomed into certain bridewells is that there were reports of these institutions becoming highly profitable brothels (Zedner, 1995). Within these mixed institutions there were numerous examples of women being encouraged or coerced to provide sexual services. It was the visibility of this 'immorality' and 'lewdness' which evangelical reformers found so distasteful and which motivated them to campaign for separate prisons for women. Separate prisons, it was argued, could reduce exploitation, improve morals and be tailored to gender-specific needs.

In Britain, the Jail Act of 1823 required that women be held separately from men, that they be supervised only by women, and that men were only to be allowed to visit the female part of the prison if they were accompanied by a female officer. In the nineteenth century a limited number of prisons were established specifically for women, but in most cases women were in segregated wards or wings of men's prisons.

There were, however, separate institutions for women in existence in the seventeenth and eighteenth century, in the form of Magdelen houses for 'repentant' prostitutes. In these institutions, which sprang up across Europe in this period, the emphasis was upon penitence and religious instruction. Work was designed to be educational, reformative and 'cleansing'. And consequently the principal tasks tended to include textile manufacture, handicrafts and domestic service, as well as cleaning and laundering. In this way these 'fallen women' could be reformed and returned to their 'proper' female role.

For many reformers, separate prison establishments was seen as a more effective way of controlling women. It was widely felt in the nineteenth century that women required different treatment from men, while it was the case that a system of silence and separation was thought to be particularly suitable for women, since they were held to be more impressionable and needed more protection from contaminating influences than men. The role of labour however was felt to be less important for women. They were not subjected to the treadmill and were excused from some of the more onerous tasks. However, they had to endure regimes of greater tedium, and were subjected to more intrusive forms of surveillance (Dobash *et al.*, 1986).

As women were placed in adapted buildings or the wings of the men's prisons, the influence of architecture was less evident and a greater emphasis was placed upon personal influences. That is, while the emphasis in men's prisons was on impersonal disciplinary techniques of reform, women's prisons were regulated primarily through interpersonal relations and the power of religion, as well as through forms of 'medicalisation'.

Towards the end of the nineteenth century women were often given short sentences for trivial offences such as theft, drunkenness and disorderly conduct. Prostitutes still filled the prisons (but a significant percentage were confined in hospitals for the treatment of syphilis and other sexually transmitted diseases) and there was a growing number of habitual offenders who were regularly recycled through the prison system. By 1872 there were three women's prisons – Millbank, Fulham and Woking – which between them had just under 1400 places. But in the last two decades of the century the number of women imprisoned began to decrease at a faster rate than the male population (Zedner, 1991). This declining rate of imprisonment continued throughout the twentieth century. The reasons for this seem to be a combination of a number of factors, including the increasingly widespread view which surfaced in the last decades of the nineteenth century that prisons are not suitable places for the vast majority of female offenders. There was also a change in the perceived nature of female criminality in this period, as well as the development of a number of alternatives to custody which were designed to divert certain types of women away from custodial institutions.

THE WELL-ORDERED PRISON

The limits of transportation and the growing concerns about crime and disorder at the end of the eighteenth century encouraged the development of new and more effective forms of punishment. The mounting critiques of the existing penal institutions, with all their abuses and inadequacies, persuaded the authorities that a well-ordered, disciplined, clean and properly managed form of confinement was required. These new and refurbished prisons were developed in the first half of the nineteenth century. They introduced new codes of discipline, more bureaucratic forms of organisation and management and changes in prison design.

Prisoners were to be differentiated and new systems of classification were introduced. The aim was to develop a system based on solitary confinement, silence, religious instruction and labour discipline. The 'moral architecture' of the prison was to express and incorporate these aims, while improving order, health and conditions. The ultimate aim was to turn incorrigible prisoners into model citizens. Prisons would be a mechanism, as Bentham put it, 'for grinding rogues honest'. Through specially designed institutions it would be possible, reformers believed, to produce a rationally organised space which would foster the development of reason and the self-regulation of inmates. Importantly, these redesigned prisons had to deal with what was perceived as the contagious nature of crime. The threat of contagion was dealt with by separating the young from the old, men from women and the vulnerable from the predatory. In contrast to the eighteenth-century penal institutions in which prisoners were allowed to congregate freely, the new nineteenth-century prisons were built with separate cells of a uniform size. Rules of silence were imposed upon prisoners, and in some prison inmates were made to wear masks, to ensure that they would not be recognised either in the prison or when they left.

The design and layout of the new nineteenth-century prisons was a hotly contested issue. The central debate among reformers concerned the degree and type of segregation that should be imposed and there was considerable discussion in the 1820s in America and Europe about the merits of segregating prisoners. While many of those engaged in this debate agreed upon the fundamental principles of individual containment and separation, the central issue was whether or not prisoners should remain totally isolated or be allowed to work together during the day. This debate crystallised around the competing systems in the Auburn and Pennsylvania prisons in America.

The Auburn state prison in New York, which was established in 1823, adopted a regime in which prisoners were to sleep alone in their cells at night and labour together in the workshop during the day. In the Pennsylvania prison, which was built in 1829, the prisoners were kept totally separate, in order to reduce the possibility of 'contamination'. Left in total solitude and divorced from evil influences, the prisoners would have the opportunity to reflect on the error of their ways and to examine their consciences. Inmates remained in solitary cells for eating, sleeping and working. 'They saw and spoke only to carefully selected visitors and read only morally uplifting literature – the Bible' (Rothman, 1971: 85). It was felt that this strategy, if rigorously pursued, would allow the prisoner to be cured of vice and idleness through a combination of hard labour and contemplation.

After a prolonged debate and much soul-searching the Auburn system won out. Advocates of the Auburn system argued that total isolation was unnatural and that it bred insanity. The case in favour of the Auburn system was enhanced by the fact that it cost less to run and potentially brought greater returns from convict labour. Consequently, the Auburn system came to be widely adopted both in America and in most of Europe.

Underlying these debates was the shared premise that incarceration was the proper response to criminal behaviour and that there should operate a silent system with a minimal diet and strict discipline. Prisons became more militaristic in style and although they contained a considerable percentage of vagrants, poachers, petty thieves and public drunkards, a strict regime of prison discipline was vigorously enforced. Alongside the introduction of military practices and military personnel, there was a growing presence of other professionals in the form of medical doctors and psychiatrists, who were introduced to diagnose, treat and cure offenders. Crime, like madness, was seen by many medical professionals as arising from a lack of self-control, and as a deviation from the path of reason. According to one influential medical practitioner, writing in 1806, 'criminal habits and aberrations of reason are always accompanied by certain organic peculiarities manifested in the external form of the body, or in the features of the physiognomy' (Cabanis, quoted in Ignatieff, 1978: 68). It was a short step from this assertion to the measuring of skull shapes and sizes, which is often associated with the founding father of criminology, Cesare Lombroso, and the development of the science of phrenology.

This vision of the criminal as a pathological subject stood in stark contrast to the classicist conception of the rational citizen choosing between good and evil, maximising pleasure and avoiding pain. The apparent contradiction between free will and determinism, and between the utilitarianism and reformative theory, was overcome in the neo-classicist doctrines through a reformulation of the relation between guilt and punishment. Thus:

> Reformative theory presented punishment to offenders as being in their own interests while utilitarian theory cast it as an impartial act of social necessity. In rejecting retributive theory, the reformers sought to take the anger out of punishment. As it was legitimised by the prisoner, punishment was no longer to be in Bentham's words

'an act of wrath and vengeance' but an act of calculation, disciplined by consideration of the social good and the offenders needs. (Ignatieff, 1978: 75)

In many respects these new ideas of prison design and the stress on silence and solitude were realised in the construction of Pentonville prison in London in 1842. Pentonville itself quickly became a model for prison architecture and discipline, not only in England but also across Europe. The prison held 520 prisoners in separate cells. Four wings radiated out from a central point from which each cell door could be observed. Both the prisoners and the guards were forbidden to talk and the thick walls and individual cells ensured that other forms of communication between prisoners would be kept to a minimum.

Between the 1830s and 1870s the average daily prison population in England climbed steadily, partly as a result of the decline in the use of transportation. Also between 1848 and 1863 prison was transformed from an institution which was used mainly for summary offences and petty felonies into the predominant form of punishment for all major crimes, except murder.

According to the prison rules, 'Every prisoner shall be required to engage in useful work for not more than ten hours a day, of which so far as it is practicable, at least eight hours shall be spent in associated or other work outside the cells'. The principal forms of work available were sewing mailbags, rag-stripping, mat-making, tailoring, cleaning and basket-making (Morris and Morris, 1963). The commitment to work discipline was evident in those prisons where productive and useful labour was not available. In these prisons the treadmill was widely used. Its attraction to the prison authorities was that it provided a form of exercise that could be used by the uneducated, while the pace and resistance of the wheel could be controlled.

One of the major problems in providing useful work for prisoners was that many prisoners were unskilled and the period of time which the average prisoner spent in prison was relatively short by current standards. Nearly two-thirds of those sentenced by magistrates in the 1860s were given terms of a month or less, while in the higher courts over half were sentenced for six months or less. Approximately 20 per cent of those convicted were sentenced to the harshest penalty, penal servitude (McGowan, 1995). There was a growing disparity between the aspirations and ideals of reformers and the reality of prison experience. Increasingly, towards the end of the nineteenth century

critics were claiming that prisons were failing in relation to the twin
objectives of reforming and punishing offenders.

THE DEMISE OF THE PRISON?

The possibility of prisons achieving the objective of turning unruly
offenders into law-abiding citizens was always somewhat utopian.
Even if the nineteenth-century prisons had not suffered from overcrowding, corruption and cruelty, the degree of individual transformation which could be expected in short periods of confinement was
always likely to be limited. The objective of designing out malicious
influences within the prison was undermined by the fact that the prisoners found ways to communicate and there were obvious limitations
to the enforcement of rules of silence in shared cells. The cells themselves were small, and confinement in these restricted spaces for long
periods of time was increasingly seen as being detrimental to the physical and psychological well-being of inmates. Reports of brutality were
widespread, although there was evidence of greater professionalism
and accountability among prison staff. Many prisons were dirty and
the food was poor. There were breakdowns of security and control,
with repeated escapes and riots. In the word of the Gladstone
Committee in 1895, the evidence of the operation of the prison system
was that it had demonstrably failed, and that 'a sweeping indictment
had been laid against the whole of the prison administration'.
  Prison, it appeared, had little apparent effect on criminal behaviour: recidivism was rampant and there was a reported increase in
violent crime. The emerging Eugenics movement raised concerns
about whether imprisonment was the proper response for the 'feeble-
minded' and the 'degenerate'. On another level, various radical
reformers pointed to the fact that very few prisoners were drawn from
the middle and upper classes, and that prison appeared as a form of
punishment which was reserved almost exclusively for the poor and
the destitute. The claim of the doctors and the psychiatrists that they
could 'cure' offenders were also seen as being largely exaggerated.
  Given these limitations, the question which historians have asked
is: why did the prison persist into the twentieth century? Was it the
case, as David Rothman (1980) has suggested, that good intentions
went wrong and the ideals of 'conscience' were undermined by 'convenience'. Or was it that prisons were performing other less visible functions? As Michael Ignatieff (1978) has argued, the prison had to offer

something to justify the enormous expense. The persistent support for the penitentiary, he suggests, 'is inexplicable so long as we assume that its appeal rested on its functional capacity to control crime'. Rather, support for the prison rested on its role as part of 'a larger strategy of political, social and legal reform designed to re-establish order on a new foundation'.

Michel Foucault (1977), in contrast, argues that it was the general deterrent effect of recycling the same offenders through the penal system which became the main rationale of incarceration. Thus for him recidivism was not so much a failure as a method of producing what he calls an 'enclosed illegality' of petty criminals who can be held up to the 'respectable' poor as an example of the dangers of non-conformity, and also a vehicle for gathering information and engaging in the surveillance of certain populations. Foucault asks:

Can we not see here a consequence rather than a contradiction? If so, one would be forced to suppose that the prison, and no doubt punishment in general, is not intended to eliminate offences, but rather to distinguish them, to distribute them, to use them; that it is not so much that they render docile those who are liable to transgress the law, but that they tend to assimilate the transgression of the laws in a general tactics of subjection. Penality would therefore appear to be a way of handling illegalities, of laying down the limits of tolerance, of giving free rein to some, of putting pressure on others, of excluding a particular section, of making another useful, of neutralising certain individuals and profiting from others. In short, penality does not simply 'check' illegalities; it 'differentiates' them, it provides them with a general 'economy'. And, if one can speak of justice, it is not only because the law itself or the way of applying it serves the interests of a class, it is also because the differential administration of illegalities through the mediation of penality forms part of those mechanisms of domination. Legal punishments are to be resituated in an overall strategy of illegalities. The 'failure' of the prison is to be understood on this basis. (Foucault 1977: 272)

Although the prison persists, it is clear, as Rusche and Kirchheimer (1968) point out, that throughout Europe and North America the use of imprisonment decreased from the end of the nineteenth century until the beginning of the Second World War. The decline of the prison population, they suggest, is bound up with the changing nature of productive relations involving new forms of manufacture: namely

Fordism and Taylorism. In this form of production-line manufacture the discipline of the worker is contained *within* the production process itself (Lea, 1979; Melossi, 1979). Moreover, the shift in this period towards 'welfare capitalism' produced other regulatory mechanisms, with the consequence that the prison shifted from being a punishment of first resort to a back-up sanction serving as a punishment of last resort.

THE WELFARE SANCTION

Towards the end of the nineteenth century a new modality of punishment emerged, in which the dominant forms of segregative control were supplanted by new forms of regulation centred around social integration and inclusion. For whole sections of the population, particularly the young and the vulnerable, forms of welfare intervention arose which aimed to deal with 'social problems' and 'problem populations' within the family and the 'community'. Intervention hinged on the perceived needs of certain individuals and involved a shift of emphasis from legal control to normalisation (Garland, 1985).

If it were the case that the nineteenth-century prison had been concerned with disciplining labour and regulating production, the emerging forms of welfare intervention appeared to be more concerned with the process of reproduction and the quality of labour power. The family became a central focus of intervention, and the establishment of a range of new agencies and institutions, particularly social work, probation, the borstal and the juvenile reformatory, signified the emergence of a new welfare complex.

The important characteristics of the shift towards the 'welfare sanction', in which welfare interventions were always conditional on compliance, was that they marked a shift away from the act to the offender. The aim of sanctions was not so much to address guilt but to identify needs and inadequacies (Garland, 1981). Sanctions therefore needed to be flexible, personalised and, where appropriate, continuous. The emphasis upon continuity can be critical, since repairing the perceived damage to the individuals requires not their removal from the locality, but working with families in the community in order to improve the process of socialisation and thereby to produce less-damaged subjects.

Social work is a key element in this process. The new forms of state-sponsored social work replaced the Victorian emphasis on personal charity and philanthropy to meet the needs of the poor. Instead professional social workers could deal with 'cases', and if necessary the whole family, since deviancy in one member might signify the breakdown or malfunctioning of the family as a whole. As part of the development of these normalising strategies, newly-developed agencies such as probation were able to provide more continuous forms of supervision and surveillance, either as an alternative to custody or as part of a post-release strategy. The Probation Act 1907 encouraged the development of non-custodial penalities, while the establishment of a separate system of juvenile justice in 1908 directed the newly-formed juvenile court to take account of the child's welfare in making disposals. From the outset the remit of the juvenile court extended beyond criminal offences, and was to include cases where children were deemed to be 'in need of care and protection'. Juvenile reformatories and borstals were designed both for punishment for wayward juveniles and as 'child-saving' institutions providing education and training. Sentences in relation to these institutions tended to be indeterminate; release was decided not only by the judge but also by the Prison Commissioners, and was dependent upon an individual's progress and reformation. The development of various interventions and the availability of alternatives to custody, as well as the removal of certain categories of offenders from prisons, meant that the 'welfare sanction' had a significant impact upon the composition of the prison population and the role which the prison was deemed to serve.

CONCLUSION

This brief overview of the emergence of the modern prison has been necessarily schematic and selective. The histories which emerged during the 1970s and 1980s have moved us a long way forward from the administrative and technical accounts that were previously available. They have also encouraged us to think more critically about the assumed humanitarian impulses which were once widely assumed to lie behind the development of the prison. However reassuring we might find such accounts, they do not square very well with the evidence. By the same token, 'revisionist' histories have forced us to rethink the claim that prisons arose as a direct response to the growth of crime and disorder. The critical questions which the revisionist historians raise are: why did punishment come to take the specific form of imprisonment in a certain period and what were the social determ-

inants which produced and shaped this response in different countries? Similar questions arise in relation to the emergence of the
'welfare sanction' at the end of the nineteenth century. The relative
decrease in the use of imprisonment in many Western countries
during the first half of the twentieth century raises the question of the
factors which affect the scale of imprisonment, as does the subsequent
increase in the use of imprisonment in recent years.

In attempting to explain these historical changes, we are drawn
ineluctably into the central debates over structure and agency, and by
implication into questions about the sources and exercise of power.
Few historians, with one or two notable exceptions, believe that these
development are either simply a reflection of the 'needs of capitalism',
or are purely the product of the campaigns of well-meaning reformers.
However, even if we avoid the twin excesses of functionalism and vol-
untarism, there are a number of unanswered questions and contested
issues which require serious consideration. Michael Ignatieff (1981),
in a critique of revisionist histories in which he includes the work of
David Rothman and Michel Foucault as well as his own, argues that
these authors incorporated three major misconceptions in their work:
'that the state controls a monopoly over punitive regulation of behaviour, that the state's moral authority and practical power are the
major sources of social order, and that all social relations can be
described in terms of power and subordination'. Ignatieff is particularly critical of those forms of overly conspiratorial class analysis which
see the prison as a response to class fear or as a form of punishment
imposed by the ruling class on the poor. Instead, he argues that
though the development of the prison may have important class
dimensions, the conspiratorial view presents ruling-class views as
being too unified, while paying little attention to the genuine support
for incarceration among sections of the working class. Also, such
accounts tend to play down how the prison relates to other forms of
regulation, both formal and informal. Consequently he has called for a
substantial reassessment of these revisionist histories and the ways in
which they deal with the critical issues of the state, power and class.
Other historians have also accused the revisionists of an endemic masculinist bias, and of underestimating the significance of race in the
development of imprisonment. Nevertheless, revisionist histories have
provided some important conceptual tools for uncovering the conditions which made the emergence of the modern prison possible, and
have identified some of the critical processes which shaped its development. These processes, however, require further investigation.

Figure 1.1 Some key dates in the history of imprisonment in England and Wales

1556	The first Bridewell opened in the City of London.
1717	The Transportation Act provided for transportation to the American Colonies.
1776	The hulks were introduced.
1779	The Penitentiary Act included proposals for improved diet and paid labour in prisons.
1783	Public hangings moved from Tyburn to Newgate prison.
1787	The first fleet of convicts set out for Botany Bay.
1823	The Gaol Act imposed new systems of classification involving the separation of male and female prisoners.
1835	The Penal Servitude Act was passed under which women were to be governed by the same rules and regulations as applied to male prisoners.
1838	A separate juvenile prison was established in Parkhurst.
1840	Transportation to New South Wales ended.
1842	Pentonville prison in London opened.
1853	A separate wing for women prisoners was established at Brixton.
1857	The last prison hulk taken out of service.
1861	The Whipping Act abolished whipping for virtually all offences.
1863	The Carnavon Committee was appointed to re-examine discipline in local jails.
1865	The Prison Act formally amalgamated the jail and the house of correction.
1867	Transportation ended.
1868	Public ceremonies of execution ceased.
1877	The Prison Act transferred control of local jails to central government.
1895	The Gladstone Committee on Prisons reported.
1898	The Prison Act introduced new categories of imprisonment based on the characteristics of the offender.
1901	A Borstal scheme was established in Rochester prison.
1907	The Probation Officers Act created the professional probation officer.
1908	The Children's Act created a separate system of juvenile justice.

2 Space, Time and Labour

INTRODUCTION

An examination of the conditions which underlay the emergence of the modern prison reveals that its development was bound up with the changing nature of three essential elements – space, time and labour. The particular forms in which these elements combined gave the prison its specific characteristics and differentiated it from other forms of punishment. Although a number of contemporary and historical studies have alluded to the significance of one or more of these factors, their triangulated and interdependent nature has not, as yet, been fully explored. The seminal writings of Michel Foucault (1977), Rusche and Kirchheimer (1968), and more recently Henri Lefebvre (1991) and Anthony Giddens (1984), as well as a number of other sociological thinkers, have begun to examine how these elements have developed historically and in particular how they have conditioned the organisation and the functioning of social institutions such as the prison.

SPACE

The coercive segregation of offenders in designated institutions is one of the main hallmarks of the modern prison as a form of punishment. The separation of prisoners from the rest of society represents a clear statement that physical and social exclusion is the price of non-conformity. High exterior walls and reinforced doors which divide the rows of cells of uniform dimensions from the designated areas of work and recreation are familiar characteristics of many of our prisons. Dispersal prisons, for example, are secured by very high perimeter walls that allow for areas of open space within the prison and a freedom of movement which is normally unavailable in local prisons. In open prisons, on the other hand, the thick, high walls are replaced with wire mesh and metal gates so that the separation from the outside world is less clearly demarcated, both physically and ideologically.

Within the prison itself space is used to differentiate between different types of prisoners, and to set boundaries on disciplining practices.

Whether prisoners are held on normal location, in segregation units, or in hospital units, they will be subject to different forms of control and different sets of rules. By the same token, being moved from one space to another, or alternatively being placed in isolation or segregation, is routinely used in prison as a method of control and as part of a repertoire of rewards and punishments. Thus, selected prisoners may be moved without warning from one location to another if they are deemed 'troublesome' or 'at risk' of engaging in some form of disruption, while others may be moved to more open prisons as a reward for good behaviour.

Prisons epitomise the ambiguous nature of notions of 'public' and 'private' space. Prisons are 'public' institutions in that they are run by or on behalf of the state, but they are 'private' in as much as they involve exclusion from the 'public' domain. The distinction between private and public space carries its own messages of difference, and provides the material basis for the construction of ideologies which portray the prison population as a unique and distinct group of people. Significantly, in Britain at least, there is no 'private' space as such within prison, since prisons are 'public' institutions. This means, for example, that all acts of homosexuality, although they may involve acts between consenting adults, are by definition illegal, since they cannot be carried out in 'private'. In contrast, in some European countries areas of private space have been constructed in prisons in order to allow conjugal visits. Thus within the prison various activities which may be legitimate or normal on the 'outside' become redefined on the 'inside' (Rose, 1987).

Space is, therefore, never neutral. It establishes social divisions. It defines and redefines behaviour. It sends out messages. It provides the basis for the construction and dissemination of ideologies. It is a mechanism through which the distribution and circulation of bodies is achieved. It reflects and defines social relations and finally, it is a mechanism through which order is realised.

Henri Lefebvre (1991) makes a distinction between 'real' and 'ideal' space. Real space refers to material phenomena such as buildings, rooms, and furniture. Ideal space, on the other hand, is more abstract, referring to different forms of social ordering produced through the formulation of mental categories which involve, for example, different architectural designs and forms of organisation. Prisons are complex social constructions which embody a mixture of real and ideal space. They are at once material, functional and ideological. The organisation of space in the modern prison allows for the supervision and control of prisoners, while providing a means for differentiating and mapping them. It also provides for the routine supervision of inmates, the monitoring of dangerous communications and the possibility of achieving subjection through detailed and regular inspection.

In the development of the modern prison a new consciousness of space was realised. The design of the prison was widely seen as critically important to the formulation of different objectives. Issues concerning the design and layout of prisons in the eighteenth and nineteenth centuries were debated with great fervour among reformers and social commentators. Which distribution of space would be most effective in minimising the risk of contagion, allowing self-reflection and facilitating the maximum degree of surveillance? How could the distribution of space help to achieve these different objectives? Did the existing structures create the right rhythms, allow appropriate movements and foster desirable relations? How could prisons be designed to achieve the reform of the prisoner? These were the questions posed by penal reformers.

The proper ordering of space, it was recognised, could produce better communications, and allow easier movement and a better use of time. The proper use of space should, according to Michel Foucault (1977), 'eliminate the efforts of imprecise distributions, the uncontrolled disappearance of individuals, their diffuse circulation, their unusable and dangerous coagulation'. The same spatial logic has been applied historically to other institutions, such as schools and hospitals. According to Foucault, the construction of these institutions is designed to effect the most profitable distribution of bodies and simultaneously to facilitate the processes of examination and inspection. Institutions such as schools and hospitals resemble the prison not only in that they look like them physically, but also because they are designed to allow the deployment of certain forms of discipline. Thus for Foucault the strategies and objectives of regulation are, as it were, built into the very bricks and mortar of institutions; once materialised in this form, they have definite effects, although these effects are not always those which were anticipated.

As Robin Evans argues (1982), the construction of the modern prison was conditioned by a number of different objectives: security, ventilation, reformation, classification, inspection and labour. Security was to be achieved by high, thick walls and regular surveillance. The preoccupation with ventilation was a product of the widespread belief that gaol (typhus) fever was generated and disseminated in the atmosphere, and that good ventilation was required to encourage the continuous flow of air. Reformation was seen to require the separation of prisoners, and it was felt that prison design was potentially the most effective way of creating and enforcing demarcations and divisions between prisoners. The aim of prison architecture was to segregate prisoners from the wider community and to keep them, as far as possible, from each other. Closely related to the aims of reform was the formulation of ever more detailed systems of classification which divided prisoners up into different types. At the beginning of the nineteenth century the Society for the Improvement of Prison Discipline had created 20 categories of prisoners: 6 for houses of correction and 14 for gaols. The formulation of these categories and the more detailed separation of prisoners was designed to limit the spread of wickedness and corruption. Significantly, by 1818 the Society for the Improvement of Prison Discipline decided that it was not the *crime* that prison punished but what they described as the 'habits and inclination of prisoners'. The objective of segregation had, however, to be balanced against the growing emphasis upon the need for inspection. From 1800 onwards inspection became an increasingly dominant theme in prison.

Providing space for different forms of labour has been a continual preoccupation for prison architects. A major focus of the debate which took place in the mid-nineteenth century concerning the relative advantages and disadvantages of the Auburn and Pennsylvania systems was centred around the arrangements for work in the prison. The introduction of the treadwheel, the crank and other imaginative devices designated to replicate 'hard labour' placed new pressures on the distribution of space within prisons. Each of the six imperatives that Evans identified helped to influence the design of the modern prison. Each, however, had different requirements in relation to design. Some required enclosure and compartmentalisation, others required exposure and association. The competing models that were proposed provided various responses to these imperatives and those which gained political favour were those which were seen to combine the designated aims in the most economical and effective ways.

Historically, the architectural design of the prison has been conditioned by the dominant views of human nature and criminality in any period, combined with the changing objectives associated with the process of imprisonment. A review of the changing design of prisons since the beginning of the nineteenth century indicates that four main styles have been developed in different periods: radial, Panopticon, telegraphic pole, and the 'new generation' prisons, which incorporate a podular design.

The Radial Design

The dominant style of prison architecture in Europe in the nineteenth century was the radial design. This construction, which involves a number of wings panning out from a central point, was seen to be the most appropriate way to divide prisoners into different groups located in their respective wings, while allowing control and co-ordination to be located at the pivotal point. Thus, in a period in which prisoners spent virtually all their time confined to their cells, a single officer could, by standing at the centre, observe each of the various wings in turn by simply turning his head through 180 degrees.

A classic example of a radial design is to be found in Pentonville prison in North London. Pentonville was run on the principles of non-communication and strict separation, which it was held would encourage meditation and self-reflection while reducing the possibility of contamination by limiting the spread of bad habits. It was felt that these silent and austere institutions would maximise the deterrent effects of incarceration, although this aim had to be balanced against growing demands for improvements in diet and hygiene. Reformers like John Howard, however, emphasised that there was no necessary contradiction between improving conditions in prisons and maintaining their deterrent value, since: confinement in a prison, though it may cease to be destructive to health and morals, will not fail to be sufficiently irksome and disagreeable, especially to the idle and the profligate' (Howard, 1777: 44).

When it was opened in 1842 Pentonville held 450 male prisoners, who were housed in cells of a uniform size, spaced along tiers within the three wings which radiated out from a central point (see Figure 2.1). Within each cell there was the necessary equipment to carry out work and the basic requirements for daily living:

> His cell was thirteen-and-a-half feet from barred window to bolted door, seven-and-a-half feet from wall to wall, and nine feet from floor to ceiling. Its contents were sparse; a table, a chair, a cobbler's bench, hammock, broom, bucket, and a corner shelf. On the shelf stood a pewter mug and a dish, a bar of soap, a towel and a Bible. Except for exercise and chapel, every minute of his day was spent in this space amongst these objects. When the prison opened in 1842 convicts spent eighteen months in solitude. As the authorities became familiar with its effects, the period of solitude was reduced, first to twelve and then to nine months. (Ignatieff, 1978: 4)

Figure 2.1   Radial design prison

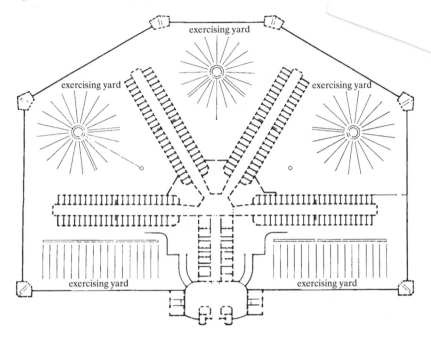

Spatial segregation involving solitary confinement produced a series of negative effects over and above those which might have resulted from segregation from the wider society. Total segregation within the prison produced disturbingly high rates of death, insanity and suicide. Although the system of solitary confinement eventually fell into disfavour, the radial design used in the majority of Victorian prisons still remains in evidence.

The Panopticon

Michel Foucault (1977) has suggested that the design which provided the most efficient system of surveillance and regulation was the Panopticon, developed by Jeremy Bentham (1791). Bentham's aim was to develop a design for the prison which would maximise surveillance. The Panopticon, he felt, provided the ideal structure, since a guard positioned in the tall, central control tower could exert continuous surveillance around the prison. Narrow viewpoints in the tower would make it impossible for prisoners to see the guard and to know at any one particular moment whether or not they were actually being watched. For Bentham, the dual attraction of the Panopticon lay firstly in the possibility that regulation could operate independently of any particular controller, and secondly in that those upon whom control was exercised were caught up in a power relation in which they themselves were the bearers. Panoptic power, therefore, has the essential characteristic that it is unverifiable, continuous, and brings both those who exercise it, and those who are subject to it, into a relation in which parties are complicit, although

Figure 2.2   Panopticon

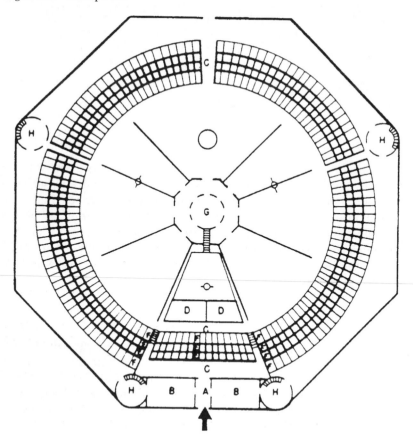

not necessarily actively engaged. It is the way in which the Panopticon appears to transcend the traditional opposition of coercion and consent, and the way in which this depersonalised form of regulation is built into the structure and design of the institution, which fascinates Foucault.

Much to Bentham's disappointment, however, the Panopticon was never widely used as a basis for prison design, or for that matter as a model for other types of institution. Two of the few prisons which were built upon this design were Stateville Prison in Louisiana, built in 1919, and the Western Penitentiary in Pittsburgh. Both prisons incorporate the central features of the Panopticon, with a tall central tower overlooking circular rows of cells (see Figure 2.2). However, the fact that Bentham's model has not been widely adopted suggests that the primary functions it was designed to achieve did not accord with the objectives of prison administrators in the nineteenth century. By implication, this raises the issue of just how significant the Panopticon is as the ideal model of control in contemporary society (Shearing and Stenning, 1985).

'Telegraph Pole' Model

Victorian prisons, which were built largely on the radial design, continued to operate and dominate the prison estate into the twentieth century, despite the fact that the theories and attitudes around which they had been constructed had fallen into disfavour. It was not until the 1930s in America that a new principle of construction emerged. This involved a number of individual oblong cell blocks arranged either side of a linking control corridor or hallway. This design, which has become known as the 'telegraph pole' model, was adapted from various pioneering prisons, such as that built at Fresnes in France in 1898, and the separate block plan which had been used some years earlier at Wormwood Scrubs in London.

The emergence of the telegraph pole model reflected the demise of the separatist philosophy. Rather than focusing on the separation and isolation of prisoners, prisons became designed to allow a greater degree of inmate socialisation, movement and activity. In this model the use of the central point, which had been a dominant feature of radial and Panopticon-type constructions, was rejected in favour of the separate control of each block (see Figure 2.3). To some extent the development of prisons with separate blocks reflected changes in the system of prisoner classification in relation to the perceived risk to

Figure 2.3   'Telegraph pole' design

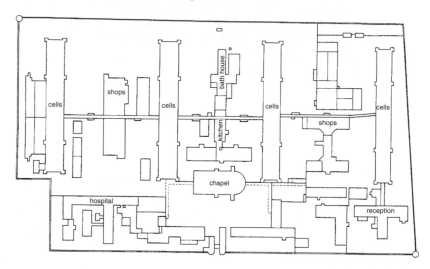

security that different types of prisoners were seen to pose. It was also felt, particularly by American prison administrators, that separate blocks joined by short corridors made administration and supervision easier, while improving the conditions in which prisoners lived.

The Podular Design

The trend towards the construction of a number of units, each containing a relatively small number of inmates, has been developed into the podular design, in which prisons are divided into a number of small buildings that open onto a central multi-use area, enabling staff to observe both the living and recreational activities more easily (see Figure 2.4). These 'new generation' prisons, as they are often called, extend the principles of classification of different types of prisoner, and reflect changes in the form of organisation towards a more decentralised system of unit management, which aims simultaneously to reduce the levels of staffing and to allow the more effective transfer of prisoners within the between institutions (Home Office, 1985).

In these new generation prisons the emphasis is upon the provision of accommodation and association rather than employment. There is less evidence of the traditional cells, bars and doors, and a greater emphasis upon improved circulation and movement. They involve a

Figure 2.4   Podular design

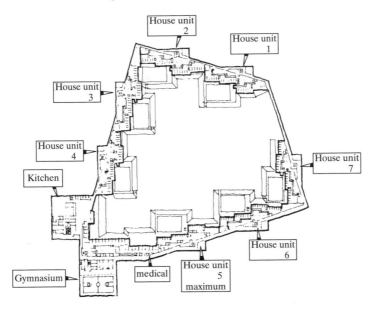

simultaneous shift towards normalisation and increased surveillance. A central aim is to provide improved security both for staff and inmates. The construction of these prisons, which incorporate new forms of 'soft architecture' by using bright colours and less hardware, has raised questions about whether they are able to achieve an environment which is simultaneously more secure and less damaging (Canter, 1987; King, 1987).

In an examination of Oak Park Heights, an American 'new generation' maximum security prison, Roy King (1991) points to differences in the systems of surveillance, the movement of staff and prisoners, and the levels of internal and external security which this type of prison displays in comparison to those employed in a typical dispersal prison in England and Wales, such as Gartree. The organisation of new generation prisons tends to be centred around a control 'bubble', in which video and other surveillance equipment is placed, and from which the guards are able to co-ordinate the movement of prisoners. A distinguishing feature of this form of prison design is that areas of work are built directly above the prisoners' rooms, and the construction of separate corridors and stairways for staff and prisoners allows inmates to move more freely from one section to another, while the staff are able to gain access quickly to certain strategic areas that are denied to the prisoners. The net result, King concludes, is that Oak Park Heights is 'perceived to be safer, more secure, and more trouble-free', offering 'a fuller and more highly rated programme of treatment, industry, and education, and better contact with the outside world'. The important distinction between these new design prisons and dispersal prisons is that the security is shifted from the design of the buildings themselves to the perimeter, the corridors and to the more extensive use of technology.

These four designs have historically reflected the changing attitudes and objectives of imprisonment, and demonstrate how space has been employed in different periods. Thus, it is evident that the deployment of spatial divisions in the prison is conditioned by theories of human nature, concepts of criminality, the changing objectives of imprisonment, forms of classification, management practices, and principles of control and surveillance. The fact that various prison designs have mirrored the social relations and attitudes which gave rise to them in particular periods has resulted in an ongoing tension between what prisons were designed to achieve and what they are commonly used for. This tension is most pronounced in relation to the competing objectives of deterrence and rehabilitation. Just as the early separatist designs were seen in practice largely to negate any rehabilitative role that was assigned to prisons, so the new podular design prisons based on a number of small units were built to promote rehabilitation rather than deterrence. However, by the time the podular design prisons became established, the rehabilitative ideal had fallen into disfavour with prison administrators and was widely replaced by a warehousing strategy, for which these small, low buildings were particularly unsuitable.

In this context a number of critical questions about the design of prisons have arisen. These questions concern the possibility of combining improved levels of control and surveillance with the realisation of rehabilitative goals, including the provision of training and education. They also raise the linked question of the relationship between the external security of the prison and the internal safety of prisoners. As John Ditchfield has noted:

> With the disappearance of separation (which itself had made escape rather difficult) and the growth of social regimes, the need of internal control and external security was expressed more functionally (and less aesthetically) by an increase in the amount of internal

hardware in prisons and by an increase in perimeter security, both physically and in the sense of separating it from the rest of the prison. The result – in America at least – has been a tendency to 'over-build' prisons both physically and technically, largely because it has been much easier to design for escape proof security than to design and build for good regimes. (Ditchfield, 1990: 94)

The tendency to 'over-build' has also been evident in Britain, particularly following a number of celebrated escapes in the 1960s and 1970s, as well as more recent incidents at Gartree, Parkhurst and Whitemoor, which have all served to increase the emphasis upon the external security of the prison (Home Office, 1995).

The sociological focus on the use of space as an instrument for producing order and facilitating control within prisons draws attention to the relatively subtle but effective ways in which social regulation is achieved. Just as in other areas of daily life, the most effective forms of regulation in prisons tend to be those which are less visible and less dramatic. Overt forms of coercion and brutality, although not absent from the prison, always carry the danger of generating resistance. In recent years a growing number of criminologists have come to realise that spatial forms of control are generally more subtle, less controversial and often more effective ways of regulating different populations (Clarke, 1992). This is not to suggest that spatial divisions are not contested, or that forms of spatial control are not resisted. The fact that riots in prisons involve the objective of controlling certain spaces and redefining their use underlines the fact that spatial control is critical to the exercise of power (Adams, 1990).

TIME

Space and time have historically been closely linked. But at a certain juncture social space and time became disconnected and appeared increasingly unrelated. This separation occurred at a point in which time itself became commodified and functionally specialised. In the transition to industrial capitalism, lived time loses its form and its interest, except for the time spent working. Time from this point on is recorded primarily on measuring instruments – clocks and watches – that are as isolated and functionally specialised as time itself. The expulsion of 'lived' time Henri Lefebvre (1991) suggests, is one of the hallmarks of modernity. He argues that time: 'which is the greatest of all goods is no longer visible to us, no longer intelligible. It cannot be constructed. It is consumed, exhausted, and that is all'.

In a similar vein, Anthony Giddens has argued that the commodification of time is one of the most significant developments associated with the emergence of capitalism. He states that:

> Time as lived time, as the substance of lived experience of durée of Being, becomes 'formless duration' with the expansion of capitalism, this is what time seems to be, just as money seems to be the standard value of all things. Time as pure duration, as disconnected from the rationality of existence, comes to be perceived in direct opposition to the actual state of things, as real 'objective' time, because like money it is expressed in a universal and public mode. This universal and public mode, again like money, is nothing less than its own quantification as a measure of standing at the axis of a host of transformation/mediation relations. The commodification of time, and its differentiation from further processes of the commodification of space, hold the key to the deepest transformations of day-to-day social life that are brought about by the emergence of capitalism. (Giddens, 1981: 131)

E. P. Thompson (1967) has argued that the Industrial Revolution not only brought about a change in the form of production but also promoted the tyranny of the clock. With the rise of industrial capitalism time was no longer 'passed' but 'spent'. The changes in manufacturing technique demanded a greater synchronisation of labour as well as a greater degree of punctuality and exactitude in the routine of work. The twin processes of the social dislocation of time and its technical calibration provided the basis on which labour time could more easily be calculated, while non-work time became seen as 'spare' or 'free' time. Importantly, time itself became compartmentalised in space, and took on a linear quality which superseded the cyclical forms of time that had dominated in pre-capitalistic periods. Linear time became an established feature of modernity, underpinning notions of progress and individual transformation. These two notions were in turn associated with the conception of prison as a mechanism for reforming offenders.

As an institution which could enforce the deprivation of liberty for a designated period of time, the prison appeared as a 'natural' form of punishment. This occurred for a number of reasons. The first important attribute of a time-centred mode of punishment was that it appeared universal and independent of each individual. Time and liberty, it was held, were commodities which all citizens possessed in equal amounts and could dispose of freely. In fact time was one of the few attributes which both the rich and the poor were seen to possess in roughly equal quantities. What therefore could be more reasonable than that those who transgressed the law should be given a form of punishment whose effects would be experienced equally by all?

The second major attribute of time-based punishments is that they have an objectivity and solidity not found in those forms of punishment that were widely used in the Middle Ages, such as shaming and the expression of remorse. The length of sentence can be calibrated directly in relation to the seriousness of the offence, and the severity of punishment can be tied to the principle of proportionality in clear and precise ways.

The third attribute of time-based punishments is that because time itself is essentially a social construct it confers on imprisonment a quality which is truly social. The prison may therefore appear as the consequence of human endeavour, or as the outcome of a 'civilising' process standing in contrast to the 'barbaric' forms of punishment which were prevalent in previous periods (Franke, 1992; Spierenburg, 1984).

The fourth attribute of time-based punishments is that as time becomes commodified it can be 'traded', 'gained' or 'lost'; that is, the period of time served can be adjusted and linked to the performance of the prisoner. Good behaviour, hard work and reform can all, in principle, be traded off against the length of sentence.

In reality, however, time inside prison was never the same as time on the outside. Institutional confinement changes the ways in which time is experienced. Time served in prison is not so much 'spent' as 'wasted'. The process of imprisonment, rather than channelling and redistributing time, involves the negation of time. Individuals removed from the workplace and the labour market – the principal sphere of 'lived' time – and simultaneously removed from their families and communities, are no longer able to spend 'free' time. Thus, although imprisonment is in essence about time, it is experienced as a form of timelessness, with prison terms often being described as 'doing' or 'killing' time. This paradoxical relation between time and imprisonment is explicable to some extent by identifying the different forms of time that are experienced both inside prison and in the wider society. There is a need to make a distinction between physical, mental and social time (Lefebvre, 1991).

Physical time is the duration taken to perform certain tasks, and is gauged essentially in terms of the activities and experiences of the body. This is linked to biological rhythms and to the natural movements involved in seasonal change. In the prison setting the daily rhythms of the body are often influenced by the change of daily routine, while the seasonal changes are muted and less relevant. Mental time or 'inner' time refers to the processes of reflection or imagination. These are the subjective processes which nineteenth-century prison reformers felt were critical to the processes of introspection and personal reform. But, as the experience of solitary confinement showed, the preoccupation with introspection can lead to depression, insanity and suicide, rather than rehabilitation.

Social time involves the continuous movement between the past, the present and the future. Although a complex process, the construction of social time is an everyday activity by which individuals try to understand the process of change. For the prisoner, however, because the present is placed in suspension, the ability to link the past to the future is limited, since the meaning of time itself is 'lost'. For some long-term prisoners for whom the future is an unthinkable and terrifying prospect, time is reduced to a continuous present and therefore lacks any proper chronology. These prisoners are in danger of losing a sense of personal development or purpose (Cohen and Taylor, 1972).

Paradoxically, the more time you have, the more it decreases in value. Therefore a recurring problem of linking imprisonment to the principle of proportionality is that the 'value' of an eight-year sentence is not necessarily twice that of a four-year sentence. By the same token, the effect which the period of confinement has on each prisoner will be a function of the individual's own mental and social time scales, and these in turn will dramatically affect the ways in which imprisonment is conceptualised and experienced (von Hirsch, 1992).

As the world speeds up and social time is accelerating, physical time appears to slow down. Thus a five-year sentence given in 1950 would tend to be experienced as a significantly longer sentence in 2000. Therefore the overall increase in the average length of sentence in real terms in recent years has an even greater significance than might at first appear. As social time continues to accelerate and physical time slows down in relation to the past, and as the present and future lose their continuity, it is probably not surprising to find that many prisoners turn to 'inner time' and become more involved with their own inner experiences. In this context, drug-taking, particularly of hallucinatory drugs, is likely to become particularly attractive, since it is able to place time into further suspension and thereby release the prisoner, albeit temporarily, from the apparent timelessness of prison life. Drugs do more than tranquillise or anaesthetise the prisoner: they readjust time. For those who were regular drug users before entering prison, drugs normalise time, in that its passing corresponds to those forms of social time which were previously experienced on the outside. By the same token, the drug subculture that has been found to be prevalent in many prisons also provides a way of organising daily life and giving meaning to the prison routine that for some approximates to the normal routines of life outside the confines of the prison. Thus by engaging in an activity whose objective is to create what we might call 'fantasy' time, prisoners can spend their days involved in activities – buying, trading, hustling, scoring – which correspond to familiar 'real time' activities conducted on the outside (Devlin, 1998). Thus physical, mental and social time can be conceptually differentiated and analysed by specialists in different fields – principally sociologists and psychologists – but the prisoner cannot afford the luxury of such strict divisions. Instead, he or she must move constantly between these levels and explore their implications and live their contradictions.

A central feature of prison life is the timetable which provides a regular programme of activities and a semblance of structure and order to the day. But, as Foucault (1977) has argued, the timetable is an essentially negative and limiting device designed primarily to eradicate idleness. Modern systems of discipline require, he argues, forms of regulation which are also positive and which involve inducements and incentives. For Foucault, the prison is not just an institution of punishment but is also designed for the production of discipline, and one of the aims of discipline is to increase speed and efficiency. The objective is to make the use of time as productive as possible, extracting from every hour and every moment the maximum utility.

So for Foucault discipline is a way of capitalising on time. This is achieved through graduated processes of training such that individuals can learn tasks of ever greater complexity and perform them with increased proficiency and dexterity. He suggests that these processes allow new forms of regulation:

> The 'seriation' of successive activities makes possible a whole investment of duration by power; the possibility of a detailed control and a regular intervention (of differentiation, correction, punishment, elimination) in each moment of time: the possibility of

characterizing, and therefore of using individuals according to the levels in the series that they are moving through; the possibility of accumulating time and activity, of rediscovering them, totalised and usable in a final result, which is the ultimate capacity of an individual. Temporal dispersal is brought together to produce a profit, thus mastering a duration that would otherwise elude one's grasp. Power is articulated directly onto time, it assures its control and guarantees its use. (Foucault, 1977: 160)

Thus, as Foucault explains, the distribution of time is usefully associated with both training and the development of certain skills and competences in prison. The organisation of time, like space, is inextricably bound up with the establishment of order and control, and both are linked, directly and indirectly, with the organisation of labour within prisons.

The nature of time-based punishments changed, however, around the end of the nineteenth century, with the greater use of indeterminate sentences. In place of fixed penalties greater flexibility was introduced into the sentencing process by setting maximum and minimum periods of confinement. The growing emphasis on treatment and rehabilitation encouraged the use of more open-ended forms of sentencing which would allow greater discretion in the release of prisoners. This development increased the powers of prison administrators and provided a useful control mechanism within the prison itself. It also increased the demand for more information on prisoners, since clearly the provision of proper treatment required detailed knowledge not only of their offending but also of their personal and social characteristics. The therapeutic encounter, as David Rothman (1981) has argued, works to a different clock from industrial or even medical time. Overcoming resistance, trauma, or more simply denial can take a long time. A proper 'cure', psychiatrists insist, is never quick.

The 'stretching' of time through the use of indeterminate sentencing became particularly pronounced in America in the first half of the twentieth century. However, over the last three decades it has come under repeated attack for inadvertently extending the average length of sentences – creating unnecessary anxiety for prisoners, who remain uncertain about their release date; injecting considerable discretion into the penal system, and creating injustices by exacerbating discrepancies in time actually served (Bottoms, 1980; Rotman, 1990). Over the past two decades the relation between time and punishment has been reappraised, with a consequent shift back towards forms of determinate sentencing.

LABOUR

Labour is tied to the process of imprisonment on two interrelated levels. On one level, labour has historically been a core feature of imprisonment, oscillating between productive and commercialised forms of industry on the one hand, and training and rehabilitative strategies on the other. On another level, the significance of labour relates to the nature of work outside the prison and particularly to free wage labour as well as the operation of the labour market. The operation of labour both inside and outside the prison has shaped the nature of imprisonment in different historical periods.

Inside the prison, prison labour performs a number of functions. It provides goods and is a source of revenue. It provides training and the possibility of rehabilitation through work. It provides a vehicle for instilling time and work discipline in those who were unable or unwilling to find proper paid employment and it is a mechanism of control, providing a way of ordering time and keeping prisoners occupied (Simon, 1993).

In the eighteenth and early nineteenth centuries prisons were often run as profit-making institutions and a number of establishments paid for themselves through the goods produced by prisoners, while some even made a profit. However, the profit-making capacities of prisons were always limited. During the nineteenth century there was growing opposition to prison-made goods because they could undercut the price of commercially-made goods, and entrepreneurs complained of unfair competition. Objections to the exploitation of prison labour came from free labour too, particularly in periods of recession or unemployment. They argued that the employment of prisoners restricted available employment and pushed down wages. Objections also arose from various prison reformers, who disliked the fact that certain prisoners were receiving a wage which approximated commercial rates. Indeed, the prospect of prisoners earning significant sums of money was seen as transgressing the principle of 'less eligibility' by some commentators, who were concerned that prison labour might be better paid than free wage labour. They were also concerned that the living conditions of prison labour exceeded those of the poorest worker, with the consequence that the deterrent effect of imprisonment would be undermined (Melossi and Pavarini 1981; Rusche and Kirchheimer, 1968).

It was also the case, as Rusche and Kirchheimer (1968) point out, that prison labour was itself anomalous, in that forced labour has no economic justification in a capitalist system of production. In consequence prison labour can only be fully justified in relation to its educative and rehabilitative roles. Moreover, the ability of prison managers to sell goods at less than the market price undermines the exchange value of commodities, and simultaneously breaks the critical connection between time, production and price. Time is the mediating link between labour and exchange value, since it is the units of time that make values of commodities divisible and quantifiable and permit their common existence as interchangeable items.

The organisation of prisons militates against efficient production. However fundamental the relationship between labour and imprisonment might be, prisons are not factories. The different forms of spatial distribution within prisons have not always easily accommodated manufacture. Indeed the historic trends in the design and construction of prisons have to some extent been away from a preoccupation with manufacture and towards other concerns.

Prison labour suffers from a disadvantage, in that it lacks the type of co-operation that has been an important feature of free labour. As Marx (1970) pointed out, free labour working in co-operation with others acquires an increased productive power. In short, Marx is arguing that the combination of social labour working in a factory produces more than the sum of its parts. Prison labour on the other hand, it could be argued, produces less than the sum of its parts. Because prisons are not factories, and because prisoners are not part of the organised working class, the productive potential among prison labour is organisationally limited. To put it another way, production and manufacture in prison is likely to be inefficient and in many respects is 'primitive' and 'pre-capitalist'. Thus if the forms of labour which are prevalent in prison are pre-capitalist, they are unlikely to embody the forms of 'discipline' that are required for a capitalist form of production. Prisoners may work side-by-side, but they do not work in 'co-operation' as in factory production, or within an organisation whose prime purpose is the extraction of the maximum amount of surplus value.

The combined effect of these restrictions on the use of prison labour historically has been to limit the range of goods which could be profitably produced. These restrictions made it virtually impossible for prisons to be run as commercial, profit-making institutions, particularly as there are other impediments which have served to limit the quality and quantity of goods that can be produced. One major impediment to the use and profitability of prison labour is that the majority of those incarcerated enter the prison with few skills and low educational levels. The general removal of financial incentives and the repetitive and monotonous nature of prison work provide little intrinsic interest. Consequently, attitudes towards work and prisoners' motives for engaging in work in prison are different from what they would be on the outside. The concept of 'job satisfaction' is fairly alien to prisoners, and the interest in work is often associated with the perks, mobility and autonomy which different tasks offer. Given that the majority of prisoners are imprisoned for relatively short periods of time, the interest in a 'career' of employment within the prison is likely to be of limited relevance to the average prisoner (Hawkins, 1983).

One innovative response to the limited productiveness of prison labour was developed in the mid-nineteenth century by Alexander Moconochie, who was the governor of Birmingham prison. He suggested that, instead of paying prisoners wages, it would be preferable to instigate a system of credit, which he called the 'mark' system, by which the productiveness of prisoners could be linked to the acquisition of 'marks', which could then be used to 'purchase' reductions in the length of sentence. He explained:

I think that … time sentences are the root of very nearly all the demoralisation which exists in prisons. A man under a time sentence thinks only how he can cheat that time, and while it away: he evades labour because he has no interest in it whatever, and he has no desire to please the officer under whom he is placed, because they cannot serve him essentially; they cannot in any way promote his liberation. Besides this, in his desire to while way his time, he conjures up in his mind, and indulges, when he has the opportunity, in every sort of prurient and stimulative thought, and word, and where he can act … Now the whole of these evils would be remedied by introducing a system of task sentences. A man under a task sentence would strip his coat to work, he would set a proper value upon time, which under a time sentence is hated, and he would exert himself in such a way that he could not but improve, *he must improve*. (Moconochie, 1850; quoted in Webb and Webb, 1963: 167)

The conception of the mark system, involving a 'task sentence', can be seen as the precursor to the policies of early release for good behaviour and to what Americans call 'good time' laws. However, the actual implementation of the mark system in the mid-nineteenth century was associated with scandal and abuse, particularly in Birmingham and Leicester prisons, following reports that various acts of cruelty as well as illegal methods of inducement were applied in order to persuade prisoners to engage in more demanding forms of labour.

The limitations on the use of productive labour in prisons resulted in the short term in the widespread introduction of modes of unproductive labour in the form of the treadwheel and the crank, and in the longer term in a shift in emphasis towards the training and possible rehabilitative value of prison work. The adoption of the treadwheel and crank was at first met with widespread enthusiasm among reformers because it was felt that the drudgery and monotony of this form of labour would enhance the deterrent value of prison, while the physical exertion involved would keep prisoners occupied. After a few years, however, the negative consequences of the treadwheel became apparent to observers, since long periods on the 'everlasting staircase', as it was known, caused serious physical damage to both men and women, and it was seen as a depressing and degrading form of punishment which did little to stimulate the mental capacities of inmates or encourage any kind of emotional regeneration.

The longer-term shift towards training, and a growing emphasis upon preparing the prisoner for employment after leaving prison, was more positive and less destructive. In the Departmental Home Office Enquiry of 1933 it was stated that: 'The main object of prison employment should not be the exploitation of prison labour so as to secure a return to the State, but the rehabilitation of the prisoner'. The problem with this objective is that it assumes employment is a major cause of crime and that offenders engage in crime because they do not have the necessary skills to undertake legitimate forms of employment. It is also the case that the types of skill which can normally be acquired in prison are of limited utility. In conjunction with these limitations, the costs of proper training are considerable, particularly given the uncertainty of the outcome (Cooper and King, 1965).

There have been in the post-war period a number of attempts to run prisons as commercial and profitable institutions. In America in the 1970s, attention shifted towards the introduction of 'Free Venture Prisons', while in England and Wales there were similar attempts to move back towards the creation of industrial prisons, or 'factories with fences' as they have been called (Weiss, 1986). The general aim was to introduce a full working day for prisoners, increase financial and other incentives, and exercise a 'hire and fire' policy in order to remove unproductive prisoners, while using the profits to offset the costs of incarceration and to contribute towards the cost of supporting dependants and compensating victims.

Although there was a surge of activity in England in Wales in the 1970s, and despite the fact that on both sides of the Atlantic a range of new occupations have been introduced, productive work in prisons has been in general decline in recent years (King and McDermott, 1989). Apart from the problems of low skill and educational levels among prisoners, the continuous turnover of inmates, the general lack of motivation and incentives has made competitive and commercial forms of production difficult to sustain. Moreover, in those prisons in which a more commercially-orientated wage structure has been introduced, the established nature of staff–prisoner relations has been brought under pressure and the sub-cultural relations which were in place have been undermined by the development of a sub-economy in which divisions of wealth may change the balance of power within the prison, leading to new forms of instability.

A continuing constraint on the recommercialisation of prison industries is the spatial dimensions of the prison. The old Victorian prisons have cramped workshops and the new generation prisons are not designed for large-scale production. The type of work which is probably most viable in contemporary prisons is low-skill service work, but although this is potentially profitable, it offers little in the way of training and carries limited rehabilitative value.

Thus the history of labour in prison is plagued with apparently unresolvable tensions. The very prospect of forced labour within prisons appears as an anomaly in a capitalist society, while the spectre of idleness is viewed as an unnecessary waste. Work in prisons is not fully 'disciplinary' in the sense that it lacks normal incentives, proper training, and the experience of co-operation and collectivism which has been a characteristic of free labour. When work is at its most commercial and profitable it tends to have a low rehabilitative or educational value; and when the training and rehabilitation are emphasised, prison labour is at its least productive and efficient. It may be the case, however, as a number of commentators have argued, that the real significance of the relation between work and imprisonment is more to do with the relation between imprisonment and the wider labour market.

It was Rusche and Kirchheimer's (1968) central contention that the form of punishment is conditioned by the changing nature of productive relationships and the organisation of labour. Thus for them it was the creation of free wage labour and the changing nature of the labour market which shaped the use of imprisonment and gave it its historical specificity. From this vantage point, they suggest that prison acts as an institution for absorbing and ideally recycling those who are unable or unwilling to participate in the labour market, while providing a general deterrent for those who are tempted to engage in illegitimate activities. The crux of this argument is that with the development of industrial capitalism the traditional ties of support and dependence are broken down, and the worker becomes separated from the means of production. The increasingly atomised individual is then free to sell his or her labour on the market, but is nevertheless forced to sell his or her labour power or starve. It is this atomisation and consequent vulnerability in the face of the market which Marx identified as the central locus of social control in capitalist societies. As labour appeared in its 'pure' form in the nineteenth century through its separation from the household and from private property, the significance of the labour market as a regulatory mechanism became even more pronounced (Offe, 1985).

The control exercised by the labour market has a number of similarities to the type of ideal system of control developed by Jeremy Bentham and presented by Michel Foucault. It is impersonal. It involves a form of continuous surveillance. It is both a cause and an effect of the atomisation and differentiation of individuals; and finally, it incorporates a form of power which is not simply excised *on* individuals but also *through* them. It is the knowledge that each worker is potentially replaceable and that the value of labour power is constructed independently of each individual that constitutes the 'invisible threads' of control in capitalist societies (Lea, 1979). The experience of imprisonment has a dual effect on the individual in relation to the labour market: one immediate and the other long term. The immediate effect is the deprivation of liberty and a loss of certain rights for a specified period of time. The longer-term effect involves a changed relationship to the labour market itself, since the sanction of imprisonment carries a certain stigmatisation which affects the individual's future marketability.

Thus, in general, the prison serves three related roles in relation to the labour market: (1) it compensates for the imperfections of the market mechanism by increasing incentives to participate in a legitimate occupation, even at low rates; (2) it reinforces the division between the respectable and non-respectable working class by pointing to the potential dangers of non-participation in the labour market; and (3) it serves the market by absorbing some of those who are socially or economically marginalised or are unable to compete effectively, thus increasing the overall competitiveness and quality of available labour power. However, the more effective imprisonment is in reducing the marketability of individuals in relation to the labour market, the more unlikely it is to be successful in imposing labour discipline on those who are incarcerated.

The changing nature of labour at the end of the nineteenth century and the development of welfare capitalism persuaded Rusche and Kirchheimer (1968) that the social and regulatory roles of the prison would diminish throughout the twentieth century and that the fine would become more widely used as a form of punishment. The advent of Fordism and its associated forms of work discipline, they believed, would render the established forms of prison discipline anachronistic. The evidence that the prison was increasingly becoming an institution of 'last resort', with a consequent overall decline in prison populations in both Europe and America, suggested that the use of imprisonment would continue to decline during the twentieth century. In the postwar period, however, the rate of decline has been halted, and in some countries reversed. In response to Rusche and Kirchhiemer, Ivan Jancovic (1977) argues that there are two critical questions which have now to be answered. These are: (1) In what ways do the changing forms of custodial and non-custodial forms of punishment correspond to contemporary productive relationships? and (2) What functions does the prison perform in advanced capitalist society?

CONCLUSION

The modern prison emerged at a point of intersection between three changing lines of force – space, time and labour. This development, however, should not be read as the bringing together of three 'variables' which just happened to combine in an accidental and contingent fashion. Rather, the modern prison was a product of a particular historical configuration which involved the commodification of all three elements, the separation of space and time, the stimultaneous technical quantification of time and the formation of a capitalist labour market that involved new forms of freedom and unfreedom.

As Anthony Giddens (1990) has argued, the buying and selling of labour time is one of the most distinctive features of modern capitalism, while the 'dynamism of modernity derives from the separation of time and space and their recombination in forms which permit the precise time–space 'zoning' of social life'. The implications of these observations is that it is the precise seriation of time and its compartmentalisation which makes the possibility of 'doing time' as a form of punishment possible, while the development of time in evolutionary and linear terms underpins notions of progress and an associated belief in the possibility of individual reform through the application of scientific knowledge and disciplinary techniques. Based upon these conventional distinctions between time and space, the prison takes on a naturalness and appears as an 'obvious' form of punishment. And what could have been more natural during the rise of industrial capitalism than subjecting aberrant populations to the rigours of labour discipline?

Just as these three elements combined to give imprisonment its unique historical character, by an extension of the same processes and an application of the same logic, space, time and labour became the central organising principles of the prison and an intrinsic part of its regulatory mechanisms. But its functioning has never been harmonious. The very construction of the prison was underpinned by a number of competing and at times incompatible objectives. The determinants of design, the organisation of time, and the attempts to engage in productive labour came into continuous conflict, with each one placing constraints upon the realisation of the others.

3 Order, Control and Adaption in Prison

INTRODUCTION

It is normally only when a major disturbance or riot occurs in prison that the issues of order and control become an object of concern. At these times the response is predictably to enhance physical security, identify and remove 'troublemakers' or impose a tougher system of control. The fact that, despite the frequent use of these familiar practices, the number of disturbances and riots in prison continues to increase in England and Wales suggests that, individually or in combination, they have a limited effectiveness or may even be counterproductive. There is, no doubt, always a pressure at the moment of conflict to repair the damage as quickly as possible and to return to 'business as usual'. But the reliance on immediate and pragmatic responses often represents a failure to examine the more deep-seated and enduring processes which generate disorder. Consequently, these forms of crisis management only tend to work in the short term, if at all. Thus, the problem of penal pragmatism is that it often turns out not to be very practical.

In contrast to penal pragmatism, sociologists have emphasised that, just as social order is sustained through a complex process of human interaction, so order in the prison is a social and practical accomplishment (Wrong, 1994). Studies of imprisonment, however, have the distinct advantage that the prison involves a more contained and manageable object of analysis. The prison has a number of characteristics which makes it a unique social institution. As we have seen, it has been historically shaped through the key elements of space, time and labour, and these have also played a critical role in its internal control and organisation. But alongside these processes there are other factors which serve to affect the nature of order in prisons. Identifying these various processes has been a central task of the sociology of imprisonment. Many of the earlier contributors in this tradition focused primarily on the processes of subcultural formation and adjustment to imprisonment (McCleary, 1961).

51

EARLY SOCIOLOGIES OF IMPRISONMENT

The starting point of enquiry for much of the early sociological literature on imprisonment was the question of why prisons which contain
large numbers of people who are detained against their will are not
the sites of continuous hostility and conflict. Why is it the case that, in
an alien environment in which the number of prisoners at any one
time will outnumber the guards, they do not overthrow their captors?
Particularly in those situations in which guards are unarmed, or where
prisoners live in overcrowded conditions and are subject to extreme
deprivations, it might reasonably be expected that they would make
strenuous efforts to free themselves.

Among the early sociologies of imprisonment the aim was to
address these issues by analysing the changing patterns of authority
within the prison, as well as through an examination of the relation
between the prison and wider social and cultural movements (Bowker,
1977). The focus upon these changing social relations was stimulated
by the fact that imprisonment itself was undergoing some marked
changes in America during the period between 1940 and 1960, when
much of this work was being produced. These studies constituted both
a contribution to and a reflection of these developments.

The major changes which took place during this period involved
firstly a transition from authoritarian styles of management towards a
more open 'bureaucratic–lawful' system (Barak-Glantz, 1981). That is,
towards a style of management which is less reliant on the authority of
a single prison governor and operates with a more differentiated,
flexible and bureaucratic form of organisation, which is able to admin-
ister a growing number of treatment and training programmes within
an expanding prison system. This process of opening up the prison
and providing more flexible, and in many cases more liberal, regimes
was accompanied paradoxically by an increase in the number of riots
and disturbances in prisons. There were also a changes in the types of
prisoners who were entering the prison system in the 1950s and 1960s.
They became increasingly younger, and were drawn disproportionately from ethnic minority groups, and certain prisons became dominated by offenders who had strong allegiances to particular gangs
(Jacobs, 1977).

In his study of a maximum security prison in Menard, Illinois,
Donald Clemmer (1940) attempted to show that the social organisation of prison subcultures was based on the 'wishes, ambitions, drives
and habits' which inmates had acquired before entering the prison.

Clemmer claimed that despite the regular turnover of inmates there was considerable continuity in the internal culture of prison, and that this was a function of the social groupings from which the prison population was drawn. He claimed that the inmate subculture was largely 'imported', that it reflected the predominantly male, lower-class, and poorly educated nature of the prison population, and that these inmates operated an 'inmate code' which embodied the norms and values of these particular social groups. This inmate code involved an emphasis on loyalty among inmates and provided a set of guidelines about how they should ideally behave towards each other and to staff. This code of conduct, Clemmer argued, provided a degree of cohesion within the prison and, though the code was formally pro-inmate and anti-authority, it was also conducive to the securing of order. Moreover, just as prisoners developed an inmate subculture, the guards also developed an occupational culture which reflected their background and value systems and which provided a stable point of reference for the development of a system of informal controls, within which working practices could operate with some predictability and coherence.

The prison, according to Gresham Sykes (1958), is to be viewed as a microcosm of the wider society, except that the 'threat of force lies close, beneath the surface', and also that control lies in the 'hands of the ruling few'. However, he notes that the requirements of prison labour, and the emphasis on treatment and on individual reform, place limits on the exercise of this power. As a result, rather than the custodians being omnipotent, they are engaged in a continuous struggle to maintain order. Constraints on the exercise of power are also produced by the bureaucratic nature of the system, such that its exercise needs to be based on legitimate authority and consequently must operate in accord with social norms, laws and sensibilities. In this context the use of physical force is both inappropriate and may be counterproductive. Thus, rather than rely on crude forms of coercion, prisons employ systems of rewards and punishments, although the 'rewards' that are available in the segregative world of the prison are necessarily limited.

For guards to carry out their work, Sykes argues, they require some degree of co-operation from the inmates. Evaluations of the guards' performance will be measured by the activities and attitudes of the prisoners. Guards are therefore compelled within this 'society of captives' to tolerate minor infractions and to exercise considerable discretion in the enforcement of prison rules. At the same time prisoners have an interest in maintaining some level of predictability and stability in their daily lives and in maintaining a reasonable degree of personal security.

According to Sykes, all prisoners are subject to a number of basic deprivations. These include the deprivation of liberty, the deprivation of goods and services, the deprivation of heterosexual relationships, the deprivation of autonomy and the deprivation of security. To this list could be added other deprivations, including the loss of certain rights. The 'pains of imprisonment', as he calls them, are not necessarily experienced by all prisoners in the same way. They are all to some degree negotiable, and implementing these forms of deprivation provides some of the 'sticks and carrots' available to prison authorities. Things which are taken for granted in the outside world can become perks and privileges in the prison.

Prisoners are seen to develop a system of norms and a variety of roles which are aimed at mitigating the 'pains of imprisonment'. Alongside these roles a special language or argot is developed in order to generate an effective system of communication within the inmate social system. A framework of formal and informal codes develops, which not only provides a philosophy for doing time, but also establishes patterns of interaction and stabilises staff–inmate relations.

One of the dominant themes in the early sociologies of imprisonment was the relationship between the outside culture from which prisoners were drawn and the prison subculture itself. This form of enquiry paralleled the development of subcultural theory within criminology and the growing number of studies which analysed how subcultures arise in response to collectively experienced problems and situations (Downes, 1966; Hebdidge, 1979). The process of 'prisonisation', as Clemmer called it, involves the adaption by different social groups to imprisonment. This 'importation' model challenged the 'deprivation' model, which claimed that it was the restrictive nature of imprisonment that was the dominant factor in inmate adjustment. Within the sociological literature on imprisonment these two models have been cast as competing alternative explanations, but, as Thomas (1977) has demonstrated, they are not theoretically incompatible, since it is likely that the prisoner's social and cultural background will provide the conceptual framework through which the deprivations of imprisonment will be perceived and experienced. However, there still remains some disagreement over the explanatory power of both these models, and the priority which should be accorded to each in accounting for the processes of adjustment.

Within the various contributions to the literature on the sociology of imprisonment different forms of individual and collective adaption have been identified. Although various authors place a different emphasis on different types of adaptation, most agree that modes of adaption are not static and that different individuals and groups may move between them during their period of confinement. There are considerable variations in the modes of adaptation which sociologists have identified, but they tend to boil down to three essential types.

1. *Co-operation or colonisation* In this mode of adaptation prisoners will aim to keep out of trouble and do their time with the minimum degree of conflict and stress, and with the intention of working towards their earliest release date.
2. *Withdrawal* This can take a number of different forms, including physical separation from other inmates, engaging in minimum degrees of communication, depression, or self-mutilation and suicide.
3. *Rebellion and resistance* This may involve engaging in riots or disturbances at one extreme, and forms of non-coperation at the other. The form which rebellion or resistance takes will depend upon the pressures placed on offenders, their background and experiences and the extent to which they feel that their confinement or treatment in prison is fair and just.

David Ward's and Gene Kassebaum's (1965) account of women's prisons suggested that women tend to adapt to imprisonment in significantly different ways from men. Their removal from their family and children and their greater geographical dispersal and consequent isolation often means that the experience of confinement is particularly difficult for many women. They note that the level of solidarity and loyalty which has been reported in men's prisons was less evident in the women's prisons that they studied, although they suggest that: '[the] solidarity of the male prisoner community, even in maximum security institutions, has been overestimated'. They also observe that the range and nature of roles which women adopt in prison are different from those of men in prison and that 'merchants' who traded in goods, 'politicians' who organised the interests of inmates, as well as 'toughs', were less evident in women's prisons. They conclude that the social structure of a female prison community differs from the male prison community:

The inmates of Frontera respond to the experience of imprisonment not only because they are reacting to deprivations and restrictions, but also because they have internalised, to varying degrees,
the values of delinquent sub-cultures, of prisoner codes, and of the
conventional criminality and finally they react as *women*. (Ward and
Kassebaum, 1965: 58)

Other authors examining the ways in which different groups deal with
imprisonment have argued that the growing number of black prisoners in America experience imprisonment differently from their white
counterparts. In some of the early literature it was strongly suggested
that black prisoners would be more resilient to the 'pains of imprisonment' because of their experience in the urban ghettos and because of
their greater levels of solidarity. Ghetto life is held to harden the individual, while the hostile environment of the streets is seen to make
the experience of imprisonment less painful (Irwin, 1970; Wright,
1989). The evidence to support these contentions is mixed. Taking
reports of aggressive behaviour, the propensity to self-mutilation,
depression and suicide as indicators of 'adjustment', studies have
shown inconsistent results. Some of the discrepancies in the findings
are a product of the different definitions of the key terms that have
been used, such as 'aggressive' and 'anxiety', as well the adoption of
different statistical techniques and sampling strategies. In one recent
study, which set out to test 'deprivation' and 'importation' models of
adjustment, Miles Harer and Darrell Steffensmeier (1996) found in a
survey of 58 Federal prisons that black inmates have significantly
higher rates of violent behaviour but lower levels of alcohol and drug
misconduct than white inmates. They interpret their findings as
lending support to the 'importation' model of prison adjustment.

James Jacobs (1979), examined the changing racial composition of
the American prison population during the 1970s, and found that
prison subcultures were characterised by racial polarisation and
conflict. Up until the 1960s a system of segregation by race was in
operation in American prisons. In Attica, for example, in the early
1970s, there were black sports teams, different barbers for blacks and
whites, and separate ice buckets for black and white inmates on 4 July.
Black protests against segregation and discrimination in prison was
actively proselytised by the Black Muslims, who provided the organisational and conceptual tools for challenging the existing structures of
the prison system. At Stateville penitentiary in Illinois the growing
politicisation of black prisoners under the influence of the Black

Muslims during the 1970s challenged the authority of the prison guards and the legitimacy of the prison system itself. Consequently there developed a greater solidarity among black prisoners (Jacobs, 1977). Jacobs claims that by the end of the decade race had become the most important determinant of the individual's prison experience. The greater solidarity of black inmates, according to Jacobs, served to tilt the balance of power within the prison and posed new problems of control for prison authorities, as the established individualised forms of control became increasingly difficult to mobilise. The Black Muslims rejected the notion that all prisoners should be treated the same or that prisoners should 'do their own time'. In opposition to some of the earlier sociological studies of prison subcultures, Jacobs suggests that:

> The view of prison as a primitive society governed by its own norms and inhabited by its own distinctive social types, was always somewhat exaggerated. Racial divisions are not the only changes that exist within the prisoner subculture, but in many contemporary prisons racial politics set the background against which all prisoner activities are played out. Taking race relations into account will help correct the overemphasis on the uniqueness of prisons and will lead to a fuller understanding of the prison's role as an institution of social control. No prison study of any kind can afford to overlook the fact that minorities are over-represented in the prisoner population by a factor of five, and that prison, ironically, may be the one institution in American society which blacks 'control'. (Jacobs, 1979: 24)

Thus, although the early sociologists of imprisonment had made the important observation that relations in prison are linked to wider social processes there was a tendency to emphasise the cohesion and conformity of the inmate subculture rather than to identify divisions and antagonisms. At the same time they provided an overly rational conception of inmate adjustment, which made critical appraisal of prison subcultures difficult to formulate. The emphasis upon the authenticity of adaptions, the rationality and the functional role of subcultures left little room for critical comment. This was 'zookeeper' sociology with a vengeance: many sociologists were content to describe and admire their subjects (Gouldner, 1968; Young, 1970).

These descriptions of subcultural adaption, as Ward and Kassebaum (1965) noted, tended to overestimate the level of inmate solidarity, while presenting men's prisons as the norm. The exaggerated levels of solidarity painted a picture of the prison population as a homogenous group and the social system in prison as being in a stable state of equilibrium. From this functionalist perspective, the processes of conflict and change within the prison system became difficult to explain, as did the growing number of riots and disturbances which occurred throughout the 1970s. The increasing politicisation and polarisation in prison, as well as the growing emphasis upon prisoner rights in the 1970s and 1980s, shifted attention away from the examination of prisoner subcultures and modes of adaptation to the more general issues of discipline and control.

Stanley Cohen and Laurie Taylor (1972) have argued that in the early sociological accounts of adjustment to imprisonment routine forms of resistance engaged in by prisoners are played down in favour of an undue stress on the passivity and adaptability of inmates. Resistance, they argue, can take a number of forms: self-protection, campaigning, escaping, striking and confronting. They also argue that forms of adaption will be dependent on prisoners' ongoing links with the outside world, as well as on the social class and background of offenders. They quote Bettelheim's (1960) study of concentration camps, in which he showed that political prisoners managed to endure the camps much better than non-political middle-class groups, who were unable to cope with the shock of incarceration. Upper middle-class prisoners, on the other hand, who segregated themselves from the rest of the prison population, were unable to accept what was happening being convinced that they would soon be released because of their importance.

John DiIulio (1987) has argued that the level of abstraction at which many of these early sociological accounts were pitched meant that they were not very informative about the precise mechanisms by which riots and disorder might occur in prisons. His rejection of these sociological approaches, however, does not lead him to argue for a more sophisticated form of theorisation. Like other 'right realists', he is sceptical of the analysis of 'deep structures' and prefers a more pragmatic approach, focusing on the more immediate situational factors which may lead up to breakdown of control. In this way he aims to promote more effective forms of managerialism and to represent a growing body of criminologists, practitioners and policy-makers who have little time for theorising, and have instead gravitated towards more administrative and technical responses (Currie, 1998; Feeley and Simon, 1992; Matthews and Young, 1992). However, it has been suggested that this managerialist approach is of limited utility and is far less 'realistic' than its advocates claim. A more productive approach to the problem of social order in prisons is provided by a number of more recent sociological contributions that have turned their attention to the analysis of 'total institutions', bureaucracies and power.

TOTAL INSTITUTIONS, BUREAUCRACY AND POWER

Alongside the literature on prison subcultures and forms of adaption to imprisonment, there is another strand of sociological theorising that has focused on the prison as a particular type of state-regulated bureaucratic institution. This body of literature, which became increasingly influential in the 1970s, was generally more critical and reflexive than the earlier writings. The investigation into the bureaucratic nature of the modern prison has led in turn towards a more detailed consideration of the nature of power relations operating both inside and outside the prison.

Gresham Sykes (1958) pointed out, in *The Society of Captives*, that: 'The prison is not an autonomous system of power, rather it is an instrument of the State, shaped by its social environment, and we must keep this simple truth in mind if we are to understand the prison'. Sykes, however, failed to develop this insight fully although he was clearly more aware than most that the prison, along with the school, the asylum and the hospital, represented a new type of state institution which had its origins in the nineteenth century.

According to Max Weber (1948), the growing division of labour and the increasing differentiation of tasks in modern society called for a new type of bureaucratic institution that could handle complex tasks in a rational and co-ordinated way. The perceived advantage of this type of organisation lay in its capacity to carry out a range of tasks in a way which was impersonal, but nevertheless subject to legal controls and public scrutiny. The degree of legitimation the prison commands will affect the ways in which control is exercised in prisons and how it is responded to by prisoners. Power can be seen to be legitimate to the extent that: (1) it conforms to established rules; (2) the rules can be justified with reference to beliefs shared by both the dominant and subordinate parties; and (3) there is evidence of consent by the subordinate party to the particular power relation (Beetham, 1991). Thus the legitimacy of the prison may be called into question either by

changes in the nature of wider social political and economic developments or by the failure of prisons to adhere to established rules and
procedures. Thus:

> [E]very instance of brutality in prisons, every casual racist joke
> and demeaning remark, every ignored petition, every unwar-
> ranted bureaucratic delay, every inedible meal, every arbitrary
> decision to segregate and transfer without giving clear and well
> founded reasons, every petty miscarriage of justice, every futile
> and inactive period of time is delegitimising. (Sparks and Bottoms,
> 1995: 607)

Although Weber saw the development of bureaucracies as inevitable
because of their technical superiority over other forms of organisation, he was highly sceptical of this impersonal form of organisation,
since he believed that the discipline of bureaucracy would eventually
encroach into every sphere of life. Indeed, it was the administrative
and organisational techniques that were developed in bureaucratic
institutions like the prison which later spread into the private sector.
Thus it was not the organisation of the prison that was in this sense
derived from the factory, but rather it was the factory which came to
adopt the bureaucratic and administrative strategies that were originally 'perfected' in state institutions (Clegg, 1990; Melossi and
Pavarini, 1981).

The defining characteristics of modern bureaucracies, according to
Weber (1948), are that they are impersonal, rule-governed organisations with a hierarchical command which allows: 'precision, speed,
unambiguity, knowledge of the files, continuity, discretion, unity, strict
subordination, reduction of friction and of material and personal
costs; these are raised to the optimum point in the strictly bureaucratic administration and especially in its monocratic form'. These
characteristics are embodied in the modern prison in its hierarchical
organisation, separation of tasks, rules and procedures, impersonal-
ity, development of surveillance techniques and systematic gathering
of information on prisoners. But the question which was raised by
Blau and Scott (1963) is: who benefits from the operation of these
bureaucratic institutions? They suggest that there are basically four
possible beneficiaries: the owners and managers; the employers in the
organisation; the clients, customers or inmates within the organisation; or the general public. An assessment of the benefits and effectiveness of a bureaucratic institution like the prison needs to consider

these options. Correspondingly, when asked the question, 'Does Prison Work?', the answer must necessarily be: 'Work for Whom?'

Other writers have questioned the presumed efficiency and effectiveness of bureaucracies. Robert Merton (1957), for example, demonstrated how executive pressure for reliability and predictability in the actions of organisational members can lead to formalisation and standardisation. In a similar vein, Alvin Gouldner (1954) pointed out that the rules which are supposed to guide bureaucratic decision-making always have to be interpreted and implemented by members of the organisation if they are to have any meaning. In doing so, he made an important distinction between the issuing of rules and their enactment, and by implication between formal and informal rule-following processes.

One powerful example of the ways in which bureaucracies can work in one particular, albeit extreme, context involving mass confinement is provided by Zygmunt Bauman (1989) in his analysis of the Holocaust. Bauman argues that the Holocaust and the atrocities which were carried out in concentration camps were not just a consequence of the activities of a few psychopathic Nazis, but were made possible by a developed bureaucracy and its associated forms of rationalisation. Behind every camp commander was a body of bureaucrats gathering information, collating files and making decisions. It was the breakdown of the overall process into a multiplicity of discrete tasks that created a form of 'moral blindness', such that the outcome was not attributable to any specific agent, as all agents could rationalise their specific contribution. If the SS strategy had relied on direct force, it would have required more troops and more time, involved more expense and might well have generated more resistance. It was, however, the collection of detailed information, the production of incentives and disincentives, the formulation of systems of classification and prioritisation, as well as the forging of co-operation with the Jewish organisations themselves, which made the Holocaust possible.

Thus, in many respects, the Holocaust represents the 'dark side' of modernity, but it is not an irrational aberration or deviation. It was, Bauman suggests, disturbingly 'normal':

Considered as a complex purposeful operation, the Holocaust may serve as a paradigm of modern bureaucratic rationality. Almost everything was done to achieve maximum results with minimum costs and efforts. Almost everything (within the realm of the possible) was done to display the skills and resources of everybody involved, including those who were to become the victims of the successful operation. Almost all the pressures irrelevant or adversary to the purpose of the operation were neutralised or put out of action altogether. Indeed, the story of the organisation of the Holocaust could be made into a textbook of scientific management. Were it not for the moral and political condemnation of its purpose imposed on the world by the military defeat of its perpetrators it would have been made into a textbook. There would be no shortage of distinguished scholars vying to research and generalise its experience for the benefit of an advanced organisation of human affairs. (Bauman, 1989: 149–50)

The suggestion that rationalised bureaucratic organisations have a propensity to produce undesirable and unanticipated effects was imaginatively developed by Erving Goffman (1968), in his classic account of 'total institutions' such as the asylum and the prison. Goffman defined a 'total institution' as a 'social hybrid, part residential community, part formal organisation'. These institutions he describes as: 'forcing houses for changing persons, each is a rational experiment in what can be done to the self.' Within those institutions which claim that their objective is to rehabilitate or cure individuals, the actual effects of institutionalisation is more likely to result in debilitation and to produce what he calls the 'mortification of the self'.

Goffman argues that the specific effects of confinement in these establishments derives from the separation of work and home, the distance between inmates and staff, limited opportunities and restricted communication, combined with a lack of personal security. On entering the total institution inmates are stripped of their familiar social and cultural supports, around which their personal identity had previously been centred. The implication of this process is that any programme of rehabilitation within prisons must first overcome these negative and debilitating process. Within this 'egalitarian community of fate', as he calls it, a fundamental revaluation of the self and others takes place which provides a basis for solidarity, sympathy and support between inmates. In this situation the criteria by which inmates judge each other may have less to do with the offences they have committed and more to do with the personal qualities of each individual. At the same time the forms of protection which might have been available in the outside world are increasingly absent within the total institution, and the prisoner may experience new forms of vulnerability and victimisation.

However, Goffman's powerful analysis failed to differentiate clearly between different 'total institutions' and the different dynamics that operated in each. Clearly there are marked differences between the processes of degradation and adaptation in prison and those in mental institutions. Moreover, it was precisely at the point when prisons were becoming less 'total' and were beginning to become open that Goffman's writings began to circulate. The important implication of Goffman's analysis is that the newly-developed inmate 'self' will be constructed through interaction with other people in prison and by engaging in the daily rituals which operate in these institutions. However, on leaving the prison, ex-prisoners are likely to revert to their previous selves in as much as they engage with the same significant others and become involved in the same type of activities that occupied their time before they entered prison. These transformations of the 'self' may go some way to explain the apparent paradox that the behaviour and attitudes of people in prison is a poor predictor of their post-prison attitudes and activities (Ditchfield, 1990).

The difficulty of achieving the rehabilitation of offenders within the confines of the prison was advanced by Norval Morris (1974), who questioned the means by which the reform of individuals was being attempted in different prisons. Morris's critique was both theoretical and practical. On the theoretical level he challenged the 'medical model' that was circulating in the penal sphere at that time, which considered rehabilitation in terms of 'curing' offenders. On the practical level, he was critical of many of the methods being used, such as tranquillising drugs and behaviour modification techniques. In general, he argued that you cannot effectively rehabilitate people by force, and that within the confines of the prison it was necessary to move away form what he called 'coercive cure' towards 'facilitated change'. That is, rehabilitation programmes should be made available and inmates should be made aware of the possible benefits of engaging in these programmes, but participation should, as far as possible, be voluntary and should not be linked to incentives such as early release.

Although Morris's contribution almost certainly encouraged greater accountability in relation to the use of certain forms of treatment in prisons, there remains an unresolved tension in his critique. If it is the case that the medical model is badly flawed, and the very notion that prisons can serve rehabilitative purposes constitutes what David Rothman (1973) calls 'the noble lie', then it is difficult to see why Morris would endorse prisoners engaging in rehabilitative programmes at all – even on a voluntary basis. Thus what appears at first sight to be a 'liberal' and humanistic critique of the use of unwarranted forms of 'treatment' in prisons and of employing illegitimate means to achieve certain ends, turns out to be a thinly veiled anti-humanism which questions the possibility and desirability of offering rehabilitation programmes in prisons at all (Cullen and Gilbert, 1982; Rotman, 1990). The dilemma is that offenders are unlikely to have a spontaneous interest in engaging in rehabilitative programmes which aim to reduce their propensity to offend, unless they are given incentives to do so. At the same time the state and the general public have a vested interest in prisoners leaving prison no more of a social burden than they went in. Reducing the period of time served is one of an array of incentives prison authorities regularly use to encourage or persuade prisoners to engage in the available rehabilitative programmes and co-operate in other ways. By posing these available options in terms of a strict duality of coercion or consent, Morris creates a dichotomy which is neither theoretically tenable nor practically applicable. There is clearly a considerable array of options which lie between the extremes of coercion and consent.

The prospect of going beyond the identification of control strategies, either within the crude oppositions of coercion and consent or as deliberate conscious strategies, has been opened up by Michel Foucault (1977) in his analysis of power. It was Foucault's consideration of space and time in relation to the development of the modern prison that, as we have seen, played a critical role in the development of his analysis of power. Like Goffman, Foucault is interested in the ways in which power relations in society become crystallised in its institutions – particularly state institutions – and, how once having taken shape, institutions act back upon society and the populations they were designed to regulate. Thus in his analysis of prisons, hospitals and asylums, he traces out how different institutional structures emerge and how they then come to define, differentiate and even create 'individuals'.

Foucault's approach is similar to Weber's in a number of ways. Like Weber (1948), Foucault examines in detail how bureaucratic and administrative processes operate within these segregative institutions and how they sustain order and secure compliance. Foucault also focuses on the way in which a bureaucratic institution can become an 'iron cage' which eventually constrains its creators. A further feature of Foucault's approach which draws on the work of Weber is his examination of the processes by which bureaucracies dominate through the gathering of information, the development of surveillance techniques and the formulation of specific knowledge(s). Foucault (1982) is also interested in the process of rationalisation but, unlike Weber, he argues that the aim of investigation should be the analysis of specific rationalities as applied to madness, medicine, sexuality or crime, rather than rationalisation in general.

In analysing the process through which order and discipline is routinely achieved in prison, Foucault is drawn into a wider examination of power. Although the analysis of power that he develops in *Discipline and Punish* was later modified and subjected to a degree of self-criticism, the conceptual schema he presents and the processes he identifies provide an invaluable starting point for understanding the dynamics of control within segregative institutions (Foucault, 1979; 1982). In opposition to those accounts which see power as something 'possessed' by one group and directed at others who are 'powerless', Foucault argues that, even within settings such as the prison, power is not a thing which is possessed, but a strategy whose effects are realised through a network of relations and tactics. This network is in a constant state of tension, since its effects are never certain and the exercise of power is always subject to the possibility of resistance. For Foucault, then, power is always 'in play' and even prisoners and captives are 'inside' power relations. In the same way as Gresham Sykes (1958) identifies order in prisons as the product of a process of negotiation between staff and inmates, Foucault sees guards and prisoners in a power relation which is mutually defining and constraining. This does not mean that these power relations are symmetrical, but that it is never a zero-sum game.

The analysis of these power relations, Foucault came to realise, is central not only to any appreciation of how order is achieved and maintained in prison, but also to an understanding of the role of the prison in wider society. The exercise of disciplinary power since the end of the eighteenth century, he argues, has been concerned with reforming, educating and moulding individuals. These strategies, however, have not necessarily made individuals more obedient. Rather, they have sought to construct a better invigilitated process of adjustment (Dreyfus and Rabinow, 1982).

What is important about Foucault's analysis of power is that it operates on a number of levels and aims to link micro and macro processes. At one level he analyses the changing power relations in society in general, involving the control of groups and populations. At another level he examines how the pursuit of order in institutions is

Doing Time

bound up with the detailed regulation of the body. Taking the body as the target of power and discipline, Foucault argues that, unlike previous forms of sovereign power which aimed at the mutilation of the body, modern 'disciplinary power' is productive, in that it aims to train and discipline the body in order to prepare it to carry out tasks, increase its capacities and improve its efficiency.

The exercise of power, then, is not simply to control in the sense of repression, but rather seeks to objectify and differentiate subjects. Disciplinary power aims to create subjects by making them the specific focus of intervention, and seeks to differentiate them through the formulation of systems of classification, thus providing a foundation for the construction of their 'individuality' as subjects in their own right. Power also creates Truth. Truth is not a pre-given entity, waiting to be discovered, but a product of political processes and power relations that create a series of rules – legal, scientific and conventional – according to which we distinguish the true from the false.

Foucault also claims that power can be 'intentional but not subjective'. By this he means that all power strategies have aims and objectives but the subjects who display them may be interchangeable. That is, control strategies which are exercised in prison may be a function of the structural and situational relations between prisoners and guards, and these strategies or tasks will remain in place even when the personnel concerned change. In developing this approach, Foucault is not offering a theory of power, but what he calls an '*analytics*' of power. It is a grid or a conceptual matrix designed to analyse the subject of power in ways which arguably takes us beyond conventional ways of thinking about this issue. He also offers some suggestions about how we might go about analysing power relations in institutions such as the prison, and even in different types of prison (Foucault, 1982). Having mapped out a conceptual field, it is possible to begin to interpret power relations through detailed empirical investigation, taking moments of conflict and resistance as a point of departure, since all power relationships involve at least a potential for antagonism and resistance. The aim is to identify the strategies and tactics in play, locate their position and their genesis, find out their point of application and analyse their effects. Specifically, there is a need to examine the different economic and social positions of those concerned, the types of objective being pursued, the means of bringing the power relations into effect, the forms of intervention and how they are bound by external rules or laws, and finally the forms of rationalisation involved.

In this way the asymmetrical nature of power relations can be analysed in relation to their actual material functioning, and we can thereby overcome the illusion that power is 'held' by some and not by others, or that power is only applied by those 'at the top' to those 'at the bottom'. In the prison both the guardians and the prisoners are located within the same concrete field of power relations, and both are tied in principal to the formal objectives of the institution and bound by the laws and rules which operate within it.

Since the publication of *Discipline and Punish*, it is impossible to see the operation of prison in the same way or to conceptualise the issues of power and control as before. Foucault, however, has not been without his critics, and his analytics of power has been criticised for underestimating the role of coercion in underpinning and structuring power relations (Dews, 1979); for not developing an adequate analysis of the state (Rose and Miller, 1992); for neglecting the gendered character of disciplinary techniques (McNay, 1992); and for his implicit functionalism (Poulantzas, 1978). Most of these critiques have, however, sought to refine rather than to reject Foucault's analysis of power, and in general they recognise that Foucault's analysis is the most suggestive and provocative account available.

Drawing on Foucault's work and subsequent critical commentary, as well as the insights from the literature on the sociology of imprisonment, it is possible to begin to construct a composite picture of the diverse processes through which order is maintained in prisons. Some of these processes, as we have seen, are linked to a wider set of power relations, and are tied to issues of legitimacy – not only of the prison itself, but also of the wider political processes. Within the prison we can distinguish between the operation of direct and indirect control strategies. Indirect control strategies involve the use and distribution of space and time and the deployment of work and other activities involving the differentiation and organisation of prisoners. It is these forms of control, which are built into the very structure and organisation of the prison, that are most pervasive and, although they are in many respects hidden, they remain central to the construction of order.

It is in relation to these indirect forms of control that we should consider the effects of overcrowding in prison. From a control perspective, overcrowding undermines the established spatial and temporal structures of control within the prison by interfering with the distribution of bodies and the organisation of activities. Overcrowding has a domino effect in that it has a propensity to upset routines, to create bottlenecks, and to reduce the flexibility of decision-making. The combined effect of these impediments is to render some of the more pervasive but less visible forms of control inoperable. The degree of bureaucracy and styles of administration which operate in this context will also have an effect on control strategies, through the separation and ordering of tasks, the degree of impersonal rule-following behaviour and the ways in which formal and informal rules are interpreted and implemented.

Direct control strategies can be seen to operate in relation to two related oppositions: incentives and disincentives; privileges and punishments. These oppositions, although overlapping, are not identical. Systems of incentives and disincentives tend to be more informal and discretionary and involve, for example, decisions regarding the allocation of work or lengths of visits. Privileges and punishments, on the other hand, involve a more formalised set of options, such as the granting of early release or the imposition of disciplinary procedures.

The recurring questions which have been raised by sociologists and policy-makers are how these different control strategies relate to each other and how they link to different models of adaption for different populations. One method of addressing this question is to construct a matrix with control strategies on one axis and different types of prison, or prison regime, on the other (see Cohen and Taylor, 1972; Sparks *et al.*, 1996). Typologies of this kind are based on the underlying assumption that forms of adaptation within prisons are structured and patterned and that this patterning is a function of different prison regimes. It is also assumed that there tends to be an 'elective affinity' between different types of regime and the control strategies which they are most likely to adopt. Thus more authoritarian regimes are normally associated with a greater reliance on physical security, rigid adherence to timetables, and extensive use of internal disciplinary procedures, including the use of segregation and isolation of 'difficult' prisoners. At the other extreme those prisons which involve a considerable degree of self-management rely on forms of dynamic security, shaming and forms of collective responsibility. The clustering of these various elements in different types of prison raises the further question of whether particular regimes and their associated strategies of control are more likely to encourage particular forms of adaption and discourage others.

It is possible to explore these questions by taking two modes of adaption, or rather maladaptation – suicide and riots – and examining the extent to which they are likely to occur in particular types of prison employing particular control strategies. These issues have practical as well as theoretical significance and consequently they are of interest to a number of prison reform groups and prison administrators. Taking Foucault's suggestion that a useful point of departure in analysing power relations and the processes of control is through the identification of points of conflict and resistance, suicides and riots appear to be suitable starting points for investigation.

MODES OF ADAPTION TO IMPRISONMENT

Suicide

Is there any discernible pattern to the incidence of suicides in prison? Is there a relationship between the personal and social characteristics of those who commit suicide and the ways in which they experience different regimes? In answering these questions we must begin from a recognition that what appears to be the ultimate expression of individualism is, as Durkheim pointed out (1952) in his classic study of *Suicide*, a profoundly social act. People, according to Durkheim, attempt or commit suicide because the social conditions in which they live and when the social relationships in which they are enmeshed become 'anomic'.

Various sociologists following Durkheim have, however, pointed to the methodological difficulties in identifying suicides and attempted suicides both in society in general and in prisons in particular (Liebling and Ward, 1994). A distinction is made in the official literature, for example, between suicides and 'probable' suicides, which include those cases in which suicide seemed on inspection to be the likely cause of death but which might have been recorded by the coroner as 'accidental death' (Home Office, 1984). Bearing these definitional problems in mind, there does appear to be some forms of patterning, since suicide is more common per capita among the male population (although self-injury appears more prevalent per capita among the female population) and among those under 21 years of age, while it tends to occur early in the sentence and is more prevalent among remand prisoners living in poor conditions. Interestingly, the type of offence or length of sentence has not been found to have a significant effect on the incidence of suicide. There is, however, a tendency to attempt to explain the incidence of suicide in prison as a function of the mental instability of some prisoners with histories of psychiatric disorder. The Report of the Working Party on Suicide in Prison (Home Office, 1986), for example, concluded that suicide was more prevalent in the remand population because there was a 'higher proportion of prisoners exhibiting factors known to be associated with suicide risks such as mental disorder'. But even in those cases where a clear link between mental disorder and suicide can be demonstrated, this would account for only about 30 per cent of the suicides which occur in prison. As Alison Liebling (1992) has shown, those committing suicide in prison are less likely to have a history of psychiatric disorder than those committing suicide among the general population. Whereas some 90 per cent of the recorded suicides in the community have a history of psychiatric disorder, only a third of those who commit suicide in prison have similar histories.

The tendency to 'explain' suicides in prison in purely individualistic terms means much less attention has been paid to the effects of regime factors or the role of control strategies. One consequence of these predominantly psychological accounts of suicides in prison is that forms of prediction based on them have been relatively unsuccessful (Lloyd, 1990). At the same time, one unfortunate consequence of the limited ability to identify the patterning and processes leading to suicide has been a steady increase in the number of recorded suicides in prison in England and Wales, rising from 21 in 1986 to 64 in 1996 (Prison Reform Trust, 1997).

The research which has considered regime factors has pointed mainly to the nature of depersonalisation in prison, the range of available activities and the degree of social stimulus. Regimes which are smaller and which allow regular contacts with family, friends and members of the community all seem to be less likely to have a high incidence of suicide. There is evidence of an 'isolation effect', both physical and social, which appears to be related to suicide. Strangely, however, the isolation or transfer of prisoners deemed 'at risk' of suicide are among the main strategies to have been adopted by prison authorities (Home Office, 1986). Research on suicides among young prisoners has found that they tend to cluster in particular institutions, and involve the more vulnerable sections of the prison population. Many of those who have attempted suicide have reported that they had been provoked by threats, teasing or bullying (Liebling, 1992). Typically, those most likely to attempt suicide are those who are physically and socially isolated in prisons with few activities and with little contact with home and family.

The reluctance in the past to address these social, institutional and regime factors can be seen as the result of the adoption of a number of 'techniques of neutralisation' among prison administrators by which they distance themselves from these acts and minimise responsibility (Sykes and Matza, 1957). These 'techniques' have taken the following form:

1. denying the role of incarceration by focusing predominantly on the biological and psychological backgrounds of those concerned;
2. denying the 'rationality' of suicide or attempted suicide, thus keeping the 'rationality' of the institution intact;
3. claiming that the suicide or self-injury was merely a manipulative strategy aimed at drawing attention or gaining advantage;
4. 'blaming the victim' by claiming that the suicide occurred because the person did not know how to cope or respond;
5. refusing to discuss the problem openly, with an emphasis upon secrecy and security in order not to promote the idea among the prison population in general;
6. presenting suicides as random and impulsive events with no discernible pattern; and
7. claiming that suicides are the outcome of a number of factors and there are no identifiable causes.

These rationales for distancing the problem, outlined by Simon Page in his study of suicide and self-injury in Armley Prison (1993), could be extended. His analysis demonstrates the ways in which these discourses have provided an obstacle to a fuller understanding of the causes and processes which promote suicides in prison. As Stephen Tumim points out in his report for the Prisons Inspectorate on *Suicide and Self-Harm in Prison Service Establishments in England and Wales*:

Current Prison Department policy fails to communicate the social dimensions of self-harm and self-inflicted death. It does not stress sufficiently the significance of the environment in which the prisoners and staff are expected to live and work, or the importance of constructive activities in helping inmates to cope with anxiety and stress. Above all, it fails to give weight to the need to sustain people during their time in custody, the importance of relationships between inmates and between staff and inmates in providing that support. The danger of targeting suicide prevention as primarily a medical problem is that the Service may have become conditioned to the view that all the answers lie with the doctors. This is not the case. (Home Office, 1990b)

Despite Stephen Tumim's pronouncements, suicide is still seen predominantly in medical and individualistic terms. This may in part be because taking his recommendations seriously would necessarily involve a major reorganisation of the prison system and a fundamental review of its control strategies.

Riots and Disturbances

It is necessary at the outset to make a conceptual distinction between riots, disturbances and violent incidents in prison: whereas riots and disturbances are collective actions, violent incidents involve individuals. The level of violent incidents in prison is disturbing. As Table 3.1 shows, in any one year there is an enormous number of incidents of different levels of violence and hostility. Although these individual and collective actions are not totally unrelated, it is the case that there is no necessary or direct relation between these two levels. Riots and disturbances may also be differentiated from each other in that, though both riots and disturbances involve collective protests, riots involve the attempt to take command over certain areas of the prison through the use or threat of force. A disturbance, therefore, may involve a collective protest over conditions, in which prisoners refuse to eat the food or decide to stop work, whereas a riot will typically involve the attempt to capture and control space. These distinctions are important, although there may well be an overlap both strategically and organisationally between disturbances and riots.

There has been a long history of riots and disturbances in prison, but since the 1950s in America and the 1960s in Britain they have become much more prevalent. In his review of riots in Britain and the USA, Robert Adams (1992) has usefully periodised the recent history of riots in both countries. In the immediate post-war period, although prisons were run in a generally authoritarian manner, with a personalised and centralised system of command and general polarisation of guards and prisoners, there was little room for riots and other forms of conflict. Paradoxically, it was during the 1950s and 1960s, when prisons were becoming more open and more facilities and programmes were being made available, that the number of riots increased, many of which were centred around a growing dissatisfac-

Table 3.1   Reported incidents in prisons in England and Wales, 1995–7

Incident	1995	1996	1997
Absconds	976	1142	1120
Assaults	3453	3588	4265
Attempted suicides	773	902	214
Attempted escape from escorts	81	81	152
Attempted escapes	117	97	90
Barricades	16	66	126
Bomb explosions/threats	20	38	28
Concerted indisciples	93	75	85
Death of an inmate	67	56	109
Dirty protests	39	45	12
Drugs	9541	7995	6835
Escapes	43	28	23
Escapes from escorts	80	109	113
Fires	649	506	599
Food refusals	403	189	222
Hostage incidents	10	9	17
Key/lock compromises	50	58	70
Miscellaneous incidents	641	1268	1085
Recapture/surrender	1639	1403	587
Rooftop protests	20	12	19
Suicides	60	64	68
Tool/Implement loss	258	142	153
Temporary release failures	234	432	567

Source: HM Prison Service.

tion with prison conditions. From the end of the 1960s through to the end of the 1970s, during what has been referred to as the post-rehabilitation era, riots and disturbances became more frequently associated with demands for rights and took a more political charac-ter. These riots raised issues of legitimacy and treatment in prisons. Riots in Folson and Attica prisons, in 1970 and 1971 respectively, were among the most violent in American penal history. The Attica prison riot, which left 43 men dead and more than 80 wounded, was seen as the result of a combination of poor conditions, understaffing, a sense of injustices and the brutal methods adopted by the guards to deal with the rioting prisoners. In the UK the riot in Albany prison in 1972 was widely seen as a turning point, since it involved a level of violence not previously seen in British prisons. The decline of the rehabilitative ideal was marked by a series of 'crises' and the increasing polarisation of staff–inmate relations. In the recent period riots appear to have become more diverse in their location and in the populations involved, although their frequency has continued to increase (see Figure 3.1). In many cases riots themselves do not have clearly articulated objectives but may be a way of drawing attention to, or halting, certain practices within the prison. Alternatively, they may be aimed at undefined 'improvements', although these may not be clearly identified at the time. This does not necessarily make them any less rational or purposeful activities.

In many respects the 'techniques of neutralisation' adopted in official discourse in relation to suicide up to the end of the 1980s have been paralleled by the official views on the nature and significance of riots in prison. These take the following form:

1. a denial of the existence of prison 'riots' and a willingness to acknowledge only 'disturbances';
2. claims that there is no pattern to these disturbances and that they are random, spontaneous or contingent events;
3. claims that all riots and disturbances over the past few decades have been resolved without any major damage occurring;
4. the assertion that riots and disturbances are isolated incidents and are limited to certain parts of the prison system;
5. the repeated claim that riots and disturbances are the outcome of the activities of a few trouble-makers or a particular 'toxic mix' of prisoners'; and
6. claims that riots and disturbances occur mainly as a result of overcrowding or a lapse in security, or both.

Events during the 1980s and 1990s rendered these 'techniques of neutralisation' largely redundant. The growing incidence of riots in different types of prisons, including those without overcrowding and even newly built prisons, revealed the transparency of these official explanations. The apparent limitations and increasing costs involved in adopting 'get tough' policies has prompted an exploration of different types of regime, particularly those in which prisoners take more responsibility for their actions an engage in forms of self-regulation. Two notable examples of this development are the Barlinnie Special Unit in Glasgow and the Maze Prison in Northern Ireland.

In 1973 a small number of the most disturbed, disruptive and violent offenders in Scotland were decanted into a Special Unit in

Figure 3.1   Riots and disturbances in prison in England and Wales, 1985–97

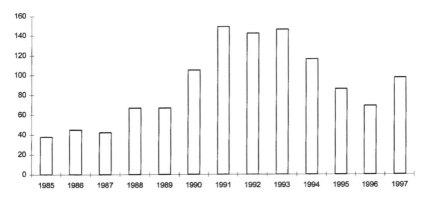

Source: HM Prisons Department.

Barlinnie Prison. The unit was run as a 'therapeutic community', in which prisoners participated in decision-making and were responsible for their own behaviour and for that of their peers. Prisoners who did not co-operate could be transferred by the community meeting of staff and inmates to other prisons. Prisoners were given some extra privileges and greater responsibility for the internal day-to-day running of the unit (Whatmore, 1987). Between 1973 and 1989 only two assaults and seven serious incidents occurred. This extremely low level of interpersonal violence has been attributed to the features of the regime, and particularly to the quality of staff–prisoner communication (Cooke, 1989). Despite this success, the Barlinnie Special Unit was closed down in 1996, following a report which, while noting the merit of prisoners taking more responsibility for their actions and being more directly involved in collective forms of decision-making, suggested that in this case 'liberalism had been taken too far', and objected to what was seen as a lack of 'physical and mental stimulus' in the unit (Scottish Office, 1993).

Equally remarkable developments have taken place in the Maze Prison in Northern Ireland in relation to forms of control and management. In a prison in which the majority of the population are political prisoners, and in which prisoners are segregated according to paramilitary allegiances, each section has its own command structure through which the authorities regulate and manage the prison. In each of the segregated wings prisoners have a large degree of autonomy and exercise considerable control over the internal running of the prison.

During the late 1970s and early 1980s the political status of the prisoners was denied and they were treated like ordinary criminals. In response to this strategy of 'criminalisation' prisoners engaged in various forms of resistance, including hunger strikes and the 'dirty protests'. As a result of these actions the existing power relations in the prison were called into question. Subsequently, a strategy of 'normalisation' was introduced, whereby the political status of paramilitary prisoners was recognised, and they were allowed a considerable degree of self-regulation, and were held collectively responsible for their actions. This more flexible system of control, which involves a reduction of petty restrictions and conflicts and allows political prisoners a range of concessions, has fostered a considerable degree of co-operation with 'the enemy'.

An extraordinary feature of this process of 'normalisation' is that prisoners are allowed to have five days home leave over Christmas and two weeks in the summer. This means that hundreds of 'prisoners of war', with a formal duty to escape, voluntarily walk out of the prison and walk back, twice a year. As strange as this strategy appears at first sight, it provides a convenient point of collaboration between supposed opponents, since:

> This scheme relies of course on the discipline of paramilitary prisoners. They will return, for a failure to do so would deny the privilege to their comrades. There is some anecdotal evidence that some paramilitary organisations actually police the return of their own prisoners. It is recognised by the organisations that a breach by a paramilitary prisoner of release conditions could jeopardise the whole system. For the same reason they are unlikely to engage in any obvious illegality. It is a scheme which offers obvious benefits to prisoners and their families and to prison authorities in terms of happier prisoners and an important privilege unlikely to be put at risk by violent protest. (Gormally, McEvoy and Wall, 1993: 103)

As in the case of Barlinnie, forms of self-regulation provide more flexible forms of control, and allow greater autonomy, increased responsibility and improved staff–inmate relations. These arrangements appear to have worked to reduce the levels of violence and conflict in both these settings.

It was, however, not until the eruption in Strangeways Prison in Manchester in 1990 that a major re-examination of the possible causes and conditions that might lead to riot in prisons occurred. The Woolf Report (1991) provided one of the most comprehensive reviews of this issue which has ever been carried out in Britain. It examined the causes, conditions and the processes which led up to the riot in Manchester, and concluded that, if riots were to be avoided, there needed to be a proper balance between 'security, control and justice' within prisons, although it emphasised the primacy of control and made it clear that the delivery of 'justice' was dependant upon the maintenance of an adequate level of security. Lord Justice Woolf made a number of recommendations, including the improvement of conditions, the creation of smaller and more local 'community prisons', a revised judicial process in prison and the formulation of 'contracts' for each prisoner, setting out expectations and responsibilities.

The recommendations of the Woolf Report have as yet only been partly acted upon, while the number of riots in prisons in England and Wales has continued to increase since 1991. These developments have raised the question of whether these riots could have been prevented if the recommendations of the Woolf Enquiry had been fully implemented; or alternatively, whether it was the limitations of the enquiry in terms of the way it conceptualised these processes that prevented it from being adopted (Morgan, 1991; Sim, 1994).

The precise causal processes which produce riots have as yet not been identified, and clearly mono-causal explanations are unlikely to account for the complex processes through which riots occur. At the same time multi-factor explanations in which different variables are seen to combine in apparently accidental ways are also of little explanatory value. Moreover, explanations which account for riots purely in terms of absolute deprivation and poor conditions appear to be undermined by the fact that in many cases riots appear to occur during periods in which conditions are improving. It would seem that it is often the degree of 'relative' rather than 'absolute' deprivation that is critical. In the same way, responses which simply call for more physical security, improved environmental conditions, the removal of 'troublemakers' and the like tend to conflate 'triggers' with causes, and focus predominantly on observable events rather than the underlying generative mechanisms which produce these outcomes (Pawson and Tilley, 1997). Explanations of riots, like explanations of suicide, need to begin from a recognition of the social, structural and institutional contexts in which they take place, the causal mechanisms which underpin them and the 'triggers' which set these mechanisms off.

Drawing on the examination of riots and disturbances presented in the Woolf Report (1991), Rod Morgan (1997) has formulated what he refers to as a 'disorder amplification spiral', in which the aim is to understand disorder not as an event but as the outcome of a process (see Lea and Young, 1984). Within this model the established control strategies become problematic. This can occur for a number of reasons, including problems of legitimacy, change of organisation, and a sense of worsening conditions or of unfair treatment. Once this dynamic is set in motion, it is likely to create greater polarisation between staff and inmates, a growing sense of antagonism and insecurity and a decreased level of tolerance on both sides. At this point any number of 'triggers' may serve to turn anger and frustration into a riot. This model can be expressed diagrammatically (see Figure 3.2).

Figure 3.2   Disorder amplification spiral: riots and disturbances

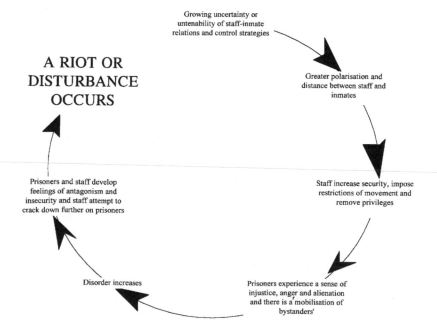

Growing uncertainty or untenability of staff-inmate relations and control strategies

A RIOT OR DISTURBANCE OCCURS

Greater polarisation and distance between staff and inmates

Prisoners and staff develop feelings of antagonism and insecurity and staff attempt to crack down further on prisoners

Staff increase security, impose restrictions of movement and remove privileges

Disorder increases

Prisoners experience a sense of injustice, anger and alienation and there is a mobilisation of bystanders'

This amplification spiral can also be applied to suicides and self-injury, although it would take a slightly different form. The major difference between the two general processes is that in the case of suicide and self-injury the untenability of control strategies produces a growing sense of anomie and insecurity among inmates, which results in stronger prisoners exercising more control over the vulnerable and weaker prisoners, rather than directing their hostilities towards the staff. In response to these developments, the staff engage in a series of interventions ranging from isolating and moving prisoners to reducing prisoner activities and visits. All these responses may encourage certain vulnerable prisoners to escape from the sense of normlessness and isolation in the only way that seems available. These two processes exemplify the ways in which a breakdown of the existing system of control may occur, and how certain dynamics can set in motion a series of self-reinforcing processes which appear to have their own momentum and logic.

CONCLUSION

Order in prisons does not arise *sui generis*. Like social order in general, it is achieved through a complex interplay of forces and a variety of control strategies which work in combination, but whose effects are never certain. We have learned from the early sociologies of imprisonment that there is an important relationship between the social and cultural backgrounds of those who enter prison, and that these backgrounds provide a framework that mediates the ways in which the deprivations, or 'pains of imprisonment', are experienced. The work of Erving Goffman (1968) and Norval Morris (1974) has sensitised us to the role of 'total institutions', the relation between ends and means and the importance of accountability. The work of Michel Foucault (1977) and Zygmunt Bauman (1989) has drawn our attention to the problems of bureaucracies and the complex and often subtle ways in which power relations operate. They both emphasise that if segregative institutions were to attempt to operate around a simple dichotomy of coercion and consent, they would have limited effectiveness, require more staff and be more expensive to run. Understanding something about the modern prison, they point out, requires a more detailed examination of the 'analytics' of power and the combination of direct and indirect, conscious and unconscious strategies through which control is exercised and order is achieved. In particular, they emphasise the ways in which forms of 'moral blindness' can be achieved through the separation of tasks in bureaucratic institutions such as the prison, with the consequence that no one appears responsible for the outcomes.

Through an examination of two modes of (mal)adaption – suicide and riots – it is evident that though disorder can take a number of forms, it is patterned. Disorder may occur as a result of a breakdown in controls, their limited acceptability or their perceived inappropriateness in certain prisons at certain times. This may involve acts of refusal and rebellion or an unwillingness to tolerate injustices or, in some cases, 'rioting for rights'. However, the experience of disorder and a breakdown of controls are not in themselves necessarily progressive or liberating, as the evidence of suicide and victimisation in prisons testifies.

Thus the official response to many of these critical issues has, in Britain at least, involved a mixture of denial and distancing, with the consequence that there has been a growing reliance on penal pragmatism. As we have seen, however, pragmatic responses are often of limited utility, mainly because they are unable to grapple with the more deep-seated and less visible causes of disorder. Sociological approaches, in contrast, offer little in the way of instant solutions, but they do serve to alert us to the various dimensions of the processes of control in prison, while sensitising us to the unanticipated consequences of bureaucracies and different types of power relations. They have also usefully drawn our attention to the wider issues of legitimacy. Finally, they have made us aware of the interplay between control and adaption in prison, and their relation to the wider network of power relations which circulate in the social, political and economic arenas.

4 Prison Profile: Data, Trends and Analysis

INTRODUCTION

Official statistics, we are continually reminded, have to be treated with extreme caution. It is often the case, however, that many of those who issue such warnings subsequently proceed to employ the data as if it were unproblematic. The dilemma is that there is a need to use official statistics because they provide an important source of information, but it is difficult to scrutinise every figure and to assess each table and graph critically. The reality is that we have to develop a critical orientation to the data that makes us continuously aware of its limitations and at the same time allows us to interpret and decode its meaning. This no easy task. Interpreting the official statistics on crime and punishment is a precarious business and even experienced criminologists fall victim to its many traps (Bottomley and Pease, 1986; Coleman and Moynihan, 1996; Levitas and Guy, 1996; Walker, 1995).

These dilemmas are compounded by the fact that even those criminologists who are rightly suspicious of the official criminal statistics tend to give more credence to prison statistics, on the basis that they are seen as being a generally more reliable form of data. Because prison statistics focus upon 'captive populations' who appear to be more clearly identifiable, they are treated as being less problematic. The reality, however, is that prison statistics both embody and compound many of the problems associated with criminal statistics, since they refer to processes which are further along the line, as it were, in the criminal justice process. Prison statistics also introduce a number of new problems which affect their general reliability.

The familiar problems associated with criminal statistics concern the relationship between the 'objectivity' of crime and the processes of reporting and recording which suggests that crimes are not simply 'events' but the product of a complex process of definition and negotiation. Criminal justice agencies play a critical role in interpreting the significance of reported incidents, and therefore the values, priorities and interests of these agencies are critical in deciding who is processed through the criminal justice system and who is diverted.

Obviously, these decisions will be conditioned by the perceived seriousness of the incident and the characteristics of particular offenders, but there is considerable latitude in the ways in which different offences and offenders are dealt with. As self-report and victimisation surveys have demonstrated, the official criminal statistics present a very selective picture of 'crime', and serve to underline substantial discrepancies between the ways in which victims and members of the general public view 'crime' and how it is ultimately represented in the criminal statistics (Jupp, 1989). The issues involved in the collection and presentation of data in the official criminal statistics reappear in the prison statistics. Although by the time offenders appear in court it might appear that the problems of definition and interpretation are largely resolved, they are in fact often intensified, while additional problems arise at the later stages of the process.

Alongside the limitations of the official statistics, there has been until relatively recently a paucity of prison research in the UK. As one Home Office researcher, writing a review of research on imprisonment in the mid-1980s, put it: 'the most significant conclusion from this review of the results of published or otherwise readily available research on adult prisons and prisoners in England and Wales since 1970 is how little there has been' (Mott, 1985). The limited nature of informative research on imprisonment has meant that we have become extremely reliant on official publications, and in particular on the annual Prison Statistics, to identify developments in both the size and composition of the prison population.

CHANGES IN THE PRISON POPULATION

Although the number of people in prison in England and Wales has increased steadily in the post-war period, from just under 20 000 in 1948 to 32 641 in 1968, rising to over 55 000 in 1996, the rate of increase has not been even over this period. It should also be noted that in certain periods the prison population has actually decreased (see Figure 4.1).

But examining the changing use of imprisonment in relation to the number of people in prison at any one time (average daily population) is only one way to look at these changes. It is also common to identify the number of people who are *sent* to prison in a given period (receptions into custody). These two forms of measurement allow us to distinguish between the *stock* and the *flow* of the prison population, and

Figure 4.1   Average daily prison population in England and Wales, 1898–1996

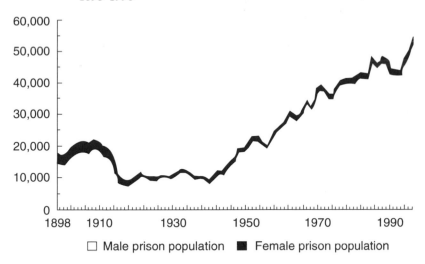

Source: Research and Statistics Directorate, Home Office.

involve differences between what some penologists prefer to call *static* and *dynamic* populations. Clearly, there is a relation between the number of receptions into custody (RIC) and the average daily population (ADP), but this relationship is not invariant, since its nature will be conditioned by the changing lengths of prison sentences and the period of incarceration actually served. For example, in 1995 some 20 000 people were sent to prison in England and Wales in default of payment of fine, but on any one day there were only approximately 1000 people imprisoned for this offence. This is because the length of sentence imposed for this offence in the vast majority of cases tends to be less than one month. Another way of looking at this relationship is that, while fine defaulters accounted for 32 per cent of receptions under sentence in 1995, they constituted 1.3 per cent of the prison population in that year. For those forms of confinement in which the period of detention is relatively short, as in the case of remand, greater attention may be directed towards the rate of admissions rather than the average daily population.

The figures showing the changing number of people sent to prison and the number of people in prison, which appear regularly in the prison statistics, digests and the general literature on imprisonment, show a steady increase over the past two or three decades. Taking these graphs at face value, much of the penological literature has been preoccupied with explaining the apparent increase in the use of the prison in the post-war period. But evaluations of the changing ADP or RIC which do not take into account changes in the size and composition of the population in the country as a whole can be misleading. Thus representations which show these developments in terms of numbers per 100 000 of the population provide a more realistic picture of change. To be even more precise, the ADP and RIC can be presented in relation to the number of 15–60 year olds in the population, since this is in effect the relevant imprisonable population.

Taking both the ADP and RIC for males and females per 100 000 of the relevant population between 1970 and 1995 produces a distinctly different picture from that which is most commonly presented. Thus, in opposition to the image of a perennially rising prison population, the reality is that the ADP was relatively stable for both male and female populations between 1970 and 1990, although there was an increase in the early 1990s. In relation to RICs, the numbers sent to prison peaked in the mid-1980s and thereafter decreased towards the end of the decade (see Figure 4.2).

The use of imprisonment for juveniles has been similarly uneven. Even if no allowance is made for population changes, the number of juveniles in custody and received into custody has not increased year on year over the past three decades. On the contrary, the number of juveniles in custody decreased steadily during the second half of the 1980s, after increasing during the 1970s (see Chapter 7). Similarly the number receiving an immediate custodial sentence increased from

Figure 4.2 Average daily population (ADP) and receptions into custody (RIC) per 100 000 relevant population, 1970–95

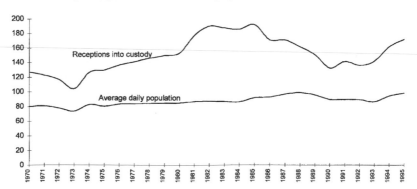

Sources: Prison Statistics 1975, 1985 and 1995 (London: HMSO), and Office of Population and Census.

6003 in 1975 to a peak of 7587 in 1981. Thereafter, the number of receptions fell gradually to 5681 in 1985 and further to 4500 in 1995 (Home Office, 1996b).

Examining the prison population in relation to the number of arrests provides another perspective from which to assess changes in the use of imprisonment. This approach has been usefully developed to demonstrate the relationship between the number of offenders who come into contact with the criminal justice system, and the numbers prosecuted and imprisoned. It shows the changes in the use of imprisonment in relation to changing inputs into the system, and is seen to provide a more 'grounded' way of assessing changing use of imprisonment (Farrington and Langan, 1992).

A review of the use of imprisonment in recent years in England and Wales from these different vantage points indicates the uneven and changing nature of prison populations. These considerations are important when assessing changes in penal policy and particularly when identifying 'watersheds' or significant changes of direction. The available evidence suggests that what may be a watershed in terms of juvenile justice, for example, may constitute a period of continuity and stability for the adult population. Needless to say, an awareness of some of these different trajectories is critical in explaining the changing nature of prison use, since the type of explanation that might accord with the developments of one sub-group might not apply very well to others (Bottoms and Preston, 1980).

SOME RECENT TRENDS

The identification of trends requires an understanding of who is sent to prison and for how long. It is also usual to distinguish between changes in the type of offenders in prison, as well as the type of offences for which people are incarcerated. The relationship between these variables will be conditioned by the length of sentence imposed in any period. Taking the available data on sentencing and imprisonment in England and Wales over the past 30 years or so, a number of trends are discernible.

Changes in the Length of Sentence Imposed

Since the beginning of the century the number of people imprisoned in England and Wales for short sentences has decreased significantly.

In 1913 over 8000 people were given prison sentences of two weeks or less. By 1948 the number given this length of sentence fell to just over 3500. Just as the use of very short sentences has declined, so the length of sentence given for more serious offences has increased. During the post-war period the number of offenders given sentences of twelve months or less has remained relatively stable, while the number given sentences of between eighteen months and five years has increased from approximately 4000 in 1948 to 5000 in 1968 and 13 000 in 1995. The number given sentences of five years or more has also risen sharply.

The tendency towards imposing longer sentences has been roughly the same for both males and females. Among adult females the proportion serving sentences of over three years doubled between 1985 and 1995. The average length of sentence, however, has been more uneven. For adult males the average length of sentence decreased slightly between 1975 and 1985, from 497 to 432 days, thereafter increasing to 549 days in 1990. Similarly, for adult females, the average length of sentences decreased from 317 days in 1976 to 287 in 1985 but by 1990 sentences for females has increased to an average of 412 days. Thus, although there have been some fluctuations in the average length of sentence handed out by the courts, particularly Crown Courts, there has been an overall increase in recent years.

Increased Proportion of Violent and Serious Offenders in Prison

A major transformation has taken place in the relationship between those imprisoned for property, drugs and violent offences. In 1985, nearly half of the male prison population was serving sentences for burglary, theft or fraud. By 1995, these offence groups accounted for only a quarter of the population. The general trend over the last decade for adult males has been an increase in the proportion serving sentences for robbery (up from 8 to 12 per cent), sexual offences (up from 6 to 12 per cent), and drug offences (up from 8 to 12 per cent).

For adult females there has also been a general increase in the proportion of prisoners serving sentences for violence, and a simultaneous decrease in the proportion serving sentences for theft and fraud. The proportion of adult females serving prison sentences for drugs offences has increased from 19 per cent in 1985 to 30 per cent in 1995. These changes are largely a function of increased sentence lengths for drugs offences, rather than the number of people sent to prison. These developments, which involve longer sentences and greater use of custody for what are deemed serious offences, coupled with a more lenient policy of non-custodial sentences for more 'minor' offences, typify a policy approach that has been described by Anthony Bottoms (1974) as a process of 'bifurcation'. This development has been particularly pronounced in recent years. It has resulted in a significant change in the composition of the prison population, with long-term prisoners coming increasingly to dominate the culture and policies of the prison system (Morgan, 1995).

An Increase in the Proportion of Ethnic Minority Prisoners

According to the 1991 census, ethnic minorities make up 5.5 per cent of the overall population, but they accounted for 16.2 per cent of the male prison population and 25.8 of the female prison population in 1994. Among ethnic minority groups those described as 'black' account for a disproportionate percentage of the ethnic minorities in prison. In 1994 black males (African, Caribbean and Other) accounted for 10.8 per cent of the male prison population, while black women accounted for 19.6 per cent of the female prison population, although the black population comprises approximately 1 per cent of the population of England and Wales. The proportion of black males in prison has increased by just over 25 per cent between 1984 and 1994, while the proportion of black female prisoners has increased by over 60 per cent over the same period (Home Office, 1994). The prison statistics also show that the level of over-representation among black men in the remand population is even greater than among sentenced prisoners (FitzGerald and Marshall, 1996).

An Increase in the Remand Population

The size and composition of the remand population is awarded particular significance by penologists because of their particular status: which derives from the fact that although they have in many cases not been convicted of a crime, and are technically innocent, they tend to be held in the most overcrowded and restrictive conditions (Faugeron, 1996; Morgan, 1994). The remand population in England and Wales increased by 20 per cent between 1985 and 1995, from 10 000 to 12 000. Among this population the numbers awaiting trial has remained fairly stable, but there has been a considerable increase in the numbers of those who have been convicted but remain unsentenced. This increase is largely a consequence of the virtual doubling of the number of receptions of convicted unsentenced prisoners between 1985 and 1995.

A Decrease in the Proportional Use of Immediate Custody

Probably the most remarkable development over the past 20 years in England and Wales has been the decrease in the use of immediate custody for those found guilty of indictable offences. This has been the case for all categories of offenders, but has been most pronounced in the case of young males between the ages of 14 and 17 years of age. Alongside the proportionate decrease in the use of custody there has been a proportionate decline in the number of offenders being convicted in the courts, which is partly a product of declining clear-up rates and a greater use of police cautions. These are among the main reasons why the increases in the prison population have been relatively modest compared to the substantial rise in crime over the past two decades.

Increased Use of Community-based Sanctions

While the proportionate use of custody has decreased generally over the past two decades, the use of community-based sentences increased by 28 per cent between 1984 and 1994. The increased use of community-based sentences has been associated predominantly with male rather than female offenders, mainly in the form of community service orders and probation orders. There has also been a considerable increase in the use of cautioning, particularly for those aged between 18 and 21, over the last decade. The fine, however, although still widely used, particularly in magistrates courts, has been deployed in a lower proportion of cases over the past few years.

Thus it is evident that, although the prison population per 100 000 of the relevant population remained relatively stable between 1970 and 1990, there have been significant changes in the composition of the prison population – both in terms of the types of offenders and in relation to the offences committed. But the prison statistics provide little in the way of social and demographic information on prisoners, and tell us little about the quality of life or social relations in prison. In 1991 the first *National Prison Survey* was carried out in England and Wales. This was designed to provide greater detail of the characteristics of those in prison and about social relations in prisons (Dodd and Hunter, 1992). Before the *National Prison Survey* was published the only detailed data available on prisoners in England and Wales were a few regional studies, together with information arising out of a limited number of research studies which had been carried out in different prisons (Home Office, 1978; King and Elliott, 1978; Mott, 1985).

PRISONER PROFILES

The general characteristics of the prison population, according to the *National Prison Survey 1991*, is that it is predominantly male and drawn mainly from manual and unskilled groups. Approximately a third were unemployed prior to imprisonment (42 per cent of those aged under 21), while 35 per cent stated that someone in their family had been imprisoned and 57 per cent had been in prison before. Approximately two-thirds had left school by the age of 16, with a generally low level of academic qualifications. Just over a quarter had been in local authority care and among those aged under 21 the figure was 38 per cent. The survey found that over 80 per cent of the prison population were under 40 years of age, with a concentration in the 18–25 age band. This prisoner profile is similar to that which was presented in the 1972 South East Prison Survey on men's prisons. This survey found that three-quarters of prisoners were from manual occupations and most of these had what were described as unstable or deteriorating work histories (Home Office, 1978).

According to the *National Prison Survey 1991*, a disproportionate number of prisoners are drawn from inner city areas (Howard, 1994). The highest proportion of prisoners came from London (1.3 per 100 000), followed by Merseyside and the West Midlands (each with 1.1 per 100 000). There were also found to be significant regional differences, with London accounting for a high percentage of those imprisoned for robbery (16.8 per cent) and a low percentage of those convicted of burglary (9.4 per cent). In other metropolitan areas the percentage imprisoned for burglary was 18.8 per cent. However, the percentage imprisoned for drug offences in London was found to be almost double that of any other metropolitan area.

The ethnic origin of prisoners was broken down in the survey into eight different categories defined in relation to country of origin, although no distinction was made in relation to their actual citizenship. However, within these categories 11 per cent described themselves as black ('Caribbean' or 'African' or 'black other'), while 4 per cent were

Asian or Indian. Among the black African and Asian prisoners drug offences were the most common type of offence (39 per cent for black prisoners); while 26 per cent of black prisoners were convicted of robbery. Interestingly, black and Asian prisoners were more likely than other groups to have been working prior to imprisonment, and both these groups tended on average to stay on longer at school.

At the time that the interviews for the survey was conducted, 15 per cent of prisoners said they were married, 20 per cent said they were cohabiting, 65 per cent said they were single, divorced or separated; 20 per cent of prisoners said that their marital status had changed since they had been in prison. Characteristically, two-thirds of prisoners lived in rented accommodation prior to imprisonment, 5 per cent lived in hostels and a further 4 per cent were homeless.

There are some significant differences between the characteristics of male and female prisoners. The female population is generally older, with a higher percentage drawn from non-manual occupations prior to imprisonment. A higher percentage of female prisoners were serving sentences of up to 18 months (36 per cent compared to 28 per cent for males). Male prisoners were more likely than female prisoners to be single, while almost half of the female prisoners had dependent children (47 per cent, compared to 32 per cent of males).

The *National Prison Survey 1991* also carries useful details of prisoners' attitudes towards imprisonment and their experience of different prison regimes. Importantly, it includes details of the nature of the relationships in prison between prisoners and staff. There are, of course, methodological issues concerning how candid people can be in interviews in this setting, but this survey does provide some useful information on different aspects of prisoners' experience, background and attitudes. Significantly, the profile of inmates in England and Wales is in most respects similar to that of the prison population in the United States, except that a higher percentage of prisoners in America are employed prior to imprisonment, while a greater proportion are drawn from ethnic minorities, particularly black and Hispanic groups (Lynch *et al.*, 1994).

It is interesting to compare the general characteristics of prisoners with those of prison officers. A survey carried out in the mid-1980s on *Staff Attitudes in the Prison Service* (Marsh *et al.*, 1985) found that prison officers were predominantly male with a conspicuous absence of women from specialist prison officer grades. They also found a concentration of prison officers in the 45–55 age range. Some 87 per cent were found to be married, and living in stable families, with the overwhelming majority being owner-occupiers, while just over 50 per cent had been in the armed forces. Although approximately 60 per cent had formal qualifications, with 31 per cent having GCSEs and 28 per cent having at least one 'A' level, some 51 per cent had previously been employed in manual occupations. Thus the profile which emerges of the prison officers is of a middle-aged, 'respectable' person interested in a career, a steady job and a stable family life.

Another important source of information on imprisonment that carries details of the operation and internal activities of different types of prison is the *Report on the Work of the Prison Department*, which is published annually. These reports carry important information on recent and current developments in work, education and welfare in prisons. They also review the activities of the Board of Visitors, as well as providing some detailed information on finances and resources. A more detailed account of conditions in selected prisons is available from the reports produced by the Prisons Inspectorate. They provide some of the most revealing accounts of the internal operation of different prison establishments. They have consistently brought attention to the poor conditions and inadequate facilities in various prisons, as well as problems of drug use, the lack of work and recreational facilities, the level of violence in prisons and the general problems of health care. It is indicative that the reports carried out by the Prisons Inspectorate are among the most revealing and informative studies of different prison establishments that are currently available. In many respects they have been more radical and informative than much of the 'independent' prisons research that has been carried out in Britain.

DOING PRISONS RESEARCH

Although there has been a growth in the volume of prison research in this country in recent years, it remains very selective and underdeveloped. The main reasons for this parlous state of affairs is the problem of access, on one hand, and the methodological problems involved in researching 'problem populations', on the other. Access has been a major issue shaping the nature of prison research. Any substantial piece of research on imprisonment in England and Wales has to be conducted with the agreement of the Prisons Department. Researchers are obliged to sign the Official Secrets Act and the Prisons Department is able to exercise considerable control over the dissemination of findings. Thus researchers who want to make careers in prisons research have to be careful not to 'abuse' the privilege. The Prisons Department is also one of the major sponsors of prisons research and therefore has a great deal of control over what is invest-igated, who does the research and, importantly, the methods used to conduct the research (Cohen and Taylor, 1972).

The Prisons Department tends to prefer a quantitative approach, and is generally sceptical about the 'scientific' nature of proposed prison research which employs qualitative methods. Studies of the qualitative kind are scrutinised in relation to sample size, the repre-sentative nature of the population being studied, and the general reliability of information gathered. However, since much of the research carried out in prisons touches on sensitive issues and the gathering of worthwhile information often requires developing a level of trust over a period of time, the use of impersonal quantita-tive methods is likely to be of limited usefulness. Developing the necessary level of trust may not be achievable within the time limits set for the research.

Whether quantitative or qualitative research methods are adopted, there are considerable physical constraints on gathering information in prisons. Interviews with prisoners have often to be carried out in uncongenial and restricted settings, which may be noisy, or interviews are interrupted (Morris and Morris, 1963). Access to the prison is nor-mally limited in practice to three or four hours a day. Thus, although the prison day may be extremely long for prisoners, it is relatively very short for researchers. In some cases prisoners, and indeed prison staff, are likely to be suspicious of academic researchers, while those who voluntarily agree to be interviewed may constitute a particular and not necessarily representative section of the prison population. The pres-ence of researchers can also affect the behaviour and responses of inmates, and there is always the danger that researchers engaging in participant observation studies may be 'drawn in' by the inmates. Moreover, the personal characteristics of researchers such as age, race and gender can also affect the research process and the research findings (Genders and Player, 1995a). Despite these constraints, however, there has emerged in recent years a small number of more imaginative and sociologically informed pieces of prison research. However, the impact of these studies has been muted by the fact that, by the time the Prisons Department has released the research findings and they have been published, the conditions which have been exam-ined have often changed considerably.

GETTING BEHIND THE DATA

So far, the data on prison populations and penal trends has been presented in a generally uncritical fashion. But interpreting and analysing this data raises critical issues of reliability. These are problems not just of sample size or statistical inference, but are associated with the ways in which data is collated and categorised, particularly since such processes have changed significantly over time. For these reasons research methodologists have argued for the need to 'get behind' the data and to be aware of the diverse processes through which data is produced (Bottomley, and Pease 1986; Coleman and Moynihan, 1996).

Like criminal statistics, interpreting prison statistics, involves an understanding of how data is generated and the purpose for which it is collected. It also involves an appreciation of the nature of the data sources and of the agencies responsible for collecting and organising the information. The standard critiques of criminal statistics apply equally to prisons data and these will not be rehearsed here. There are, however, a number of processes which are evident in the criminal statistics but which take a particular significance in relation to prison statistics, since they affect both the structure and the reliability of the data. These processes can be summarised under four main headings: categorisation, slippage, telescoping and errors and omissions.

Categorisation

Just as with criminal statistics, there are basic issues concerning the ways in which different activities are categorised. The adopted system of classifying offences and offenders is not static or always clear cut. What constitutes 'violence', for example, is differently conceived by different groups, and these definitions are themselves subject to changing definitions over time (Young, 1992a). There also seems to be a great deal of uncertainty in the official literature in relation to the offence of 'robbery', which is classified both as a form of violent crime in some official publications and as a form of property crime in others (Matthews, 1996).

Thus, when examining the classification systems for different offences, we need to ask how clear-cut are the boundaries between different categories (for example, at what point does burglary become aggravated burglary) and to examine the consistency of the underlying principles which relate to the production of different categories. For example, in terms of race the processes of categorisation are often inconsistent, in that they define subjects simultaneously along a scale of colour (black, white, and so on) and by place of birth (Afro-Caribbean, Asian). When these two scales are collapsed into one, differentials which were always somewhat arbitrary can become extremely confusing. Categories such as 'Asian', for example, are used to cover a diverse range of peoples, who may have very little or nothing in common. When nebulous categories of this kind are then added to or contrasted with 'black' populations who may be of African, Caribbean or British origin, the value of such comparisons will necessarily be limited. Further problems arise with the categorisation of young people. Up until 1992, 14–16-year-old males and 14–17-year-old females were called 'juveniles' and all 14–21-year-olds were called 'young offenders'. Since 1993, however, all 15–17-year-olds are referred to as 'young offenders'.

Slippage

Closely related to the problems of categorisation is the process of slippage. As cases proceed through the criminal justice process, they are liable to be redefined and recategorised. Thus cases which began their life as a particular type of offence may in the course of being processed become redefined in relation to other, normally lesser, offences. Through the process of 'plea bargaining', for example – by which offenders elect to plead guilty to charges with the aim of appearing 'co-operative' in the expectation of being treated more leniently by the courts – the original charges may be transformed. As a result, the data on court disposals may bear only a rough equivalence to the offences originally recorded by the police. Even in relation to the statistics on 'homicide', which is seen as relatively 'hard' data, only 86 per cent of those cases which were originally recorded by the police as homicide in 1991 came to be categorised as homicide as a result of court proceedings. Before or during the trial, cases of 'homicide' may become redefined as 'accidents', 'self-defence', or alternatively may be recategorised as a lesser offence (White, 1995). When this process of recategorisation occurs, however, the original 'case' stands and is not changed retrospectively. Thus the same case may well be categorised differently at different stages of the criminal justice process.

Slippage also occurs because each annual edition of the *Prison Statistics* does not deal with a cohort of offenders, but only captures a proportion of those moving through the system over a certain period of time. Because of bureaucratic delays, adjustments, or waiting for sentence, different offenders may not have their cases dealt with until the following year. As a result, 'inputs' in any one year do not necessarily match 'outputs'.

Telescoping

The process of 'telescoping' in the use and presentation of criminal justice statistics can take a number of forms. Its primary form involves the tendency by the principal agencies in the Criminal Justice System to record only the most 'serious' or most 'convictable' offence. Thus, when an offender has committed or been charged with a number of offences, it may only be the most serious offence for which he or she is actually tried, although once a suspect is arrested a range of offences may be 'cleared up' as far as the police are concerned. The net result of this process is that, because indictable offences are considered to be more serious then summary offences, and since only the most serious offences tend to be recorded, there is a probability that the number of summary offences published will be less than their actual values (Walker, 1995).

Just as this first form of 'telescoping' involves a tendency to collapse and undercount the number of offences, there is a simultaneous problem of overcounting, which occurs from looking through the telescope, as it were, the other way round. This arises because one offence or incident can lead to several charges or convictions, each of which may be recorded separately. The taking of a motor vehicle, for example, may lead to several convictions – unauthorised taking, no insurance, no driving licence, or driving while disqualified. Overcounting can also occur because, as they proceed from one stage of the process to another, offenders may be recounted. Thus, if a person is held on remand, his or her presence may be recorded more than once in any particular year, as he or she will be counted at the point of reception into custody as being 'untried', and possibly at a later date as 'convicted but unsentenced' or 'under sentence'.

Errors and Omissions

The prison statistics are subject to the problems of collecting accurate and up-to-date returns from the various criminal justice agencies. This can affect the quality of the data. There are a number of examples of 'errors and omissions' which can be found in the statistical data. In the *Criminal Statistics* for 1995 it was noted that:

For magistrates' courts proceedings, the number of remands and more importantly the number which are in custody, are believed to be under-recorded in total. For a number of police forces, the breakdown of remands into bail and custody cases is not accurate. The totals quoted in the chapter therefore include estimates for 11 forces (amounting to about 20 per cent of the total proceedings), based on their total proceedings and the averages for other forces. The figures quoted in this chapter should therefore be regarded as *providing no more than an order of magnitude*. (Home Office, 1996a: 186)

The police, in particular, are seen routinely to under-report certain offences. Problems of accurately recording events, incorrect entries, possible double-counting and incomplete returns are mentioned with disturbing regularity in the official statistics. For example, the proportion of the prison population whose offence is not recorded has increased from 5 per cent in 1985 to 15 per cent in 1992. This makes it difficult to gain a comprehensive picture of the overall situation, particularly if these omissions are concentrated among discrete populations. In a similar vein, the figures presented on average length of sentence are open to distortion, particularly for those serving long sentences, since the average sentence length can only be calculated for those who have already been discharged. It will therefore not reflect the actual length of sentence that someone who is currently serving a long sentence will serve (Pease, 1995).

Thus we can see from these four processes that the prison statistics are in many respects likely to compound and intensify the problems inherent in the criminal statistics, since they are the product of a complex process of negotiation and definition and must be treated with extra caution. Prison statistics tell us little about the 'process' of imprisonment, but rather provide a series of snapshots of the prison population taken from a number of different vantage points, using a number of different lenses. The pictures produced are necessarily selective and at times are blurred or distorted. Each of the agencies involved in collecting information has its own procedures and its own priorities, with the consequence that the production of knowledge is tied to interests.

A disconcerting feature of the prison statistics is that even data which appear reasonably straightforward turn out on investigation to be either erroneous or in some cases misleading. Take, for example, the monthly or annual costs of incarcerating an offender. The figure of

£2000 per month is boldly presented in the *Summary of Official Statistics, Digest 3*, without qualification, and is often quoted as an authoritative assessment of cost (Barclay, 1995). This figure is qualified in the *Annual Report of the Prisons Department*, which suggests that the current cost of incarcerating a prisoner ranges from approximately £7000 per month in a dispersal prison per month down to around £1500 per month in an adult open prison. These figures, however, although indicating a significant variations in costs between different types of institution, only reflect a proportion of the actual monthly cost. This is because they involve only revenue costs and omit capital costs. Moreover, these figures do not include the wider social costs of providing care for dependants, and other indirect costs associated with the removal of offenders from the community. Including such costs in the calculation could well double the average cost for each prisoner, and for some categories of prisoner it could well even triple or quadruple the formally stated cost. Thus the average cost of sending an offender to a high security prison is, as has been often pointed out, considerably more expensive than sending someone to Eton or Roedean. At the same time it should be noted that the marginal cost of sending an extra person to prison is only a fraction of this amount, since the cost of running a prison is roughly the same, whether the prison is full or half-empty. Thus we can see that behind this average figure there are a number of considerations which need to be taken into account, and that taking the basic figure of £2000 a month at face value gives a misleading impression of the actual costs involved.

It is clear from the example of costs that official statistics need to be critically interrogated in order to reveal the underlying assumptions, and to evaluate the methods which have been employed to produce them. Below are two 'case-studies' which bring out some of these issues, and indicate how certain items which are presented in the prison statistics can be interpreted.

ANALYSIS

1. Cross-National Comparisons in Prison Use

In recent years, prison statistics have begun to include data on cross-national comparisons of prison use. These data are derived from the Council of Europe annual survey which presents the incarceration rate per 100 000 population in a number of different countries. Among Western European countries, the United Kingdom, with just over 100 prisoners per 100 000 population, is among the highest in Europe: although it appears moderate compared to various Eastern European countries and America which has a rate almost six times greater at 592 per 100 000 (Barclay, 1995). These figures are often taken as indicating the level of punitiveness in different countries and as evidence that countries like the UK and USA use prison excessively. These comparisons, however, are seriously flawed, and as a point of comparison of the relative punitiveness of different countries, the figures are virtually meaningless (Pease, 1992). Differences in the way in which the figures on imprisonment are gathered in each country are enough to render any comparisons suspect in themselves. Some countries do not include juveniles or remand prisoners in their statistics, while others do not count various categories of detainees among the prison population. As a result of these inconsistencies the general reliability of the data has been called into question (Young and Brown, 1993).

Although the *Prison Statistics for England and Wales* notes some of these limitations in passing, and does not itself draw any conclusions about the relative punitiveness of different countries, it clearly presents the data as saying something important about prison use around the world and by design or default encourages spurious comparisons. The fact that a summary of these figures is also included in *Digest 3* indicates the level of significance the Prisons Department and Home Office attribute to them (Barclay, 1995).

Engaging in this form of cross-national comparison therefore raises issues about the relevance and significance of the different types of data. It also raises issues about the significance of studying the prison population in terms of the static measure of average daily population rather than by means of 'flow' designs which examine the number of admissions to prison and discharges from prison over a period of time. As noted above, static measures tend to over-represent the number of serious offenders with longer sentences.

Examining prison populations solely in relation to the general population tells us very little about the punitiveness, or otherwise, of the courts. The nature of court decisions and the use of custody and other sanctions makes little sense unless it is linked to the nature and level of offending in the country concerned. Clearly countries with different levels of crime would have different incarceration rate even if their sentencing practices were very similar. Taking the incidence of arrest as a point of reference and restricting comparisons to selected classes of crime while employing a form of 'flow' analysis James Lynch (1988) shows that when comparisons are made between England and Wales, Canada, Germany and the United States, the probability of incarceration given arrest is roughly the same for violent offences in the United States, England and Wales, and Canada, although England and Wales has a slightly lower rate for homicide. These three countries were also found to be roughly similar in respect to the propensity to imprison those convicted of property crimes such as burglary and theft. Rates, however, were found to be lower in Germany for both violent and property crime. However, Lynch concludes that the differences between the USA and England and Wales are largely a product of different rates of crime rather than major differences in sentencing practices.

Analysing data over a twenty-year period, Warren Young and Mark Brown (1993) found that, when the rate of imprisonment is examined in relation to relative offence rates, England and Wales is roughly similar to France and Germany. In fact, in relation to violent crime, England and Wales was considerably less punitive than France during the 1980s. Although they found considerable fluctuation from one period to another, the relationship between England and Wales and other countries has remained relatively constant since the late 1960s. These findings suggest that for specific offences the United States, which has often been held to be an excessively punitive country, imprisons a roughly similar proportion of convicted offenders to England and Wales. The higher rate of incarceration in America is therefore largely a product of a much higher level of serious and violent crime (see Langan and Farrington, 1998).

Although these figures provide a more accurate view of the relative willingness of different countries to send people to prison, there are other factors which need to be considered in order to make proper comparisons. Accurate comparisons would have to take into account the use and availability of alternatives to custody, the role of plea bargaining in reducing sentences, differences in the criminal histories of defendants, as well as differences in the organisation of different criminal justice systems in different countries. There is also a need to differentiate between the number of people sent to prison and the length of sentence imposed. Thus the United States, for example, may be similar to England and Wales in relation to the number of people who are sent to prison following conviction. However, the USA tends to impose longer prison sentences for those convicted. Thus the level of punitiveness may be measured both by the number of people sent to prison and by the length of sentence imposed for different crimes. A third measure is also relevant. This involves the length of time actually served, and invites a consideration of the use of parole and early release schemes in different countries. Ken Pease (1992), for example, after comparing the relative punitiveness of England and Wales and other Western European countries, concluded that, although in relation to length of sentence given in England and Wales was modestly more punitive than most other countries in Western Europe, in terms of the length of sentence actually served England and Wales was generally less punitive for all offences except for those causing death.

2. Reconviction Rates

According to the 1994 *Prison Statistics*, the reconviction rate of those imprisoned is 56 per cent for adult males, 40 per cent for adult females, while for those aged under 21 it is approximately 70 per cent. This measure is often taken as an indicator of the effectiveness, or otherwise, of imprisonment and other penalties. In particular, reconviction rates are often presented as evidence that prison does not serve as an effective specific deterrent.

In recent years, however, it has become evident that these widely referenced reconviction rates are a fairly crude and a somewhat arbitrary measure, which does not provide a very accurate gauge of the effectiveness of imprisonment or other sanctions. The first point which should be made in relation to reconviction rates is that they are not in fact 'rates' at all, but simply a percentage of those who have been reconvicted within a certain period (Maltz, 1984). The period of two years which has become the normal yardstick for measuring reconviction is arbitrary, and it is clear that taking different time spans produces very different results. If the aim of reconviction scores is to measure the effectiveness of various sanctions, it might be supposed that a one-year time span would be more appropriate, since the longer the period of time after leaving prison, the greater are the chances that any specific deterrent effect will have been eroded by outside pressures.

Equally problematic is the fact that until recently reconviction scores did not fully take into account either the seriousness or the frequency of subsequent offending. That is, if an offender after leaving prison commits an offence of a much less serious nature than that for which he or she was initially imprisoned, or even if the offender commits the same type of offence but less frequently, it will still appear as a reconviction and the offender will be identified as a recidivist. A further problem arises in applying these data, since reconviction is not synonymous with reoffending. Offenders may not be caught, the police may issue a caution or the Crown Prosecution Service may decide not to prosecute. In all these cases a conviction will not be registered, although an offence has been committed.

A recent study entitled *Explaining Reconviction Rates* (Lloyd *et al.*, 1994), which compared reconviction scores for different types of offenders, found that the best predictors of reconviction were age and criminal history. According to this research, these factors have a major influence on the likelihood of reconviction, whatever sanction is deployed:

> For example, the reconviction rates of middle-aged sex offenders are likely to be low whether they are imprisoned or punished in the community; and young burglars with long criminal histories are very likely to be reconvicted whether they go to prison or not. Thus a straightforward comparison between say the reconviction rates of a community penalty targeted at middle-aged sex offenders and those of a custodial sentence given to young burglars would reach the same – very possibly erroneous – conclusion that the former sentence 'worked' much better than the latter. (Lloyd *et al.*, 1994: ix)

These findings suggest that the characteristics of the sanction may be less important in affecting reconviction than the characteristics of the offender. The authors note that reconviction rates are often adopted uncritically, and rather than providing a reliable and solid point of reference they are better seen as 'artefacts constructed from (for the most part) rather dubious data'. It is not that reconviction scores themselves should be regarded as simply erroneous or misleading, but that they need to be carefully and critically interpreted.

Although bringing a greater sophistication and awareness to the issue of reconviction rates, the study by Lloyd *et al.* (1994) also displays some limitations. The principal limitation is that within its multifactor approach it does not take account of the social characteristics of offenders, such as their marital status or employment histories, which have been found by other researchers to have considerable impact on the likelihood of reoffending and reconviction. Their analysis does not explore the causal relations involved. It is therefore unable, for example, to address effectively the issue of why females should have a considerably lower level of reconviction than males, allowing for differences in age and criminal history.

In the last few years there has been a growing desire to develop a more sophisticated and reliable reconviction score and, following the recommendations of the Carlisle Committee in 1988, a revised 'Reconviction Prediction Score' has been produced, which is designed to predict the risk of future offending (Copas *et al.*, 1994). This revised version aims to distinguish between trivial and non-trivial offences, and more clearly between the point of reoffending and the date of reconviction, although it still takes 'reconviction' as its point of reference. This new predicator, which is based upon an examination of previous offending patterns, was designed to assist in the formulation of parole decisions. In this approach the attention has moved away from the measurement of reoffending within a fixed two-year period to an examination of how long the ex-prisoner 'survives' without reoffending. This form of 'survival' analysis identifies a number of key criteria that are held to affect the propensity to reoffend. These include the age at conviction, the number of previous custodial sentences, current marital status, the length of time in last job, previous employment status, and the number of previous convictions (Tarling, 1993). Although this form of risk analysis incorporates a wider range of factors than previously employed, it does not overcome the various methodological problems identified by Lloyd *et al.* (1994). It ultimately ends up by measuring the relation between reconviction and reoffending, and does not clearly differentiate the effects of offender characteristics and the effectiveness of different penalties.

CONCLUSION

A review of official statistics as well as research on prisons indicates that, while there have been some important developments in the recent past, the data and its analysis remain problematic and underdeveloped. Although the prison statistics carry a considerable amount of information, this information is selective, and has been linked historically to the needs and interests of the Prisons Department in managing the prison estate. Consequently there is little information available on the quality of life in prison, and not a great deal on the experiences of those who are imprisoned. The *National Prison Survey 1991* and the various reports by the Prison Inspectorate have provided some important insights into the nature and problems experienced by prisoners and include information about the relationships between prisons and staff. Operating within the various constraints a small body of prison researchers has begun to produce informative – and on occasions critical – evaluations of the process of imprisonment. Making sense of the available information on imprisonment is not an easy or straightforward task. Both official statistics and prison research need to be critically evaluated. It is always necessary to 'get behind' the data, and – as the two 'case-studies' demonstrate – the processes by which the various tables and diagrams are constructed within the prison statistics need to be critically analysed if erroneous and distorted interpretations are to be avoided.

5 Unemployment, Crime and Imprisonment

INTRODUCTION

Even a cursory examination of the emergence of the prison leaves little doubt that the form of labour, the operation of the labour market, and labour discipline have played a critical role in shaping its development and its functioning. But it has been suggested by Georg Rusche (1978) that the use of the prison may be conditioned not only by the form of labour but also by the level of unemployment. Following the lead of Rusche, a number of other sociologists have hypothesised that the use of imprisonment, as well as the severity of punishment, will increase during periods of rising unemployment and deepening recession (Jancovic, 1977). These two related hypotheses have been explored at length by criminologists, although the predominant focus has been on the changing size of the prison population rather than the possible relation between unemployment and penal austerity (Sparks, 1996).

Most of the major schools of criminology have addressed these issues and the overwhelming majority have concluded that increased unemployment is associated, either directly or indirectly, with the growth in crime and by implication the growth of the prison population. Marxist criminologists see the growth of crime as a function of worsening conditions, greater levels of deprivation and lack of opportunities. These sentiments are echoed in the work of writers such as Robert Merton (1957), who argued that the motivation to commit crimes will increase whenever legitimate opportunities to achieve culturally defined success, particularly material success, are reduced or closed off. An important element of Merton's theory of anomie is that there will be different responses to blocked opportunity, and this in turn will be conditioned by the meaning which different people attach to unemployment. Control theorists, on the other hand, see unemployment leading to an increase in crime as a result of the weakening of social bonds. Widespread unemployment, it is suggested, can lead to increased social tension and a breakdown of community and familial controls; while limited employment prospects can reduce the significance of schooling and education in the eyes of the young. Labelling theorists focus on the response of control agencies to rising unemployment. They suggest that because these agencies are likely to anticipate an increase in crime they will tend to extend social control and, through the process of 'deviancy amplification', produce higher rates of criminalisation and thereby intensify and exacerbate existing problems (Thornberry and Christianson, 1984).

These various theoretical accounts can be integrated and embellished. Since some focus on the motivation of the offender, while others look at the changing nature of the control process, they tend to approach the issue from a number of different vantage points which are not wholly incompatible. Despite this broad theoretical consensus on the probable links between unemployment and crime, the various studies carried out to date which examine this relationship have proved inconclusive. The majority of them have involved the use of quantitative data designed to test for a correlation between either unemployment and crime or unemployment and imprisonment. This research, which takes the form of time-series or area-based studies, has failed to find a consistent relationship between unemployment and either crime or imprisonment. These findings have led some researchers to reject the suggestion that there is any relationship between these phenomena at all. The disturbing disparity between the predictions of most of the major criminology theories and the empirical findings raises issues concerning both the conceptual adequacy of these theories and the methods used.

TIME-SERIES AND CROSS-SECTIONAL STUDIES

In a fairly comprehensive review of time-series and cross-sectional studies, Steven Box (1987) found that, although on balance there was evidence of a link between unemployment and crime, there was considerable variance in the results reported. Among 18 time-series studies he reviewed, Box found that 13 reported a positive relationship between unemployment and crime, while five were unable to locate any such relationship. Of a total of 32 cross-sectional studies examined, 19 presented evidence supporting the relationship, while 13 did not.

As Box notes, however, these studies (whether showing a positive or negative relationship) are subject to a number of methodological limitations. There is a general problem of consistency of the various measures employed. In many cases the use of data sets appears to be more a matter of convenience than the outcome of a rigorous process of selection. The first major problem is that these studies use different measures of unemployment, crime and imprisonment.

The definition of unemployment has been widely contested in recent years and there are a number of competing definitions currently circulating. It has been repeatedly redefined and there have been 32 changes in the way the unemployed are counted for official purposes over the last two decades (Levitas, 1996). Alongside the official counts there are a number of independent measures. Some of these focus on the number of jobs available, some on the number of people registered as unemployed, and some on the number of people actually looking for work at any particular time. The variation among the different measures is considerable. In April 1997 the official figures stated that the level of unemployment stood at 1.7 million. The figures produced by the International Labour Organisation put the figure at 2.4 million, while they estimated there were a further 2 million people who wanted work but could not find employment. These figures, it should be noted, do not include part-time or temporary work, those who have retired, or those claiming long-term sickness benefit.

Irrespective of which particular measure is used, these studies give little or no consideration to the meaning of unemployment among those who experience it. As the anomie theorists point out, unemployment will be experienced by different individuals and groups in different ways. Some will feel depressed and withdrawn, others may engage in sub-economies, while others may turn to crime. Whether unemployment is voluntary or enforced, or short-term or long-term can have a profound effect on how it is conceived and experienced. Whether or not unemployment is experienced as problematic will be dependent to some degree on the level of personal, social and economic support individuals receive. In many of these studies, not only are these factors not taken into consideration, but there is little or no discussion of whether or not it is those who are unemployed who are actually involved in committing crime. At the same time, it should be noted that some forms of crime (such as white-collar crime) are dependent for employment for their execution, while there are undoubtedly a significant number of offenders who mix employment with crime. The underlying and largely misguided assumption which underpins much of this research is that for those who engage in crime it is their primary or only means of support (Orsagh and Witte, 1981).

Similar problems of definition and interpretation arise in relation to the use of the other key variables – crime and imprisonment. Some studies use the officially recorded crime rates, some use arrest data, while others use victimisation statistics. Although there is some similarity in the general trends associated with these three different measures over time, the choice of definition can have a considerable impact upon the identification of 'crime' in different areas, and can make a difference in assessing its distribution. As for imprisonment, there are – as noted above – a number of different measures available, such as average daily population or receptions into custody, and each of these can be adjusted to the changing size and composition of the general population.

Time-series studies, in particular, are subject to a series of methodological problems arising from the changing definitions of crime and unemployment over time as well as, from the perceived delays between changing levels of employment and the time it can take for unemployment to be translated into the increased motivation to commit crime. In some cases researchers have used the notion of 'lags' in order to try to accommodate the problem, but it is far from clear what periods of delay should be allowed.

Different researchers have attempted to address some of these methodological issues, while others have become more preoccupied with the technical manipulation of the data. Some studies have broken down the data in order to examine more closely the relation between the level of unemployment among specific groups and the different forms of crime which have been recorded, with the result that they have generally produced a more focused and informative analysis.

After reviewing these various studies, Steven Box (1987) concluded that, while the relationship between unemployment and crime is inconsistent, income inequality is strongly related to most forms of criminal activity (with the exception of homicide). Other research, however, which has explored the relationship between economic movements and crime and imprisonment, has expressed scepticism about the centrality of unemployment in this process.

FROM UNEMPLOYMENT TO CONSUMPTION

The difficulties of finding a consistent relation between unemployment and crime using aggregate data has led some researchers to consider other economic processes. One influential account has been presented by Simon Field (1990), a Home Office researcher, who argues that there is a stronger association between the level of personal consumption and crime than between unemployment and crime. Although his approach suffers from some of the same deficiencies as other time-series studies in relation to the measurement and management of different variables, it has attracted considerable attention because it offers what appears to be a more imaginative and seemingly more rigorous approach than most of those aggregate studies which focus on unemployment.

In contrast to many other studies, Field recognises that the relation between economic variables such as consumption and crime may be subject to countervailing tendencies. That is, he suggests, following the work of Cantor and Land (1985), that different forms of crime may be differently affected by changing economic conditions and that property crime may respond differently from personal crime. In fact, Field claims that while personal crime – sexual offences and violence against the person (but for some unspecified reason not robbery) – tends to increase in line with consumption, property crime has an inverse relation to personal consumption, with the consequence that in the years in which personal consumption increases very little or reduces, property crime tends to grow relatively quickly.

Field's account is more elaborate than many previous studies which focus on unemployment, in that it attempts to account for demographic changes and changes in the operation of the criminal justice system, and distinguishes between short-term and long-term movements. Field claims that there is a strong correlation between consumption rates and crime and that his account, by focusing on personal consumption, has a greater explanatory value than previous time-series studies. To enhance the explanatory value of his account, Field claims that he intends to distinguish between purely coincidental connections and causal relations, on the one hand; and to draw on routine activity theory in order to develop a form of explanation which can account for countervailing movements as well as short-term and long-term developments, on the other (Felson, 1986).

Despite these claims, Field's (1990) study, like many previous time-series studies, collapses into atheoretical empiricism. Like other 'naïve' empiricists, Field's mode of explanation involves taking a wide variety of possible variables, which are then systematically excluded if no significant statistical relationship is found at the 5 per cent level. In this approach a number of different factors are run together, and it is the level of statistical correlation which determines how seriously the various factors are taken, rather than their explanatory potential. Once the significance tests have been carried out and the factors have been related, then the 'theory' is mobilised to account for these apparent relations (Dickenson, 1993).

Field's (1990) use of theory is therefore largely *ex-post facto*, and what is presented as an 'explanation' turns out on investigation to be more of a rationalisation. We can see how this process of rationalisation occurs by examining Field's contention that increases in personal consumption can have three distinct effects on crime: an *opportunity* effect, a *motivational* effect and a *routine activity* effect. The opportunity effect refers to the increased number and value of goods which may be available for theft. The motivational effect refers to the limited available legitimate income and the tendency to gravitate towards illegitimate sources. The routine activity effect refers to the process by which in periods of increased consumption there is a greater propensity to go out and that exposure in public places is likely to increase the chances of victimisation.

At this point, Field employs a deliberate sleight of hand in order to 'explain' differences in short-term and long-term effects. He suggests that:

> The growth in property crime, it will be recalled, has an inverse relation to consumption growth in the short run, but in the long run displays no relation. The 'motivational effect' is the only explanation cited which implies an inverse relation. This suggests that the motivation effect of consumption on property crime is dominant in the short run, but in the long run it is balanced out by the opportunity and routine activity effects, both of which involve a positive relation of consumption to property crime. (Field 1990: 33)

It is apparent from this statement how the 'theory' is adapted to fit the 'facts', as if they themselves were theory neutral. Why the opportunity effects and the routine activities effects should not dominate in the short term is unclear. Since this is the basis of Field's theoretical explanation, it dissolves into conjecture. Moreover, we are given no direct evidence that the subgroups who are experiencing changes in their level of personal consumption can actually be shown to change their behaviour as Field contends.

Similar problems arise in relation to Field's assertion that violent crime increases in line with personal consumption and that this is related to the level of beer consumption. Increases in the overall consumption of beer does not provide evidence of this relationship, and, significantly, a demonstration of this relationship is conspicuously absent from this study. Other more detailed research has found that the assumed relation between an increase in alcohol consumption and changes in the level of crime is at best tenuous (Sumner and Parker, 1995).

The weakness of Field's (1990) account is exemplified in his ambivalent attitude towards the unemployment-crime relation. Although he acknowledges that there may be a causal connection between unemployment and crime at the individual level, he dismisses the possibility of a causal relation at the national level by glibly concluding that: 'the statistical test showed no evidence of any unemployment effect on any of these types of crime'. There is a confusion here between the particular and the general, the macro and micro, and between causal and contingent relations. A further problem with Field's account is that, while national rates of consumption may be increasing, patterns of consumption will vary considerably among different social groups. That is, it may be the case that the level of consumption of the wealthiest 20 per cent of the population increases substantially in a specified period while the bottom 20 per cent – those who are most commonly associated with crime and imprisonment – may decrease. Thus in periods of economic growth in which the average level of personal consumption increases, levels of personal consumption will not increase equally among all social groups. Field takes no account of these variations.

A great deal of reliance is placed in Field's study on the use of what are seen as sophisticated statistical techniques in the form of regression analysis. However, the difficulty with linear regression analysis, as Field himself notes, is that the underlying assumptions of this approach include: 'that of normality, independence, linearity, homeostacicity, structural stability and exogeneity'. Thus within the explanation different factors have to be treated as if they were independent of one another, linear and additive. Therefore, where causal relations involve interdependence and are non-linear, they are treated as nuisances. This is particularly problematic when examining complex social processes. However, rather than analysing them as dynamic, connected and emergent movements, this mode of investigation must assume one variable to be dominant (in the short run at least), since it cannot adequately grasp movements which are simultaneously oppositional but connected. Thus, whatever explanatory value his 'routine activity' approach might potentially have, it is undermined by a statistical method which finds the existence of countervailing movements an embarrassment. What appears to be a rigorous statistical technique turns out to place unnecessary constraints on the explanatory potential of the study. Just as no amount of statistical manipulation can compensate for a poorly conceived research programme, so the use of techniques such as regression analysis in this case does nothing to rectify the conceptual shortcomings of the study. Indeed, it adds to them.

Despite the considerable limitations of this account, its continued attraction – in official circles at least – derives in part from its apparent sophistication and from the differentiation of the processes involved. It also gains attention as a result of its claim to supersede those studies which focus on unemployment, by claiming that consumption rates have a greater explanatory potential. Unfortunately, the study does not demonstrate this and, despite its theoretical veneer, it is subject to the same fundamental problems as the aggregate studies which focus on unemployment and crime. Unlike most studies which focus on unemployment, however, Field's (1990) account has the political advantage of disconnecting crime from deprivation and the labour market, and couching the problem in the more technical language of 'business cycles' which, being a 'natural' and regular feature of the economy, are not easily amenable to intervention or reform. The best that can be done to prevent property crime, it follows, is to reduce opportunities, limit exposure to victimisation and increase rates of consumption – although this might have the disadvantage of increasing personal crime.

The work of Simon Field has been considered at some length, not only because it involves an explicit critique of the contention that there is a causal relation between unemployment and crime, but also because it raises important methodological issues. Importantly, it raises issues about causality and of what constitutes an adequate explanation.

DEVELOPING CAUSAL EXPLANATIONS

A central issue which the various studies examined so far raise is the difference between correlations and causal explanations, and in particular the possibility of spurious correlations. A crucial issue in any form of explanation is being able to differentiate between causal and contingent relations. Since even a strong correlation (or some other quantitative association) need not imply causation, there are problems about the explanatory potential of this form of enquiry. The attempt to attribute the variation in one dependent variable to the changes in another also raises the issue of causality. For example, a number of researchers have disaggregated their data into different inner city areas and then proceeded to examine the employment patterns and crime rates for these areas. On finding that in some areas unemployment increases as the crime rate goes up, or alternatively that when unemployment goes down the crime rate decreases, some criminologists will want to claim that employment patterns *explain* the variation in crime, at least in this particular area, and may be tempted to generalise on the basis of these findings to other areas. The problem here is: what does it mean to say that the variation in crime is 'explained' by changes in the level of unemployment? The relevant causal links between unemployment and crime are overlooked, and the specific processes which foster crime in different contexts are played down, as are a whole variety of extraneous factors which may also affect the level of crime in different ways.

In a number of respects, therefore, statistical analysis is not neutral in relation to cause but can be seen in a sense as contrasting forms of explanation, since the value of statistics is depreciated as our knowledge of causal mechanisms becomes more complete. Although it is widely assumed that quantitative methods produce 'hard' data since they allow relations to be expressed in the more precise language of mathematics, it is the case that mathematical language tends to render explanations a-causal and a-structural. Thus other languages are needed to explain how x produced y. The aim is to find out what makes things happen and to understand the processes which bring about change (Pawson and Tilley, 1997; Sayer, 1992).

Thus empirical regularities may be useful in drawing our attention to *possible* causal relations and encourage us to look for common processes in different areas. However, it is clearly inadequate simply to note the presence or co-presence of certain variables. By the same token, the fact that event a is followed by event b does not mean that a caused b. The mere succession of events does not indicate any necessary causal relation. Causal mechanisms can operate in ways which have little to do with regularity. Causal tendencies may or may not be activated. They can be resisted or may not take effect in certain contexts. Thus, although unemployment may act as a causal mechanism in certain contexts, prompting particular individuals or groups to engage in crime, these pressures may be resisted in other contexts, and often are.

We tend to make sense of these relations through a process of retroduction and by developing an understanding of what it is about unemployment which generates particular types of criminal activity. This requires considerable effort and ingenuity. Andrew Sayer (1992) has convincingly argued that an adequate form of explanation needs to combine 'extensive' analysis which is concerned with discovering some common properties and general patterns of the phenomenon under study, with a more 'intensive' form of research which focuses on the identification of how causal processes work out in a particular case. 'Intensive' explanation can take a number of different forms, but in relation to the debate on unemployment and crime there are two notable examples: one involving longtitutinal analysis and the other involving a detailed area study.

Longitudinal Studies

One of the best-known longitudinal studies which has been carried out by criminological researchers is that conducted by David Farrington *et al.* (1986). They examined the effects of unemployment on criminal activity among a cohort of 399 18-year-old London boys. Although the survey was initated in 1971, during a period of relatively low unemployment, the research found that the rate of offending was about three times as great for individuals experiencing unemployment as for those in work. Moreover, the frequency of offending increased for those who had experienced unemployment for three months or more.

It was also found that offenders were twice as likely to commit property crimes during periods of unemployment as when employed. Significantly, Farrington and his colleagues concluded that, while young people are more likely to commit crimes when they are unemployed, unemployment does not seem to cause 'basically law abiding youths to commit crimes'. The implication of this observation is that unemployment is more likely to increase the frequency and seriousness of offending of those who already have some criminal involvement, rather than transform previously law-abiding individuals into hardened criminals.

Intensive Local Studies

A very different approach to these issues has been presented by Howard Parker *et al.* (1988), whose research, which was based in the Wirral, demonstrated that the relation between unemployment and crime was mediated by drug use. In this locality, drug use (principally heroin) was found to be financed through property crime, mainly in the form of burglary and car theft. The patterning of this indirect relationship between unemployment (together with associated forms of deprivation), drug use and crime was identified through detailed qualitative analysis which revealed that in many cases there was a causal link between the despondency associated with unemployment, the gravitation towards particular forms of drug use, and the engagement in acquisitive crime in order to finance a drug habit.

An interesting aspect of this study was that the search for a causal connection revealed a circular dynamic and a mutually reinforcing process whereby the articles which were stolen were sold within an established informal economy to the friends and family of the young heroin users. At the same time, members of the community, including those who were purchasing goods through the informal economy, were putting pressure on the police and authorities to do something about the 'epidemic' of drug use in the area. Subsequent intervention by the police and other agencies, however, rather than solving the problem, tended to marginalise young drug takers further, such that it stimulated the development of a drug subculture which became more established and more committed to crime, and less likely to engage in full-time employment. Thus the causal relations were found to be neither linear nor the product of one leading variable, but were instead the outcome of a vicious circle of deprivation, drug use, crime and unemployment (Parker and Newcombe, 1987).

These two studies exemplify different approaches to the examination of the relationship between unemployment and crime, which – through the adoption of 'intensive' forms of investigation – identify different causal connections. Other studies which have attempted to identify causal relations have focused on the operation of the criminal justice system and the ways in which unemployment may influence the decision-making process.

UNEMPLOYMENT AND DECISION-MAKING WITHIN THE CRIMINAL JUSTICE SYSTEM

Because a high proportion of those who end up in prison or on the books of probation officers have poor employment records or were unemployed at the time they committed their last known offence, it does not necessarily follow that unemployment causes crime. The aim of analysis is to show the way in which unemployment affects different groups, not only in relation to offending but also in the way in which it influences the responses to that offending.

As Ian Crow *et al.* (1989) suggest, one probable consequence of the strong historical link between the criminal justice system and the work ethic is that unemployment prior to arrest may well affect the ways in which offenders are treated. Crow *et al.* suggest that unemployment is likely to influence decision-making in the criminal justice system in a number of ways. Having a job or the prospect of a job is often seen by the court as a pointer to the stability and character of the offender. Employment status can therefore become a relevant factor in sentencing in certain cases. through the presentation of social enquiry reports, detailed information on the employment status and the history of the offender is normally included. This information can influence both the type of sentence and, in some cases, the length of sentence.

The offender's relation to employment, however, can influence court decisions in both positive and negative ways. Thus:

> Employment information was sometimes presented to the court as relevant to the circumstances of the offence. Occasionally it was aggravating: theft from an employer, for instance, would be very much frowned upon by the bench. Much more commonly it was suggested in investigation that the offending was partly due to unemployment or had occurred in connection with the offender's efforts to work. Alternatively, a steady work history or current job would be advanced as evidence of good character in a plea for mitigation of the sentence. (Crow *et al.*, 1989: 41)

Importantly, Crow *et al.* point out that the focus on unemployment takes attention away from the fact that a great deal of criminal activity takes place in work and that employment offers a range of opportunities for various crimes, particularly white-collar crime.

Those who are unemployed or on low incomes are less likely to receive a fine. This is because in many cases in which fines are given to unemployed offenders, they end up in prison as a result of non-payment. At the same time, Crow *et al.* (1989) found that courts favoured the use of community service orders for unemployed offenders, although this was not the group who were initially identified as the ideal recipients of community service orders. They appear to be widely used for unemployed offenders because they are seen as a way of giving them something constructive to do, and as a way of providing some form of work discipline. In some locations, however, where the number of places on community service were limited, the unemployed were found to be at increased risk of receiving an immediate custodial sentence instead.

Some of these themes have been taken up by Steven Box and Chris Hale (1986) but with a slightly different emphasis. They suggest that in periods of recession it is not simply that crime increases and that this puts more pressure on the courts, which in turn leads to more people being sent to prison. They are critical of this orthodox or common-sense account:

> According to this orthodox perspective, there is a very mechanistic relationship between unemployment and imprisonment. It proposes that rising unemployment pushes up the crime rate as more individuals are tempted to break the law, a temptation many of them are unable to resist because they lack sufficient moral fibre. (This personal failing is also a major convenient explanation for their being unemployed.) As the rate of crime increases, and assuming a constant rate of reporting crime by the public, and arrest and prosecution by the police, so there is an *automatic* increase in the work-load of the judiciary. As this work-load increases and as more people are convicted of crime, so naturally the judiciary send more people to prison. (Box, 1987: 157)

While they accept that there is an element of truth in this model, they argue for a more radical perspective, which recognises that during periods of recession the increase in crime will be stimulated by greater fear of crime and a probable increase in the number of police, who are likely to be tougher on the unemployed because they, like members of the public, *believe* that unemployment causes crime. The judiciary, in turn, will increase the use of prison sentences because they feel that this is necessary to reduce growing anxieties about crime in the country.

In line with labelling theory, which holds that if people believe things to be true they will tend to be true in their consequences, Box and Hale (1986) argue that the belief that unemployment causes crime (whether it does or not) affects the response of the police, the judiciary and the probation service in deciding whether or not to arrest or prosecute offenders. It will also affect the type of sentence given. It is suggested by Box and Hale that during periods of recession various 'problem populations' may well become the object of criminal sanctions as official intolerance of certain activities increases – particularly those which are seen to undermine or negate the work ethic. They also intimate that changing economic circumstances may influence the severity of punishment.

UNEMPLOYMENT AND THE SEVERITY OF PUNISHMENT

Explaining the relationship between unemployment and the severity of punishment raises a number of problems. On one side, there are issues about the definition, level and distribution of unemployment which have to be considered; while on the other side, the severity of punishment has been measured in a number of ways, including the proportion of offenders given prison sentences, the length of the prison sentence, the time actually served and the nature of the conditions of imprisonment.

Attempts to examine the severity hypothesis using aggregate time-series data have produced mixed results. Though there has been found to be an association in certain areas between the level of unemployment and the number of people in prison (Jancovic, 1977; Wallace, 1980), other research has found little direct relation between unemployment levels and the length of sentences given and time actually served. Although some authors have suggested that during periods of prosperity the debate about punishment tends to recede (Melossi, 1994), there is also evidence that there are oppositional tendencies. During the era of Thatcherism, for example, there was an increase in national prosperity and, although welfare expenditure was curtailed, 'law and order' became an increasingly prominent issue and more resources were directed towards the criminal justice system. Much to the surprise of many observers, there was in this period a movement to reduce prison overcrowding through expansion of the prison estate and through the development of alternatives to custody as well as the use of early release strategies. A programme of refurbishment was also implemented, which resulted in improved conditions in many prisons, and there was a growing commitment to the provision of internal sanitation in all prisons in England and Wales by the mid-1990s (see Chapter 6). These apparently contradictory developments can in part be explained by the fact that the decline in various forms of government spending in periods of fiscal crisis may not apply to the 'law and order' budget, since the anticipated increase in social problems, social conflict and crime which is expected to result from a decrease in the 'welfare sanction' comes to be regulated by more coercive means. Consequently, the number of prisons may increase and the general conditions may improve in prisons in a period of welfare cuts (Matthews, 1979).

One overview of trends in imprisonment during the 1980s, by Roy King and Kathleen McDermott (1989), suggests that some developments in the penal sphere transcend economic cycles and fluctuations in the level of unemployment. They argue that, despite the prison building programme and the increasing availability of internal sanitation, prisons in England and Wales went through 'an ever deepening crisis', with greater overcrowding, an increase in the numbers of prisoners per cell, and a decrease in manufacturing and other activities. These developments occurred during a period of relative affluence and economic expansion and continued through to the periods of recession in the late 1980s and early 1990s.

These uneven and apparently contradictory developments remind us of the need, particularly in the sphere of penal reform, to distinguish as clearly as possible between rhetoric and reality; and to be sensitive to the fact that, while politicians and prison administrators may be saying one thing, they are in fact doing another. At the same time, change is rarely unidirectional. In any period there are likely to be oppositional and countervailing tendencies. Thus during the 1980s in Britain there may have been an increased emphasis on 'getting tough' and greater penal austerity, accompanied by an attempt to resuscitate the notion of 'less eligibility'. But during the same decade the numbers of juveniles in custody decreased and the number of receptions of adults into custody also dipped (Sparks, 1996).

THE CHANGING NATURE OF EMPLOYMENT

In examining the relationship between unemployment, crime and imprisonment over the last two or three decades, it is important to bear in mind the changing nature of employment itself. In the postwar period some profound changes have taken place in the patterns of employment, the processes of marginalisation and the restructuring of the labour market. In terms of employment patterns and their effects upon crime and imprisonment there are two dimensions which require consideration. The first involves the changing composition of the labour force and the level of unemployment among different groups. The second involves the changing *form* of labour, involving a shift towards post-Fordism and systems of flexible accumulation.

Over the last 30 years we have witnessed a shift away the prospect of 'full employment' and towards structural unemployment, particularly long-term unemployment. The various unemployment figures available in the UK make sober reading. Current unemployment estimates hover around 2 million, while figures which include all those who want to work are nearer 4 million. In recent years men have accounted for the majority of those who have been classed economically inactive, while unemployment is most heavily concentrated among the black population, who have an unemployment rate two and a half times that among whites. The level of unemployment among young people has also increased dramatically, despite the significant increase in those staying on at school or going to college. Young males under 25 years of age, for example, who are not engaged in education are now ten times more likely to be economically inactive than they were in the mid-1970s (Milne, 1997).

Recent changes in the form of labour are often referred to by the phrase 'post-Fordism', which signifies a shifting emphasis away from manufacturing and towards service occupations, and the introduction of more flexible working practices, including an increase in part-time and temporary forms of employment. Correspondingly, there has been an increase in the new information technologies, which are associated in turn with more decentralised forms of labour and work organisation. There are also changes in the international division of labour and the globalisation of financial markets, linked by the communications revolution. Although there is some debate over the extent and speed at which these changes are taking place, there is a growing recognition that changes in the nature of production and in the organisation of labour markets are having the effect of weakening the old collective solidarities and social identities (Amim, 1994; Back, 1996). The changing nature of employment has been linked to changes in the level of crime and the use of imprisonment in a number of more or less direct ways.

(1) Decline in Work as a Mechanism of Regulation

Work remains a principle mechanism of regulation and discipline in advanced capitalism. But in areas in which work had disappeared, or where there has been a substantial decrease in available employment opportunities, the relevance of work and work discipline has become more remote. At the same time flexible accumulation in the form of temporary and short-term contracts has introduced new forms of uncertainty into the work contract (Wilson, 1996).

(2) Increasing Levels of Absolute and Relative Deprivation

Changing forms of employment are seen to encourage crime both by increasing poverty and by stimulating inequality. As a result of either absolute or relative deprivation, the restructuring of the labour market creates both the possibility of increased profits and financial rewards for certain sections of society and decreased real wages and benefits for other sections. The growing gap between the rich and the poor has created new aspirations and desires, while denying marginalised sectors of the population the legitimate means to achieve them (Currie, 1998). The growing regional and intra-regional disparities in the levels of crime, victimisation and imprisonment have been linked to changes in deprivation (Cullen, 1994; Sherman *et al.*, 1989; Trickett *et al.*, 1995).

(3) The Breakdown of Informal Control Networks

The restructuring of communities has in a number of areas served to break down established informal control networks. As criminologists have repeatedly reminded us, informal controls are the most pervasive regulatory mechanisms in society, and when these cease to operate the control of anti-social behaviour falls increasingly on formal agencies and on the criminal justice system (Braithwaite, 1989; Skogan, 1990). It is in this context that the issue of disorder takes on increasing prominence and challenges crime as the main object of police attention (Wilson and Kelling, 1982).

(4) Changing Gender Roles, the Family and Work

Closely related to the fragmentation and dissolution of informal control systems is the change in gender roles resulting from the changing relation to the labour market of men and women. Alongside this development has been the growth in single-parent households and the demise of the nuclear family. As males are less able to act as providers, the economic basis of the modern household has come under increasing pressure. This has resulted in increased tensions and new forms of dependency, as well as an increased exposure to different forms of crime and victimisation.

(5) Changing Patterns of Socialisation

The changing forms of employment have been linked to the growth in crime because they change the relationship between young people and work. It is often asserted that teenagers are responsible for a disproportionate amount of crime, although much of this criminal activity may be relatively trivial. However, criminologists have argued that the vast majority of adolescents 'grow out of crime' when they make the transition to work and 'settle down' (Rutherford, 1986). But, as John Graham and Ben Bowling (1995) have pointed out, the lack of available work opportunities for many young people has resulted in the extension of the period of 'youth' for certain sections of the population into the mid-twenties. As a consequence, these young people do not properly complete the transition from adolescence to adulthood, and do not 'grow out of crime'.

(6) Changes in the Level of Public and Political Tolerance

A key factor in both defining and responding to crime is the level of public tolerance in a particular period. Changes in production relations can radically affect the penal climate. Activities which were once ignored can take on a new significance and may even be the object of 'moral panics'. These 'moral panics', however, are rarely just manufactured. Rather, they resonate with the changed lived experience of the relevant populations. As Box (1987) and others have argued, it tends to be those activities which are seen to negate the work ethic that become the main objects of concern. The translation of these sentiments into official policy and the relation between community concerns and those of criminal justice agencies is always uncertain, since the agencies have their own agenda and interests.

The erosion of informal control mechanisms, through the fragmentation of community relations and the demise of the family, may be seen to have an effect upon the use of imprisonment by changing the relationship between informal and formal mechanisms of control. The undermining of the modes of discipline and regulation which were once associated with continuous employment and its effects upon communities, groups and individuals means that the regulatory processes which have been in operation in the post-war period up until the late 1970s are gradually being transformed (Young, 1998a). Central to these changes has been the greater degree of participation by women in the labour market. At the same time there has been a steady increase in the number of women imprisoned. Before falling into the trap of empiricism, however, there is a need to examine this relation in more detail.

WOMEN, UNEMPLOYMENT, CRIME AND IMPRISONMENT

In the course of their research, Box and Hale (1986) raise the issue of the relation between women, unemployment and crime, in an attempt to address the masculinist bias which is evident in the literature. They note that women and men stand in a differential relation to the 'segmented' labour market, and claim that certain groups of women are likely to become increasingly marginalised during periods of recession. In a similar vein, Pat Carlen's study, *Women, Crime and Poverty* (1988), which was based on interviews with 39 imprisoned women, found that poverty 'denied them adequate material means for alleviating their multiple misfortunes'. The women she interviewed had little material incentive to be law-abiding. Once institutionalised, their chances of employment were further diminished, and the more their options narrowed, the less they had to lose by being 'nicked', or to gain by conformity. Thus, although in many respects women are likely to experience unemployment in the same way as men, the relation between gender, employment and crime is complex:

> Rising female employment, we hypothesise, may increase crime not only by expanding criminal opportunities for employed women. Thus other reasons are hypothesised. First, rising female employment may increase criminal opportunities for males. Second, it may also increase women's vulnerabilities as *victims* of crime. Third it may increase the vulnerabilities of other members of their families to being victims and offenders to the extent that slack in traditional guardianship responsibilities is not taken up by men, childcare services and other institutions. (Braithwaite *et al.*, 1995: 9)

Thus Braithwaite *et al.* (1995) suggest that the increase in female employment is likely to increase certain forms of crime through a combination of four processes:

1. *the supervisory effect:* the absence of women from the home increases the chances of being burgled and decreases the level of supervision of children;

2. *the opportunity effect:* when women are outside the labour force, their opportunities for engaging in more lucrative forms of crime are limited;

3. *the vulnerability effect:* employment extends the range of women's possible victimisation from the domestic sphere and public sphere to the place of work; and

4. *the power effect:* the prospect of women working can change the power relations in the home and potentially lead to greater conflict.

Thus taking gender differentials into account suggests a more complex relationship between unemployment and crime. These developments have to be seen against a background in which job opportunities have contracted for young uneducated women, while expanding for the better educated. Thus there has been greater unemployment among one group of women and increased job opportunities for the other. This has been associated with greater social and economic inequality, as well as the 'feminisation of poverty' by which poor and working-class women largely carry the burden of the effects of poverty.

The increasing polarisation between the employed and the unemployed among both men and women, as well as the marginalisation of those whose relationship to the labour market has become more distant, has given rise to concerns about the emergence of a new 'underclass'. This term has become widely used to describe both the reality and the fear of an apparently growing number of individuals whose stake in society appears to be minimal and who operate outside the normal social and moral boundaries. Although definitions vary and the empirical data is far from conclusive, the prominence of the debate itself signals a growing concern that there is an increasing proportion of people who do not adhere to conventional rules and roles.

THE 'UNDERCLASS' DEBATE

In recent years there has been a growing reference by commentators from across the political spectrum to the development of an 'underclass' whose links with mainstream economic and social activity is tenuous. This group, it has been suggested, is increasingly involved in crime, and makes up a large percentage of the prison population. Thus it is argued that as the underclass grows the prison population is likely to become larger.

It has been estimated in America that on any given day at least half of the young males in the 'underclass' are in custody, and that in every household in the zones of hardened poverty one member will have been in prison or will be currently serving a prison sentence (Simon, 1993). The notion of an underclass, however, has been widely debated. Many critics suggest that there is nothing particularly new in the existence of marginalised populations and that during the nineteenth century notions such as the 'lumpenproletariat' the 'criminal classes' and the 'dangerous classes' had considerable currency. These terms were widely used to differentiate between the 'deserving' and the 'undeserving' poor and to separate the feckless from the respectable. However, there is a growing body of evidence that new social divisions are emerging, and that these are closely related to the changing nature of crime and the use of imprisonment. The term 'underclass' became increasingly used in America during the 1980s, and many of the points of reference which are used in the literature refer to American developments. The question which arises, however, is how useful this term is to understanding developments in Britain and the rest of Europe.

For those who argue for the emergence of an identifiable underclass, there are four major points of reference which are generally used to provide an indication of the speed and the extent of its development: the growth of long-term unemployment; the increase in the number of single-parent households; the concentration of crime socially and geographically; and spatial segregation.

The growth of long-term unemployment, as noted above, has become more pronounced in Britain in recent years, as hundreds of thousands of people have dropped out of the official labour market. In 1997 nearly 2 million people, which is almost half those previously counted as unemployed, were claiming long-term sickness benefit. The increase in the number of single-parent households has been well documented. The percentage of lone-parent families in Britain with dependent children has increased from 2 per cent in 1961 to 19 per cent in 1995. There is not much disagreement over these figures, but there is a great deal of controversy over their interpretation. Right-wing libertarians like Charles Murray (1996) and liberals like Angela Phillips (1993) feel strongly that the demise of the stable two-parent family has adverse social consequences and results in inadequate forms of socialisation which lead many young people into crime and drug use. Beatrix Campbell (1993), on the other hand, argues that the demise of the two-parent family has a liberating potential for many working-class women, who have become less dependent on the male breadwinner. As more women take up paid employment and become economically independent, they are under less pressure to accommodate the needs and demands of males, who were never very good at being carers and are now less able to act as providers. In this context women were more able and more willing to extricate themselves from oppressive and damaging relationships. Thus, in contrast to those who lament the passing of the present 'cornflake' family, Campbell argues that the changing nature of employment and its effects on the structure of the household may be seen as a positive development. Ironically, she points out that it is in the process of attempting to provide care that women are often scapegoated for 'failing' their children. The problem, she argues, is not so much that men and boys are facing an identity crisis and the changing forms of crime and disorder are a consequence of the loss of male identity, but rather that they represent new ways of asserting it (Messerschmidt, 1993).

The third and related criterion which has been presented for identifying the emergence of an underclass is the social and geographical concentration of crime. It is widely reported that, whereas a significant percentage of both young males and females commit one or two offences, about a quarter of male offenders and one in ten female offenders admit committing more than five offences. Overall, about 3 per cent of offenders account for a quarter of all known offences (Graham and Bowling, 1995). Charles Murray (1996) has argued that the decreasing economic activity of young males, mainly as a result of declining levels of motivation and increased welfare dependency, has created a group of persistent offenders. He claims that 'the habitual offender is the classic member of the underclass'.

What, then, is the evidence of a growing concentration of offending among a hard core of persistent young offenders who eschew social values and norms? Offender profiling, which might have helped to answer this question, has not been in operation for long enough in Britain to draw any conclusions. However, research carried out by Anne Hagel and Tim Newburn (1994) found that the term 'persistence' is subject to a number of different definitions and measures, with some studies using arrest data while others take the numbers of alleged or admitted offences as a point of reference. In their study involving a sample of 10–16-year-olds they found that those who could reasonably be defined as 'persistent offenders' tended to be persistent for a limited period of time, while others were only involved in relatively trivial offences. Characteristically, the few offenders they identified who could reasonably be regarded as persistent and

involved in serious crime had experienced residential care, chaotic
family backgrounds and problems at school or school exclusion, and
engaged in regular use of controlled drugs.

If the evidence on the concentration of crime among certain groups
of offenders is uncertain, the evidence relating to the concentration of
victimisation is much more convincing. Recent research based on
British Crime Survey data has found evidence of an increasing concentration and compounding of victimisation during the 1980s:

> Broadly, it can be said that for property crime there was an increased
> inequality in the distribution of victimisation rates between areas
> during the 1980s. This seems to have been mainly a function of an
> increasing concentration of victimisation among victims, with a
> smaller change in area differences attributable to changes in victim
> prevalence. It would appear that the distribution of property crime
> between areas during the 1980s experienced a 'double concentration'
> – a smaller number of areas during the 1980s suffered an increased
> proportion of property crime victimisation not only because they con-
> tained more victims than other areas but also because victims in those
> areas were becoming much more frequently victimised than were the
> residents of other areas. (Trickett *et al.*, 1995)

The fourth related element is that certain groups are becoming not only
more socially and economically marginalised but also more spatially segregated. In a powerful depiction of what is seen as the emerging underclass in America, William Julius Wilson (1987) has argued that processes
of marginalisation have taken a spatial and racial form that has resulted
in the formation of black ghettos and created 'hyperghettoisation'. This
refers to a process in which crime, drug use, housing deterioration,
family disruption, commercial blight and education failure take on a
qualitatively different form and serve to systematically compound and
reinforce each other (Wacquant and Wilson, 1993). Although it is clearly
the case that nothing approaching the level of racial and spatial segregation has taken place in Britain, there are signs that the spatial segregation of certain groups is becoming more evident (Hesse, 1993). The
concentration and segregation of different ethnic minority groups in predominantly inner city areas, the evidence of 'white flight' and the construction of out of town shopping malls have created new forms of
'spacism' through which different populations are regulated. In contrast
to the integrationalists there is evidence, in some communities at least,
that territorial boundaries have hardened, while the growing number of

racial attacks is one of the means by which territorial boundaries are secured, enforced and policed (Webster, 1996).

Thus there is evidence of growing social, economic and spatial divisions in the current period, as well as the concentration of crime and disorder. However, in Britain at least, there is not as yet an identifiable social group operating outside mainstream society. It is probably for this reason that many British commentators have been sceptical of the term 'underclass' and, in line with other European countries, have tended to favour the term 'social exclusion'. As Lydia Morris (1996) has argued, what is needed is a form of analysis which can comprehend these emerging social divisions, but which moves beyond familiar concept of the underclass as a group of 'outsiders' who reject the norms and values of mainstream society, and thereby move beyond a centre-periphery model of social order and social relations.

CONCLUSION

Reviewing the debate about the relation between unemployment, crime and imprisonment raises a number of important methodological and theoretical issues. Such issues are often seen to be on the margins of, or even outside, the parameters of conventional penology – which likes to enforce a clear demarcation between crime, social and economic processes and the use of imprisonment. The logic of this unwarranted separation is that the materiality of the prison is negated and the process of imprisonment is seen in predominantly 'political' terms. The possible relationship between unemployment and imprisonment has been investigated by various empiricist studies which have attempted to correlate these two phenomena. The inability of researchers using these aggregate forms of statistical analysis to find total consistency has encouraged some to conclude that there is no relationship at all. These conclusions are misguided. Changes in the level and forms of employment can be seen to have different kinds of causal effects on the level of crime and the use of imprisonment.

This is not to suggest any form of crude determinism, but to offer the more modest and realistic proposal that there are causal links between employment patterns, crime and imprisonment. These links are not necessarily unidirectional. Rather, they often involve contradictory and countervailing processes (Downes, 1993). Clearly, the simple contention that an increase in unemployment will lead to an increase in crime is banal and misleading. Underlying this contention is a form of radical positivism which holds that there are transcultural and transhistorical 'laws' which underpin the relation between these phenomena. The quest for such laws is, however, illusionary. Instead of searching for such 'laws', the aim of investigation is to uncover the causal links and to differentiate as far as possible between causal and spurious connections.

Following Steven Box (1987), it has been suggested that, while unemployment impacts upon crime in a number of different ways, increasing unemployment tends to be linked to other social processes which increase uncertainty and put pressure on existing control mechanisms; this in turn is likely to affect sentencing policies, the use of imprisonment and the severity of punishment. It would seem that in Britain in the current period the forces which are pushing up crime rates are simultaneously affecting reactions to crime.

Importantly, however, it has been argued in this debate that the meaning of unemployment has to be considered, both socially and individually. With this in mind, it would seem that the purely quantitative forms of time-series analysis, whether focusing on unemployment, inequality, recession or consumption patterns, obscure the significant changes in the nature of employment over the past three decades and how these changes may be linked to new form of marginalisation and social exclusion.

There is in the debate around unemployment, crime and imprisonment a growing tension between a more specific focus on persistent offenders, anti-social individuals, 'hot spots' and the concentration of victimisation among identifiable groups. This concentric vision uses the language of targeted deterrence and specific forms of intervention aimed at persistent 'hard core' offenders. It centres around the contention that a relatively small number of individuals are responsible for a disproportionate amount of crime and victimisation. In contrast, there is a more divergent vision which talks in terms of an 'underclass', actuarial justice and broad categories of risk assessment, and which sees the problem of crime control as the management of aggregate populations. Current crime control strategies tend to oscillate between these apparently contradictory visions (Feeley and Simon, 1992; Mathieson, 1983). The fact that one in sixteen males in the general population in England and Wales has received at least one custodial sentence by the age of 31 suggests, however, that prison is neither reserved for a 'hard core' of offenders nor used to absorb members of the underclass. Instead, it appears to cater for a population which cuts across both of these reified groups.

6 The Scale of Imprisonment

INTRODUCTION

Just as there is no single factor which fully explains the development of the prison, so there is no one factor which explains the scale of imprisonment. The examination of the relationship between unemployment and imprisonment, in fact, suggests that there are a number of causal processes in play in shaping the use of imprisonment. These may usefully be divided into *interior* processes, which operate within the criminal justice process; and *exterior* processes, which operate in the wider social, economic and political arenas. Among the interior processes which affect the scale of imprisonment are the number of arrests, prosecutions and convictions, as well as the use of diversion strategies. Among the exterior processes are those broader social dynamics which affect the definitions of crime, the framing of legislation and the development of policing strategies, as well as the wider social and political debates which can influence the penal climate. Although it is conceptually possible to treat each of these processes separately, we should not lose sight of the reality that these interior and exterior processes are related, and that they can combine in ways which produce diverse and, at times, surprising outcomes.

The immediate difficulty which arises in analysing the changing scale of imprisonment is that these interior and exterior processes may act relatively independently at certain times, with each developing at a different pace and in different directions. Thus, for example, the introduction of new legislation designed to recategorise certain activities as crimes may in practice result in no arrests or prosecutions because the police have different priorities or a minimal interest in processing such cases. There is, as lawyers often remind us, an important distinction between 'law in books' and 'law in action'.

Analysing the changing scale of imprisonment, and identifying the specific reasons for its expansion or contraction, is critical for the development of reforms. A number of competing explanations have been put forward to account for the changing size of the prison population. A central objective of much of this analysis is to identify the main determinants in order that some form of intervention can be devised to adjust the prison population to a desired level, although there is little consensus over exactly what this level should be (Zimring and Hawkins, 1991).

When measuring the scale of imprisonment it is sensible to attempt to explain not only the changing numbers of people in prison and sent to prison, but also changes in the composition of the prison population. This is not only because the types of offences for which people have been imprisoned has varied historically, but also because changes in the composition of the prison population may provide important clues about what type of offences or offenders are associated with an increasing or a decreasing prison population. At the same time it is necessary to note that those forces which act to increase the prison population at one point may not be the same as those which bring it down at a later date. Examining changes in the composition of the custodial population also draws our attention to the deployment of non-custodial penalties. The use of the fine, community-based sanctions and other 'alternatives' to custody will have a direct bearing on the scale of imprisonment, and therefore changes in their use need to be analysed within a broad framework of 'penality' which includes the whole range of custodial and non-custodial penalties (Garland, 1983).

If the conceptual and methodological issues which have been identified so far did not in themselves present a daunting enough task, there are problems arising from the interpretation of the data which are no less formidable. There are serious discrepancies in the basic data sources which are used as the point of reference in explaining changes in the scale of imprisonment. The majority of penologists use the figures for the average daily prison population, while some prefer to use receptions into custody. Few researchers in Britain, however, have adjusted these figures to account for changes in the general population over time. The time frame which is adopted is also critical, since the period over which developments are examined can radically affect the picture of change which is produced and the questions which are asked. Depending on the measures used and the time frame taken, different researchers can produce, even over the same period, conflicting accounts of the use of imprisonment. For example, if we take the period between 1970 and 1990 in England and Wales, different commentators have variously identified this as being a period of overall increase, relative stability or even (during certain periods) a decrease in the scale of imprisonment (Nuttal and Pease, 1994; Rutherford, 1986).

Interestingly, some of the most influential literature on the scale of imprisonment in the 1960s and early 1970s sought to explain the relative 'stability of punishment' (Blumstein and Cohen, 1973). This literature, which took as its point of reference the relative stability of the American prison population between 1920 and 1970, saw, in Durkheimian fashion, prisons operating as largely self-regulating mechanisms, whereby: 'The standards or thresholds that define punishable behaviour are adjusted in response to overall shifts in the behaviour of the members of a society so that a roughly constant proportion of the population is always undergoing punishment' (Blumstein, Cohen and Nagin, 1976). The plausibility of this stability of punishment thesis came under increasing scrutiny, however, as the American prison population began to increase rapidly from the mid-1970s onwards. Since then, America has engaged in a strategy of 'mass incarceration' in which imprisonment has become increasingly re-established as a sanction of first rather than last resort. This radical transformation therefore indicates not just a quantitative shift, but a qualitative change involving a redefinition of the role of the prison. This change of role has, by implication, also altered the relationship between prisons and other social institutions, particularly welfare institutions (Cullen *et al.*, 1996; Zimring and Hawkins, 1991).

The American prison population has tripled in size over the past 15 years and the population in state, federal and local prisons was in excess of 1.6 million in 1996 (Bureau of Justice, 1996). This staggering increase and the substantial differences in the nature of crime and penal policy should make us very cautious about generalising from American-based explanations of change. In comparison to America, the average daily population per 100 000 of the relevant population (15–60 year-olds) in England and Wales has undergone a relatively slow overall increase between 1970 and 1995, with periods of stability and even decline, at least until the beginning of the 1990s (see Figure 6.1).

In this review of the changing scale of imprisonment, the aim is to examine the role of both exterior and interior processes and to identify as far as possible the contribution of different processes and their points of intersection. In relation to exterior processes, demographic and political changes will be considered, as well as the impact of the prison building programme. Interior processes cover changes in crime levels as well as changes which have occurred at different stages of the criminal justice process, starting from the arrest through to the point of conviction (Sanders, 1997).

Figure 6.1   Average daily prison populations in State and Federal prisons in America and England and Wales 1970–95

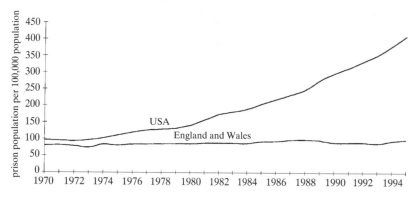

Source: Prison Statistics, England and Wales, 1975–95 (London: HMSO) and *Correctional Populations in the United States 1970–1995*, (Washington, DC: Bureau of Justice).

DEMOGRAPHIC CHANGES

Of the different accounts that have been presented in the literature, considerable attention has been given in recent years to demographic changes, since these are widely seen as influencing not only the level of crime but also the rate of imprisonment. The diverse nature of demographic trends make them difficult to measure with any accuracy. For this reason criminologists have tended to focus on, and differentiate between the changing social and geographical distribution of those who may be described as 'offender prone', 'victim prone' and 'prison prone'. These three groups can be treated as conceptually distinct, but clearly they will overlap in practice at certain points. Increases or decreases in these populations as well as changes in household composition and the location of particular populations are all seen to affect the level and distribution of crime.

The development of offender profiling in recent years suggests that not all sections of the population are equally 'offender prone' (Graham and Bowling, 1995; Tarling, 1993). Known offenders are disproportionately drawn and most heavily concentrated among the poor and younger sections of the male population who live in inner city areas. An increase or a decrease in this particular population, it is widely assumed, can have a significant impact upon the crime rate and by implication on the size of the prison population.

Between 1978 and 1990 there was approximately a 25 per cent decrease in the number of males aged between 14 and 17 in the population in England and Wales (Pratt, 1985). After a slight increase in the number of males aged 14–17 found guilty or cautioned for an indictable offence up to 1982, there was a dramatic decrease thereafter, and the number of male juveniles placed in custody fell from almost 7000 in 1979 to just under 2000 in 1989. However, this decrease has only been attributed in part to the demographic changes which occurred in the 1980s. At that time there was strong emphasis on juvenile diversion, combined with an anti-custody movement among practitioners which put pressure on criminal justice agencies to treat juveniles more informally and to divert them, wherever possible, from the mainstream criminal justice system. Consequently only about 30 per cent of the decrease in the use of custody for juveniles which occurred during this period was attributable to demographic changes (see Allen, 1991; and Chapter 7).

Alongside considerations of 'offender proneness', we should take into account 'victim proneness', as a growing body of research suggests that victimisation is also concentrated among certain social groups living in certain areas (Hirschfield and Bowers, 1997; Trickett *et al.*, 1992). A significant percentage of individuals and groups, it has been found, are subject to repeat victimisation (the victims of the same crime on a number of occasions) and multiple victimisation (victims of a number of different crimes) over a period of time (Farrell and Pease, 1993). The major determinants of 'victim proneness', according to Richard Sparks (1981), are vulnerability, accessibility and the attractiveness of different targets. Thus it might be expected that in periods of growing inequality the vulnerability of the poorest and more marginalised sections of the population would increase, while the attractiveness of certain targets would also increase. We have seen in the previous chapter how victimisation in England and Wales has become more concentrated both socially and geographically in recent years, and how these changes might be related to changes in the nature of employment and social exclusion.

Paradoxically, the more concentrated and compounded victimisation becomes, the less likely it is that it will be recorded or reported. As a result of the processes of 'telescoping', by which victims tend to discount the more minor offences when they experience high levels of victimisation, there is an increased probability that they will report only the most serious offences. This selection process is reinforced by national victimisation surveys, which normally limit the number of responses each person is allowed to make over a certain period of time, resulting in what might be called 'the suppression effect' (Coleman and Moynihan, 1996; Skogan, 1990).

It is important to note that the production of 'crime' involves the presence of motivated offenders together with available and suitable victims. Crime is not just an act, but a process of action and reaction. Therefore, crime is likely to be highest in those areas where there is both a large pool of potential offenders and a wealth of suitable victims. Where social and demographic change brings these overlapping groups into closer proximity, the level of crime can be expected to increase. A growing body of criminological research has begun to examine the relationship between demographic change, crime and victimisation, although the emphasis has been on local or regional studies focusing on either offenders or victims, rather than exploring the dynamics of offender–victim relations and how these relations are conditioned by the social environment (Bottoms and Wiles, 1997; Painter, 1992; Reiss, 1986).

In terms of 'prison proneness', we know that only certain types of offences and offenders are likely to receive a custodial sentence. According to the *National Prison Survey* 1991, there is greater use of imprisonment per head in certain locations. Prisoners are drawn disproportionately from inner city areas and regionally from the North, North West and West Midlands, to a degree which has allowed criminologists to talk in terms of 'justice by geography' and which appears to reflect the growing North–South divide in terms of work, victimisation, deprivation and urban change.

The complex nature of demographic changes makes it difficult to gauge with any precision their impact on crime rates, let alone prison rates. It is possibly for this reason that researchers have concentrated on various sub-groups and their differential involvement in offending and victimisation. A more comprehensive examination of these processes, which incorporates local, regional and national movements, and which links them to the distribution of potential offenders and victims would be necessary if the impact of demographic change on the prison population were to be fully acknowledged.

POLITICAL CHANGE

Changes in political direction are generally seen as critical in influencing the social distribution of punishment and in particular the use of imprisonment. As Rusche and Kirchheimer (1968) pointed out from their experience of fascist Germany, extreme political shifts towards authoritarian regimes have historically been associated with a reduction in legal guarantees, lack of due process, reduced accountability and an increase in the severity and duration of imprisonment.

In less extreme and more democratic situations a shift to the right politically is often associated with the introduction of more punitive policies; while shifts towards the left tend to be linked to a greater emphasis upon welfarism and the development of non-custodial options. However, the impact of political change is not always predictable. For example, the introduction of the Thatcher government in 1979, which embodied a growing preoccupation with 'law and order' and the promotion of 'get tough' policies, produced some mixed and, to some extent, unanticipated outcomes.

Certainly, the rhetoric of the incoming Conservative government was fairly punitive and the 'Iron Lady', as Margaret Thatcher became known, promised to make 'law and order' a government priority not only because she wanted it but because the public demanded it. This characteristic strategy of combining authoritarian policies with frequent reference to popular demands has been described by Stuart Hall (1979) as 'authoritarian populism'. However, as the 1980s unfolded it transpired that the term 'authoritarian populism' captured at best only certain dimensions of Thatcherism. As Bob Jessop *et al.* (1988) have argued, it was characterised by a greater selectivity in the forms of intervention as well. That is, alongside the development of tougher and more intrusive policies, there was also the rationalisation of those agencies and institutions which were seen as inefficient, while at the same time there was seen to be a need to develop forms of non-state intervention through privatisation (Matthews, 1989).

An appreciation of this differentiated and typically managerialist approach towards the issue of 'law and order' helps to explain some of the unanticipated developments which occurred in the areas of crime and penal policy in the 1980s. Over the decade the average daily population in England and Wales increased from 40 748 in 1980 to 45 636 in 1990. The increase in the number of prisoners on remand accounts for a considerable percentage of this overall increase, as the remand population increased from 5793 in 1980 to 9905 in 1990. Another way of looking at these developments is that the prison population, excluding those on remand, remained relatively stable throughout the 1980s, even without taking into account changes in the wider population.

The most significant changes which took place during the decade, however, were in relation to the number and type of people sent to prison. Receptions into custody increased from 72 290 in 1980 to a peak of 96 189 in 1985, thereafter falling to 67 510 in 1990. This increase in the middle of the decade, which involved mainly the adult population, was attributed to the increased number of custodial sentences given by the Crown Court, which generally accounts for three-quarters of the sentenced population. Importantly, despite that increase in the middle of the decade, the number of people being sent to prison annually was less at the end of the decade than it had been in 1980.

All the predictions in the early 1980s were that the Thatcher government would push up the prison population in the same way as the Reagan administration had done on the other side of the Atlantic. However, much to the surprise of many observers, the number of people sent to prison actually decreased towards the end of the decade. Although there can be little doubt that some of this downturn was a result of fewer young people being sent to prison, there was also a relative degree of stability among the adult sentenced population. Under the banner of monetarism, which stressed cost-effectiveness, the government introduced a series of strategies designed to divert or remove certain groups of offenders from custody and effectively to depoliticise the issues of crime and punishment: either by placing the burden of regulation back on the community, or by shifting the locus of control outside established state agencies.

A further indication of the implementation of this managerialism was the introduction during the 1980s of two measures designed to reduce the average period of time served. In 1984 the Home Secretary, Leon Brittan, reduced the minimum length of time that a person had to serve before becoming eligible for parole from twelve to six months, and a near-automatic parole system was introduced for short-term inmates. The result of this measure was that some 2500 inmates were released early, much to the disquiet of the popular press at the time. Three years later, in 1987, the amount of remission available for sentences of twelve months or less was increased from one-third to one-half, resulting in the immediate release of approximately 3500 inmates. These forms of early release, which were introduced as measures to reduce pressure on the prison system, stood in stark contrast to the 'get tough' rhetoric which was publicly associated with the Thatcher administration. Indeed, a series of Conservative Home Secretaries expressed publicly the view that prison was an inappropriate way of dealing with certain categories of offenders.

At the very beginning of the decade the All Party Parliamentary Penal Affairs Group produced a report entitled *Too Many Prisoners* (1980), which claimed that the prison system was clogged up with too many petty persistent offenders for whom imprisonment was not a particularly appropriate sanction. The report also claimed that there were a number of mentally ill offenders, habitual drunks and a growing number of drug addicts for whom imprisonment was seen as an inappropriate response. During the decade, although certain members of the government on the right of the party complained that prisons were becoming too soft on prisoners, and although Margaret Thatcher herself led a campaign for the re-introduction of capital punishment, a growing concern about the dangers of overcrowding was expressed by members of the government and their representatives. Critiques of the value of incarceration, both socially and economically, appeared in a number of official reports. Most reports during this period emphasised the growing costs of running the criminal justice system, and the prison system in particular. The White Paper *Crime, Justice and Protecting the Public* (1990), for example, notes in its opening paragraph that the annual cost of running the criminal justice system at that time in England and Wales was £7 billion. This, the authors of the report complained, was a 77 per cent increase in real terms over a ten-year period. The same report also states pessimistically that:

It was once believed that prison, properly used, could encourage a high proportion of offenders to start an honest life on release. Nobody now regards imprisonment, in itself, as an effective means of reform of most prisoners. If there is continued progress against overcrowding in prisons, the recent reforms should enable better regimes to be developed, with more opportunities for education, and work, and so a greater chance of turning the lives of some inmates in a positive direction. But however much prison staff try to inject a positive purpose to the regime, as they do, prison is a society which requires virtually no sense of personal responsibility from prisoners. Normal social working habits do not fit. The opportunity to learn from other criminals is pervasive. For most offenders, imprisonment has to be justified in terms of public protection, denunciation or retribution. Otherwise it can be an expensive way of making bad people worse. (Home Office, 1990a: 6)

The rejection of rehabilitation as a primary objective of incarceration in favour of retribution incapacitation and deterrence has implications for the selection of the prison population. A clear message was sent out during the 1980s that imprisonment should be used mainly for violent and serious offenders, and that forms of property crime – including burglary and theft – should be dealt with by means of community-based penalties (Home Office, 1988; Worrall, 1997). Even in more serious cases guidelines were given to the judiciary on a number of occasions that prison should only be imposed when all other available options had been explored, and if a prison sentence was given it should be for a minimal period. Throughout the decade efforts were made to control the prison population through a combination of strategies aimed at diverting offenders where possible into community-based punishments, to limit the numbers on remand, increase the availability of bail and to reduce what was generally seen by many in official circles as the over-reliance on imprisonment (Windlesham, 1993).

In fact it was not until the early 1990s, with the appointment of Michael Howard as Home Secretary, that the 'get tough' rhetoric was consistently translated into penal policy. The rapid increase in the prison population and the numbers sent to prison represented a radical break with the virtual stability of the previous decades. Even so, two considerations should be borne in mind before attributing the total responsibility for the increase in prison population solely to Michael Howard. First, there is some evidence that public opinion took a more punitive turn in the 1990s, which might explain why the anticipated public outcry against Howard's policies was so muted, and why the mass media were largely supportive of these policies (Hough, 1996). The second, related, consideration is that the various agencies involved in the criminal justice system are capable of resisting and even blocking policies with which they do not agree. They have historically demonstrated their capacity to change the direction of policy, although this has not always been in the direction of greater tolerance or leniency. If these factors are not taken into consideration, there is a danger of developing an over-politicised account of social change, and of seeing developments in penal policy as primarily the result of individual decision-making rather than as a social process.

Despite the continued calls for controlling the costs of imprisonment, and at certain times for greater penal austerity, the various Conservative governments in office between 1979 and 1997 sponsored the largest prison-building programme in England and Wales since the nineteenth century. It also instigated a major refurbishment programme, designed to end the practice of slopping-out and to improve conditions, particularly in some of the more dilapidated local prisons. The instigation of this programme was met with criticism from both fiscal conservatives, who objected to the enormous costs involved, and liberal penal reformers, who saw the expansion of the prison estate as a mechanism for encouraging the increased use of prison.

THE PRISON BUILDING PROGRAMME

During the 1980s, while the Conservative government was engaged in developing a series of measures to reduce public spending, it engaged simultaneously in a massive prison building and refurbishment programme at enormous cost. At the time the cost of building a new prison was estimated to be in the region of £30–60 million. In response to increased overcrowding, deteriorating physical conditions inside many prisons and the threat of an increase in the number of prison riots and disturbances, the government embarked upon the largest prison building programme since the Victorian period.

A number of penal reformers and criminologists, however, were sceptical of this development and claimed that as increased prison capacity becomes available it will be readily filled (Blumstein and Cohen, 1973). By making more places available, critics claimed, there is a tendency for the judiciary to resort to imprisonment more frequently and thus to fill the available places. Consequently, a number of penal reformers argued that in order to keep the prison population stable, there should be a moratorium on prison building (Nagel, 1977; Rutherford and Morgan, 1981). Thomas Mathieson (1991), for example, writing from an abolitionist perspective, argues that once prisons are built they remain in operation for many years, and thereby foster expansionist rather than reductionist goals. Instead of building more prisons, he advocates a policy of shortening prison sentences and decreasing the period of time served, thereby increasing the rate of turnover within the system.

The problem with Mathieson's strategy, however, is that, as we have seen, the Thatcher government was involved in diverting certain groups of offenders away from prison into non-custodial options, as well as shortening the sentences of minor property offenders. It also reduced the minimum period for parole eligibility. The level of reduction in prison sentences and time served that would have been

required to make any real impact on the size of the daily prison population, however, would almost certainly have been too drastic for
the government to implement, at least in the short term. In reality,
therefore, the implementation of a moratorium on prison building
would have increased overcrowding and ensured the deterioration of
prison conditions and the continuation of slopping-out into the
twenty-first century. It is therefore contradictory to argue, as many
penal reformers did in the 1980s, for the reduction of overcrowding
and the simultaneous improvement of prison conditions; and for a
moratorium on prison building in a context in which the number of
offenders being processed through the criminal justice system was
increasing annually. Such a stance, far from being 'radical', was in
that context a recipe for making conditions much worse for many
prisoners. It is also the case, as David Downes (1988) has pointed
out, that the lack of availability of places does not necessarily dis-
suade the judiciary from imposing prison sentences, and therefore
the effects of a moratorium on prison building in the 1980s would
almost certainly have been extreme overcrowding, with many prisoners living three or four to a cell. This is not to suggest, however, that
the prison building programme provided a neat solution to what was
perceived as the growing prison crisis (King and McDermott, 1989).
On the contrary, as the National Audit Office (1985) pointed out, a
number of prisons were built in the wrong places and for the wrong
categories of prisoners, which was in part a consequence of the
difficulties of finding suitable sites and partly a result of the miscalcu-
lation of the projected growth of the prison population.

The refurbishment programme also generated a number of problems and was extremely disruptive for prisoners and staff. Probably
one of the most graphic examples of the types of problem that became
associated with the programme was the refurbishment of Wormwood
Scrubs prison in west London. According to the National Audit Office
(1985), 'the partial redevelopment started at Wormwood Scrubs in
1982 but was suspended in 1984 after £6.2 million had been spent in
favour of a more comprehensive redevelopment which was designed
at the end of 1984'. The new scheme, however, which cost an estimated £34.5 million, rendered much of the suspended work obsolete.

As the costs of prison building and refurbishment began to mount
during the 1980s, and as the economic recession deepened, the
question began to be raised, as it had in America some years before,
of the opportunity cost of these programmes, particularly in relation
to the funding of education and health. Thus, although the prison

building programme had served to improve conditions for many prisoners, there were ongoing debates about whether the money could have been spent in more effective ways. One option which gained considerable support both in official circles and among criminologists in the late 1980s was to direct resources towards crime prevention, thereby reducing the flow of offenders into the criminal justice system. Reducing the growth of crime, particularly serious and violent crime, it was suggested, provided the most effective strategy in the longer term for reducing the reliance on imprisonment.

THE GROWTH OF CRIME

When Sir Leon Radzinowicz and Joan King wrote their influential account of the *Growth of Crime* in 1977, crime appeared to be increasing 'relentlessly', not only in England and Wales but also in many other Western countries. Although crime rates had been relatively stable between 1945 and 1956, they increased gradually up until 1989, and subsequently began to level off in the early 1990s. The increase in recorded crime from 2 million in 1980 to over 5 million cases in 1995 indicates the significant increase in the volume of crime handled by the criminal justice system throughout the 1980s. The sheer magnitude of the increase has encouraged some commentators to argue that the increase in the average daily population in prisons was a direct consequence of these changes (Murray, 1997). But this 'workload' model, as Steven Box and Chris Hale (1986) have pointed out, does not take account of the complex processes by which recorded crimes may be translated into imprisonment rates, or of how the scale of imprisonment is influenced by exterior factors. The limitations of the workload model is exemplified by the fact that, while the level of recorded crime began to decrease after 1990, the prison population climbed at its fastest rate in 30 years.

Taking the general increase of crime as the point of departure is therefore problematic. Clearly, much recorded crime is of a relatively minor nature and unlikely to attract a prison sentence. An examination of crime trends and their possible influence on the use of imprisonment therefore needs to look more specifically at certain forms of offending over a designated period. A review of crime trends during the 1980s reveals that, while the level of both property crime and violent crime almost doubled between 1981 and 1991, they constituted roughly the same percentage of all crimes reported at the beginning and end of the decade, with the exception of less serious forms of violence and robbery, which increased at a faster rate than other crimes (see Table 6.1). The increased number of cases being processed through the criminal justice system undoubtedly stimulated the flow of offenders through the system and increased the probability, *ceteris paribus*, that a growing number of people would end up in prison. However, the proportion of these offenders actually receiving a custodial sentence is dependent upon a number of intervening processes, including those of arrest and trial.

FROM ARREST TO TRIAL

The criminal justice process has been described by various authors as a 'funnel' or a 'sieve', in which the number of holes or outlets in the system will determine what percentage of the original input (crime) will flow through the criminal justice apparatus and at a later stage result in imprisonment. There are two critical processes which will affect the percentage of recorded offences dealt with by the courts: the proportion of offences cleared up and the use of cautions. As Table 6.1 shows, during the 1980s each of these stages of the criminal justice process was subject to significant change which affected the number of offenders who appeared in court. Firstly, the clear-up rate fell significantly, particularly for burglary, which dropped from 31 per cent to 23 per cent between 1981 and 1991, while vehicle theft decreased from 28 per cent to 24 per cent over the same period. The clear-up rate for violence, sex offences and robbery remained relatively stable over this period, with the result that a consistently high percentage of these offences ended up in court.

These divisions between property and personal offences were compounded during the 1980s by the increasing use of cautions for certain property offences. Although there is considerable variation in different parts of the country, cautions tend to be used mainly for offences involving theft, burglary and handling of stolen goods and for juveniles and first-time offenders. Thus it can be seen that property offences, particularly involving inexperienced offenders, were less likely to be cleared up or referred to court for prosecution, with the result that a far lower percentage of these cases proceeded through to the court and sentencing stage during the 1980s.

Table 6.1 Changes in crime and punishment in England and Wales, 1981–91 (adults)

	Burglary		Vehicle theft		Robbery		Assault		Rape		Homicide	
	1981	1991	1981	1991	1981	1991	1981	1991	1981	1991	1981	1991
Total offences recorded (000s)	718	1 219	333	582	20.3	45.3	98	184	1.068	4.045	1.559	0.725
Per 1000 population	14.5	23.9	6.7	11.4	0.409	0.887	1.97	3.59	0.042	0.155	0.011	0.014
Cleared/recorded	0.31	0.23	0.28	0.24	0.25	0.23	0.75	0.77	0.68	0.76	1.1	1.1
No of persons convicted	73 469	46 089	35 988	22 837	4 132	4 841	48 650	45 513	320	540	388	427
Per 1000 population	1.69	1.04	0.829	0.514	0.095	0.109	1.12	1.02	0.017	0.027	0.0089	0.0096
No of adults to custody	17 792	12 194	7 324	2 924	2 860	3 182	5 938	6 765	269	499	316	367
Per 1000 population	0.470	0.304	0.193	0.073	0.071	0.079	0.157	0.168	0.015	0.026	0.0083	0.0091
Average sentence length (months)	10.9	17.2	8.0	6.6	26.7	40.9	10.8	17.8	40.1	58.0	134.2	159.8
Average sentence served (months)	6.3	7.9	4.8	2.8	13.1	20.4	6.0	8.2	20.3	29.5	68.9	94.1

Source: Adapted from Farrington, Langan and Wikstrom, 1994.

SENTENCING POLICY

The sentencing process is widely seen as the key to the control of the scale of imprisonment, since it is apparent that the size and composition of the prison population will be a function of the numbers of people that the judiciary decide to send to prison and the length of sentence imposed. This simple calculation will therefore, of course, be moderated by the reductions in the period of time actually served, which will be influenced in turn by the availability of parole and other early release mechanisms. However, as Keith Bottomley and Ken Pease (1986) have argued, the diversion of minor offenders serving short sentences is likely to have a limited impact on the average daily population in prison. It is estimated that almost half of those currently sent to prison would have to be diverted into a non-custodial option in order to reduce the population by 17 per cent.

However, the claim that reducing the number of admissions to prison will have little impact on the average daily population has been challenged by John Walker *et al.* (1990), who argue that the changes in the prison population in England and Wales in the 1980s were not so much a consequence of an increase in crime or greater police success in apprehending offenders, but of the increased number of people sent to prison; both on remand and under sentence. A similar line of argument has been presented by Johanas Feest (1991) in relation to West Germany. Feest argues that the decreasing prison population in West Germany between 1982 and 1987 was not due to increased unemployment, demographic changes, or increased levels of crime, but a drastic reduction in the number of short sentences and the increased use of non-custodial sentences, particularly in the form of day fines. In West Germany during this period the average length of sentence was generally similar to that of England and Wales, but the substantial decrease in the numbers admitted to prison or held on remand had a significant impact on the average daily population.

Other research, however, has shown that in most Western countries it is sentence length rather than the rate of admissions which is most relevant to determining the scale of imprisonment. Evidence from Sweden and the Netherlands suggests that the relatively low levels of incarceration in these countries is a function of the generally low average length of sentences imposed and served (Farrington and Langan, 1992; Lynch, 1988). In their extensive review of recent changes in sentencing policy in different countries, Warren Young and Mark Brown (1993) conclude that it is the length of time served which has tended to play the most significant role in determining prison population trends, and in particular that reducing the average lengths of sentence has been the most common method of reducing the size of the prison population. This may be because it is politically easier to decrease average sentence lengths than to divert convicted offenders from prison. Young and Brown claim that between 1968 and 1987 the steady increase in the prison population in England and Wales was a result of the equal contribution of an increase in the number of admissions and an increase in the length of time prisoners were held on remand. These two tendencies were, they argue, offset by a decrease in sentence length for certain types of offences.

Within these broad and contrasting movements there are, however, some other more specific changes in sentencing policies which have affected the composition of the prison population. Although there was relative stability in the average length of sentence imposed during the 1980s, there was significant variation in sentencing strategies, with minor property offences being dealt with more leniently, and more serious violent and sexual offences being dealt with more severely. Consequently, while the number of offenders convicted of burglary, theft and criminal damage sent to prison decreased, the number of those convicted for a violent offence increased, and the length of sentence imposed on this group also increased. Thus at the end of the decade prisons contained a much higher proportion of serious and violent offenders than they had done in 1980.

Among the most important developments in this period was the decreasing proportion of offenders given a custodial sentence. The preoccupation with overcrowding and its associated problems, together with the debates about the possible effects of the prison building programme on fuelling the expansionist programme, deflected attention away from the growing proportion of offenders who received a non-custodial sanction. As Andrew Ashworth (1983) has pointed out, the dominant theme in penal policy at the beginning of the 1980s had been how to stabilise or reduce the prison population, and this meant providing the courts with a number of new alternatives to custody.

LIMITING PRISON USE

If the aim is to limit the use of imprisonment in a context in which the flow of offenders through the criminal justice system is increasing, then either offenders need to be diverted away from custody by 'front-door' strategies into non-custodial options; or alternatively 'back-door' strategies need to be developed which shorten the length of time actually served, through the use of parole of other forms of early release. Front-door strategies involve the development of non-custodial sanctions such as fines, community service orders, electronic monitoring and reparation, which can be used as alternatives to imprisonment. The expanded use of non-custodial sanctions during the 1970s and 1980s was reflected in the deployment of community service orders. The use of this option, which was designed to provide a form of punishment by which the offender could stay in the community and perform some useful work, increased from 30 000 in 1982 to over 40 000 in 1992. Community-based sentences in general increased over this period. The use of the fine, however, decreased.

Despite the increased use of community-based sentences and the adoption of a range of diversionary measures, the impact of front-door strategies on the prison population has been less beneficial than anticipated. Although the average daily population has remained relatively stable over the decade, there has been growing criticisms of the deployment of community-based sanctions. Rather than reduce the size of the prison population and solve the problems of overcrowding, non-custodial sanctions appeared to grow alongside imprisonment. Thus, instead of undermining the use of custody, they appear to have performed a complementary and reinforcing role (Austin and Krisberg, 1981; Cohen, 1985).

How could such an anomalous situation arise? Surely the proliferation of non-custodial sanctions served to take pressure off the prison system by diverting more offenders from the mainstream of the criminal justice system? These were the type of questions which a generally perplexed body of criminologists and policy-makers asked themselves in the 1970s. Over the following decade four types of explanation were presented to account for this anomalous situation.

The first was that development of alternatives to custody had instigated a process of 'net widening'. The proliferation of non-custodial sanctions, it was argued, had inadvertently drawn more offenders into the criminal justice system, thus expanding the system as a whole. Paradoxically, the consequence of the introduction of a range of what appeared as more benign and humane sanctions was that more and more people were drawn into the net of social control, with the result that – through the processes of stigmatisation and marginalisation –

many minor offenders became labelled as 'criminal' and were thereby confirmed in their deviancy (McMahon, 1990).

The second, and related critique of the deployment of community-based sanctions was that they catered predominantly for minor offenders rather than for those who were realistically at risk of receiving a prison sentence. Thus some alternatives were seen as largely irrelevant to the growing problem of overcrowding within prisons. For others, the use of alternatives for mainly minor offenders was seen as fuelling the prison crisis by increasing the number of recidivists who had initially been convicted of a relatively minor offence.

The third concern was that as each new 'alternative' came into operation, it drew a significant proportion of its clientele not from the potential prison population but from existing alternatives. Thus it was estimated, for example, that community service orders drew half their clients from those who might reasonably have been expected to receive a prison sentence, while the other half were drawn from the other non-custodial options (Pease, 1985). The movement of offenders between different alternatives created a situation in which many offenders were being diverted 'within' the system, rather than out of it. The consequence was thus to create a self-reinforcing system which involved not so much a policy of 'decarceration' but of 'transcarceration', through which offenders became continuously recycled by a number of different agencies through a range of institutions (Lowman *et al.*, 1986).

The fourth problem was to do with the appropriateness and availability of alternatives to custody. Fines, for example, which had been widely seen in the post-war period as a consistently suitable sanction for a whole range of offences, came to be seen as less appropriate during the 1980s, as levels of poverty and inequality increased (Allen, 1989; Young, 1989). Similar difficulties have occurred in relation to the use of community service orders, in that suitable activities are not readily available in certain areas and therefore the deployment of this sanction is limited (Carlen, 1990; Vass, 1990).

Thus by the late 1980s the optimistic assumption that the introduction of a range of non-custodial penalties would reduce the prison population was met with increasing disillusionment. It was widely felt that if measures were to be introduced to limit prison use, they would need to be directed at those offenders who were actually 'at risk' of receiving a prison sentence, and at the same time provide an option which the judiciary would see as a viable alternative to custody. The response was that there is a need to introduce 'intermediate sanctions' which could act as effective alternatives to imprisonment and not just be seen as 'soft' options (Byrne *et al.*, 1992; Morris and Tonry, 1990). However, the introduction of intermediate sanctions in the form of house arrest, electronic monitoring or forms of intensive probation still have to overcome the problem of ensuring that these sanctions are used for the types of offenders for whom they are designed, and that they avoid being used as alternatives to existing alternatives.

In relation to back-door strategies the results are equally uncertain. The introduction of parole in England and Wales in 1968 was designed to shorten the length of time actually served. As with the experimentation of front-door strategies in the 1970s, the introduction of parole was expected to have an obvious and direct effect in reducing the average daily population in prison. But its introduction has been seen as providing only a limited reduction in prison populations and creating new tensions and anxieties within the prison system. This is because some saw it as undermining the 'honesty' of sentencing policy, by introducing increased uncertainty into the lives of prisoners and their families, and ultimately being self-defeating by encouraging the judiciary to pass longer sentences which anticipate the possibility of early release (Bottomley, 1984). Despite these shortcomings, however, it has been argued with some justification that without the availability of parole in the 1980s the prison population would have been considerably higher (Worrall and Pease, 1986).

In sum, the expectations and optimism which were widely associated with the development of both alternatives to custody and parole require some reconsideration. The haphazard and often pragmatic way in which these measures have been implemented has produced various anomalies and uncertainties. One consequence is that, rather than simply reducing the size of the prison population or reducing the problem of overcrowding, they have resulted in the construction of a much more elaborate system of penality, in which the dynamics of control are more complex and the outcomes more uncertain. Gains have often been short term and limited to particular populations.

What is now required if prison use is to be more effectively controlled through the use of alternatives, is that they will need to be developed in a more systematic and integrated form. It is not enough simply to create more and more non-custodial penalties or new forms of early release but rather there is a need to develop appropriate sanctions for different types of offences and different types of offenders, which are commensurate with current notions of justice, fairness and culpability. One country which has been widely perceived as developing an effective sentencing strategy combined with a good use of alternatives to custody is the Netherlands. For these reasons it has become a major reference point for discussions on developing ways to limit the use of prisons.

CONTRASTS IN TOLERANCE

During the 1980s there was a great deal of interest among British criminologists in Dutch penal policy. While England and Wales were experiencing growing concerns about the numbers of people in prison, the problems of overcrowding and the apparent limitations of developing alternatives to custody, the Dutch were not only reducing the numbers of people in prison but their prison conditions were among the best in Europe (Rutherford, 1984). What was particularly remarkable about the Dutch situation was that they managed to reduce the prison population during a period in which crime was increasing at a rate which was roughly similar to that of England and Wales. Between 1945 and 1957 the Netherlands had a higher average number of people per 100 000 in custody, but by the end of the 1950s the average daily population in both countries converged, and from that point onwards the numbers imprisoned per 100 000 population in the Netherlands became progressively lower than that for England and Wales. In England and Wales between 1957 and 1975 the average daily prison population doubled, while that of the Netherlands almost halved (Downes, 1988).

The principal reason given for this divergence of prison trends in the two countries was the relatively short length of sentence imposed in the Netherlands. Over half the sentences imposed in 1975 were for less than one month, while the number of sentences of a year or more decreased from 12 per cent in 1950 to just 4 per cent in 1975 (Steenhuis *et al.*, 1983). The question for British researchers was how the Dutch managed to maintain such a mild-penal climate in the face of an increasing crime rate. The suggestion that this mild penal climate was a product of leniency was questioned by David Downes (1988), who pointed out that the Dutch imprisoned roughly the same proportion of offenders as England and Wales. Downes also examined the differences in crime between the two countries and while noting some significant differences, suggested that declining clear-up rates and widespread use of pre-court diversion strategies, as well as the use of judicial discretion not to prosecute, were among the key factors in limiting prison use.

What, then, were the differences between Dutch and English penal policy? One major difference, Downes suggests, is that the Dutch have generally adopted restitutive rather than repressive measures:

> For the prisons, these strategies have resulted in a contrast between shielding and dumping. In the Netherlands the small prison system was shielded by not only the waiving policies of the public prosecutors but also by the co-operation of the courts in lenient sentencing and the falling clear-up rate. In England, the prison system became progressively more swollen as offenders passed through the criminal justice system to be dumped inside its walls. Rising crime in the Netherlands was handled by extending the shields in even more flexible ways. In England, attempts were made to manage the growing size of the dumps more effectively. (Downes, 1988: 193–4)

Although expressing some reservations about the possibilities of transporting policies from one country to another, Downes suggests that the Dutch have proved that humane containment is possible within a reductionist framework. Drawing on the Dutch experience, he suggests a number of measures which in combination can achieve a more positive prison system. These include the drastic shortening of prison sentences, which would need to take place within a well co-ordinated penal system. Some limits would need to be placed on the penal estate, and there would need to be legally enforced minimum standards for prison conditions, combined with an attempt to divert persistent petty offenders away from custody.

Unfortunately, while British criminologists were busy discussing the Dutch situations during the 1980s in order to find out the key to the Dutch 'success', the Netherlands itself embarked on a prison building programme and the prison population increased from around 2500 in 1975 to over 12 000 by the mid-1990s. Sentence lengths increased from an average of 33 days in 1972 to 152 in 1992 and the prison population became swollen by those convicted of drug-related offences, as well as by a growing number of non-nationals (Swaaningen and de Jonge, 1995). Why this shift in penal climate occurred is unclear. The official line, which is generally accepted by Downes, claims that the hardening of penal policy in the Netherlands was a result of a process of 'depillarisation', by which the regulatory powers of the church, the trade unions and the social elite were eroded. As a consequence the existing system of informal controls was undermined, resulting in increased levels of crime, which in turn led to increased public demands for tougher 'law and order' policies. This account of developments has been challenged by Herman Franke (1990), who suggests that the more likely causes of the increasing crime rates and greater levels of punitiveness in the Netherlands were: 'changing economic conditions, rising unemployment, and increasing relative deprivation'.

CONCLUSION

An examination of the determinants of prison use suggests that the size and composition of the prison is the product of a number of competing and countervailing forces. Although there is no single determinant, the aim of this investigation has been to try to identify those processes which have had the most impact on the scale of imprisonment during the 1980s. A range of exterior processes have been examined and it was suggested that, despite the 'get tough' rhetoric and the growing concern with 'law and order' in Britain in the 1980s, this rhetoric did not automatically translate into authoritarian practices. Instead, policies were driven by a monetarist and managerialist rationale which was deeply concerned with cost-effectiveness. Quite surprisingly, the average daily prison population remained fairly stable throughout the decade, while the numbers sent to prison rose slightly between 1980 and 1985, thereafter decreasing towards the end of the decade to below the 1980 level. Thus it would have been more appropriate if the penologists who were examining changes in the 1970s and 1980s in England and Wales had posed the question in terms of the relative stability of imprisonment, rather than trying to explain an assumed increase in the prison population as a whole.

The prison building programme, which was widely perceived as encouraging expansionist policies, has generally served to improve conditions for a growing number of prisoners. The implications of not embarking on this programme without reducing the level of crime or changing the nature of sentencing policy was not, as some prison reformers argued, to limit prison numbers but to increase overcrowding. Thus 'radical' reformers in the 1980s found themselves in the paradoxical situation of arguing for improved prison conditions on the one hand, and for a moratorium on prison building on the other, without offering a realistic way of reducing the numbers in prison. Since many of them were also sceptical about the use of alternatives to custody, it was not surprising that many became disenchanted and pessimistic about the possibility of developing progressive penal reform strategies.

In terms of interior processes, the emphasis which is often placed on the growth of crime in driving up the prison population was found to be exaggerated. Although the level of crime more than doubled over the decade, different crimes increased at roughly the same rate, with the exception of robbery and certain forms of violence. Thus the 'workload model' needs to be supplemented with an examination of the changing processes of selection within the criminal justice system, whereby some offenders are increasingly filtered out of the system while others are processed with increasing vigour. Demographic shifts had an impact on the scale of imprisonment, but it is difficult to determine with any accuracy exactly how these shifts were translated into the production of imprisonable populations. The evidence which would be required to appreciate fully the effects of demographic change is not, as yet, available. However, there can be little doubt that the reduction of the number of juveniles in the population had a depressing effect on both crime and imprisonment. The 1980s also witnessed an increasing concentration of victimisation among already vulnerable groups. There was also some indication of growing regional disparities in imprisonment rates, which appeared to reflect changing patterns of crime and victimsation as well as changes in patterns of employment and deprivation.

There was a significant change in clear-up rates for different offences, with burglary and theft decreasing significantly, while violent and sexual crimes remained relatively stable (Nuttall and Pease, 1994). For the offences of burglary and theft which were cleared up, offenders were more likely to receive a caution, particularly if they were young. Of those who went to court for these offences, a growing percentage were given non-custodial penalties. At the same time, the numbers of violent (including robbery) and sexual crimes processed remained stable and those cases which appeared in the Crown Court received longer sentences on average. The net result of this policy was that the composition of the prison population changed significantly, with a greater percentage of prisoners incarcerated for crimes of violence, robbery or sexual offences; a significant percentage of those convicted of these offences were given longer sentences. The research carried out by David Farrington, Patrick Langan and Per-Olof Wikstrom (1994a), which examined changes in crime and punishment in England and Wales between 1981 and 1991, found that there were growing disparities at virtually every stage of the process between the processing of burglary and vehicle theft, on one hand, and violent crime on the other. Most importantly, differences in clear-up rates between property and violent crime were compounded by differences in the number of adults given a custodial sentence and the time actually served in prison. The outcome of these changing processes of selection was that by the end of the decade almost half of those in prison were imprisoned for violent or sexual offences. Thus, by the beginning of the 1990s there were more long-term, violent and more volatile prisoners behind bars in England and Wales than there had been 10 years earlier.

7 Young People in Custody

INTRODUCTION

During the nineteenth century two new characters appeared on the social landscape – the adolescent and the juvenile delinquent. Adolescence came to denote a new phase in personal development which stood between childhood and adulthood. Young people were no longer seen as 'little adults', but rather as persons still in the process of personal development who were not, as yet, fully responsible for their actions. Closely associated with these new conceptions of childhood and adolescence was the formation of the modern family and the introduction of compulsory education. These two agencies took on increasing responsibility for both extending and deepening the processes of socialisation (Gillis, 1974; May, 1973).

Alongside the adolescent, the related figure of the juvenile delinquent was formed. The juvenile delinquent stood in contrast to the healthy adolescent and was seen as a product of faulty socialisation, inadequate parental supervision, or a lack of proper education. He or she was someone who was predisposed towards crime as a result of under-socialisation or as a product of environmental conditions, and was therefore in need of guidance and reform (Pearson, 1983). Fortunately for the delinquent there was a growing body of experts who had already developed their expertise through their involvement in prisons – lawyers, doctors, psychiatrists and criminologists – and who were on hand with an extensive repertoire of explanations which they claimed could account for delinquency among young people.

The juvenile delinquent provided a convenient object for the growing debates on the causes of crime and the relative contribution of environmental, domestic, hereditary and other factors that were held by criminologists and psychologists to lead to criminality. Although there were differences of opinion over the primary determinants of criminality, most commentators agreed that if the problem were to be addressed, it was necessary to catch delinquents while they were young and reformable. The growing concerns about juvenile delinquency and the thousands of 'lost' children and hooligans who were becoming a more visible feature of inner city life were expressed at the end of the nineteenth century by General Booth:

The lawlessness of our lads, the increased licence of our girls, the general shiftlessness from the home-making point of view of the product of our factories and schools are far from reassuring. Our young people have never learned to obey. The fighting gangs of half-grown lads in Lisson Grove and the Scuttlers of Manchester are ugly symptoms of a social condition that will not grow better by being left alone. (Booth, 1890: 66)

In this statement General Booth identified the three key points of reference by which the processes of juvenile socialisation were to be measured in future decades: the family, education and the labour market. One of the defining features, however, of the young delinquent was precisely their marginality from all three processes. What was also evident in the pronouncements of General Booth and many of his contemporaries was that it was clearly no longer possible to rely on the established forms of philanthropy to deal with the problems affecting the poor who lived in the inner cities. Instead, the situation required a more formal and impersonal approach.

The growing concerns in the mid-nineteenth century with youthful misbehaviour and 'hooliganism' on one side, and neglect on the other, encouraged reformers like Mary Carpenter (1851) to distinguish between the 'dangerous classes' and the 'perishing classes' – vagrants, those excluded from schooling and those suffering from parental neglect. She was also influential in promoting the introduction of reformatory and industrial schools in the 1850s as specialist institutions for young offenders. The key to reformation, Mary Carpenter suggested, was to place wayward juveniles in a proper position of dependence within an organised family system so that they might be 'gradually restored to the true position of childhood'.

Up to this point young offenders had been subject to the main forms of punishment which were in use – capital conviction, transportation and imprisonment. But the decrease in the use of transportation and the consequent increase in the use of imprisonment resulted in the incarceration of some 12 000 juveniles annually in the 1850s. This level of imprisonment among young people became increasingly seen as inappropriate and counterproductive. Imprisonment for juveniles, as John Howard and others had argued, was likely to create 'schools of crime', while the relatively short periods of confinement provided little possibility for reform. In political circles it was felt that imprisoning young people had the effect of reducing rather than increasing parental responsibilities.

Attempts to separate younger from older offenders had taken place in the early part of the nineteenth century. There had been a prison ship for juveniles and in 1830 a separate prison for male juveniles was opened in Parkhurst Prison. By the end of the nineteenth century there existed a widespread system of reformatory and industrial schools were designed to accommodate children and young people previously sent to prison. By 1895 there were around 24 000 young people in these schools, which were run for the most part by voluntary associations. These institutions were designed to filter those under sixteen years of age out of the prison system and to place them in reformatories, where they could be held from between three to five years. Consequently, the number of those aged under sixteen sent to prison decreased from 10 000 in 1870 to 4500 in 1890 and to less than 1000 by 1907.

Alongside the development of specialist exclusionary strategies in the form of reformatory and industrial schools, there emerged around the turn of the century a range of inclusionary strategies aimed at dealing with young people in their own communities. These inclusionary responses, which formed part of what David Garland (1981) has referred to as the 'welfare sanction', provided forms of intervention which, rather than disrupt the process of socialisation for wayward juveniles and reduce parental responsibilities, offered a more continuous but necessarily more intrusive approach. These strategies had the advantage that they could address the situation not only of the young person concerned but also of the family as a whole (Cohen, 1985; Harris and Webb, 1987).

In contrast to the popular nineteenth century view that to 'save' and reform individuals it was necessary to remove them from the corrupting influence of their environment and community, the increasingly dominant view by the turn of the century was that if interventions were to have maximum effect they would need to take into account the background and disposition of the offender (Platt, 1969). The young offender, not being fully responsible for his or her actions, was deemed to be in need of support, supervision, guidance and control. This task required the accumulation of detailed and co-ordinated knowledge on each individual, which could relate offending to personal circumstances.

The introduction of the probation service in 1907, with its emphasis on supervising offenders in the community, was seen as a particularly suitable agency for supervising young people. By 1920 four out of five of the 10 000 people under probation supervision were under the age of twenty-one (Rutherford, 1986). In the longer term the key agency involved in developing inclusionary strategies was social work. As Jacques Donzelot (1979) has argued, the development of social work was critical to the elaboration of the juvenile justice system and the implementation of the 'welfare sanction'. He suggests that the two major historical achievements of social work are firstly that, as an agency with no institutional base of its own, it has played a critical role in linking the juvenile court, the family and the school by tracing the movement and performance of the individual through each of these settings; and secondly that, by drawing freely on the concepts of psychoanalysis, it promoted a particular form of discourse and a set of analytic categories through which the behaviour and attitudes of young people could be examined and assessed. This discourse located the problems of juvenile delinquency principally within the sphere of the individual's relation to their family, providing an approach which was complementary to that being developed by the probation service and which dovetailed with dominant legal discourses of the atomised judicial subject (King and Piper, 1990; Pearson, 1975).

Despite this element of formal compatibility, a number of underlying tensions emerged between legalistic and welfare approaches. In particular there is a tension between an adversarial system of law and the reliance on legal evidence and procedures on one hand, and the attempt to address the problems or the needs of the young person on the other. This discrepancy between 'care and control' which is located at the centre of the juvenile justice system has generated ongoing debates over rights, legal representation, due process and protection, as well as differences over what constitutes the 'best interests' of the child. These tensions and debates are played out daily in the juvenile court.

Although the industrial schools were widely used up to the end of the century, with some 15 000 children held in them, compared to 5000 in juvenile reformatories in the 1880s, their populations began to decrease during the first quarter of the twentieth century. Criticisms from the press and from the Prison Inspectorate drew attention to the perceived limitations of these institutions. In the 1920s Sir William Clarke-Hall (1926) expressed the view that 'no child should be sent to an Industrial or Reformatory School if there is a reasonable hope of reforming him by other means'. The apparent 'failure' of the reformatory and industrial schools, however, detracted from the growing belief that young people needed to be treated differently and that it was necessary to develop a penal system which could offer specialist provision for young people. Increasingly attention shifted towards strategies for dealing with troublesome young people through community-based agencies.

By the outbreak of the Great War in 1914, a modified exclusionary system of control had been constructed in the form of reformatory and industrial schools and an embryonic inclusionary system centred around the probation service and the emerging social work profession had also been established. This dual response to the traditional forms of imprisonment involved new forms of classification and changing conceptions of youth and individual responsibility. The creation of a penal system which incorporated these forms of specialist provision for young people was realised in the passing of the Children Act 1908, which established a separate system of juvenile justice and introduced the juvenile court, which was to deal with the cases of those under 16 years of age.

Around the turn of the century there had been a growing debate about how to respond to those between the ages of 16 and 21 years of age. Gladstone had expressed the view that there was a need for a different kind of regime for prisoners aged between 18 and 23, which he suggested could operate halfway between the prison and the reformatory. Influenced by the spread of reformatories for those aged between 16 and 30 in America, the first of which had been opened at Elmira in New York in 1876, Gladstone advocated a new type of institution which could accommodate those in danger of becoming habitual criminals.

BORSTAL AND BEYOND

Sir Evelyn Ruggles-Brise, who was to be Chairman of the Prison Commission for over 25 years, took personal responsibility for devising a response to the 'young hooligan advanced in crime'. These wayward young people were to be reformed by:

> a stern and exact discipline, tempered only by such rewards and privileges as good conduct with industry might earn; and resting on its physical side on the basis of hard manual labour and skilled trades and on its moral and intellectual side on the combined efforts of the Chaplain and Schoolmaster. (Ruggles-Brise, 1921: 142)

On the basis of these pronouncements, a scheme was begun at Borstal Convict Prison near Rochester, which was to give its name to the emergent 'borstal' system. Between 1905 and 1920 borstals were set up for males at Dartmoor, Lincoln, Feltham, Portland and part of Aylesbury Convict Prison was converted into a convict institution for young women. There was also a 'modified' borstal for young women in operation at Holloway Prison. The modified borstal system was designed for those aged 16–21 serving short sentences. They were segregated from adults and given physical exercise, drill and weekly lectures, followed up by a system of after care. By 1921 there were over 900 young men undergoing borstal training, and nearly 250 young women (Forsythe, 1990). Borstal training for girls had, however, fallen a long way behind that for boys by the 1920s. The institution of girls located in the former prison at Aylesbury accommodated around 200 inmates. It provided a retraining regime which was monotonous and repressive and little different in most respects from a conventional prison, despite the special physical and emotional needs which were widely seen as being associated with adolescent girls (Bailey, 1987).

Borstals were located on the custodial continuum somewhere between prisons and reformatories. Designed initially for persistent young offenders between the ages of 16 and 21 years who had been given sentences of one to three years, they offered the possibility of early release after six months. The aims of these institutions were to provide education and occupational skills and to instill the habit of hard work. Males would work in the workshops and the farms attached to the borstals and each day there would be 'silent hours' for study, religious instruction and drill to promote physical co-ordination, mental alertness and obedience. Young women, on the other hand, would learn domestic skills through participation in laundry work, housework, needlework and cooking.

In the inter-war period the borstal system was hailed throughout England and Wales as a promising and effective innovation. It was claimed that about 70 per cent of trainees were successfully 'reclaimed'. Assurances came from governors, magistrates and journalists that the borstal system improved the demeanour and attitudes of its charges, who were in many cases reformed (Ruggles-Brise, 1921). Consequently, the number of young people sent to borstal increased in the inter-war period and by 1938 the number of males detained had increased to over 1500. In fact, just over half of all institutional commitments by the end of the 1930s were for borstal sentences (Hood, 1965). Although approximately two-thirds of those confined to borstals were discharged at the outbreak of the Second World War in 1939, the number of young people in borstals continued to grow, with 2358 young people in borstals in 1946. Indeed, borstals were the only part of the prison system in England and Wales to expand in the immediate post-war period.

During the period of sustained growth, between 1920 and 1950, there were three recurring issues which arose in relation to the development of the borstal. The first was who should be eligible for borstal training. Opinions varied over the age of criminal responsibility and the age at which people would cease to benefit from the type of training available. The problem was that the older and often more experienced offenders were less likely to be reformed, while younger and more inexperienced offenders who might have derived some benefit from such a regime were not always considered suitable.

The second issue concerned the length of time necessary for borstal training. If training was to be effective, it needed to be for a period of between one and three years, it was argued. However, such long periods of confinement were at odds with established notions of justice and proportionality (Lawson, 1970).

The third issue which was repeatedly raised was the relationship between prisons and borstals. Were borstals to be an alternative to prison? If not, should they operate as 'open' or closed' institutions? Reginald McKenna, the Home Secretary, stated in 1914 that borstals should involve the deprivation of liberty only to the degree necessary to achieve the objectives of training and education. The reality, as Roger Hood (1965) has argued, was that by the 1930s borstals were increasingly coming to resemble prisons, as training became more mundane and monotonous, with few inmates learning proper skills. Periods of confinement became shorter as the level of security increased.

During the 1950s the borstal system fell into disfavour. Not only were they seen as increasingly resembling the prisons they were designed to replace, but they also offered little real prospect of rehabilitation. In 1948 the Criminal Justice Act introduced detention centres for young people seen to be less in need of lengthy training (Rutherford, 1986). Detention centres were explicitly punitive and were structured partly to offset the 'soft' implications of abolishing judicial corporal punishments and partly to take pressure off borstals and prisons. They were administered by the Prisons Department and were largely devoid of any reformative or educational component but did involve a period of after care with supervision. They were designed for young people between the ages of 17 and 21 who were seen as unsuitable for probation and for whom long periods of treatment in a borstal was seen as inappropriate.

Within the detention centres the emphasis was on hard work and strict discipline, which was designed to replicate the arrangements in prison in various ways:

> Normally the Centres have perimeter security and the boys are kept under close supervision within the establishment. They are left with comparatively little free time in an active day. Work forms part of the treatment and there is a full working day of 8 hours. The short period of detention rules out elaborate trade training, but there is sufficient time to engender a habit of consistent effort and to encourage the boys to find a sense of achievement in work rather than to regard it as mere drudgery. Pocket money depends on the marks earned each day, effort rather than output being assessed. In addition to domestic work and labouring, the boys are given constructive work of a type that can be mastered quickly. This includes making sports nets, concrete moulding, metal recovery and commercial greenhouse production as well as work on the farm or garden. (Home Office, 1970)

Although public and political support for the borstal declined in the 1950s, the number of young people sent to borstal increased from just over 2000 in 1952 to 4000 in 1965 (Millham *et al.*, 1978). However, behind its varying fortunes the borstal system brought the three key elements of the prison system – space, time and labour – into question. The borstals' more open nature offered greater freedom of movement in and out of the institution. The experimentation with time and periods of training and the greater emphasis on education and personal development counterbalanced the emphasis upon labour discipline which had been a core feature of the earlier prison system. Borstals, however, always remained in effect junior prisons, in which the time–space relationship was stretched and readapted. Although the doors between the inmates and the outside world were not always locked, the young people lived in 'houses' rather than wings, and the emphasis was on training and education rather than productive work, the borstal challenged but did not really depart from the essential structure of the prison.

In a similar way the approved schools, which had been in operation for those described as being in need of 'care and protection' or being 'beyond control' in the 1930s, despite their punitive functions, were not highly controlled custodial institutions. As Millham *et al.* (1975) have pointed out, 'they are open to the outside world, and in many ways boys are less constrained in them than in ordinary boarding schools'. Comparisons between approved schools and boarding schools have been common in the literature, with many commentators arguing that approved schools were in fact better in many respects than some boarding schools, since unlike the latter at least they were 'approved' (Dunlop, 1974; Hood and Sparks, 1969).

Thus, by the 1950s an array of custodial institutions was available in England and Wales for young people. Alongside the borstal, the detention centre and the approved school, remand centres were introduced for those aged between 17 and 21 years who would otherwise be sent to a local prison. Other forms of detention were also available for young people, including community homes, attendance centres and secure units. 'Community homes' became the generic term used to cover all those institutions which formed part of a growing system of residential care. The aim had been to introduce greater flexibility into the system in order to accommodate both offenders and non-offenders who were seen to exhibit similar personal and social problems. The flexibility of this process resulted in a more elaborate system of classification and assessment and the provision of a range of open and closed institutions (Hood and Sparks, 1969). Among these institutions were 'secure units' for those deemed to require control rather than care, although the actual differences in behaviour between those sent to secure units and those placed in care were not great (Millham *et al.*, 1978). Attendance centres were established in 1948 and were designed to deprive young offenders of their leisure time. Remand centres were set up at the same time for young people awaiting trial or sentence.

Increasingly in the post-war period the juvenile justice and child care systems became intertwined. The Children Act (1948) created local authority children's departments. This expanded the role of social work and consequently increased forms of welfare intervention aimed at promoting inclusive strategies. The blurring of the distinction between the deprived and depraved child was a feature of the 1933 Children and Young Persons Act, which stated that:

> There is little or no difference in character and needs between the neglected and the delinquent child. It is often a mere accident whether he is brought before the court because he is wandering or beyond control or because he has committed some offence. Neglect leads to delinquency. (Home Office, 1933: 6)

The tension between care and control, welfare and punishment, inclusionary and exclusionary forms of intervention took a number of distinct turns in the 1960s, 1970s and 1980s, which had profound effects on the number of young people locked up in custodial institutions and the kinds of regimes which they experienced (Morris and Giller, 1987).

THE INCARCERATION OF YOUNG PEOPLE IN THE POST-WAR PERIOD

In the post-war period the term 'youth' became widely identified as a metaphor for social change. The development of youth subcultures, particularly during the 1950s and 1960s, and the growing autonomy and affluence of certain sections of the teenage population generated different images of and attitudes towards young people (Clarke *et al.*, 1975). It was against this background that the incarceration of young people was organised in the post-war period. By the 1950s a complex system of care and control, involving different forms of custody and detention, had been established. The 1948 Criminal Justice Act was something of a landmark in juvenile justice reform. Although it had introduced remand centres, attendance centres and detention centres, it simultaneously gave financial backing to the provision of probation hostels, while abolishing corporal punishment and attempted to place further restrictions on the use of imprisonment for young people (Bailey, 1987). The attempt to place restrictions on the use of imprisonment and the encouragement of community-based sanctions can be seen as a precursor to the more general strategy of juvenile decarceration which developed during the 1960s.

In the pre-war period there had been a number of penal reformers who argued that incarceration should be used as sparingly as possible for young people. But it was not until the 1960s that these arguments found a wide audience in both official and professional circles. Thus, from the mid-1960s onwards, there was a continuous, but not always consistent, movement towards the decarceration of young people. The term 'decarceration' is meant to embrace a range of strategies, including decriminalisation, diversion and de-institutionalisation, with the aim of each strategy or a combination of strategies being to reduce the number of people in custody (Matthews, 1979; Scull, 1977). Although these strategies became particularly pronounced in the

1960s, it should be noted that there were oppositional voices which expressed deep scepticism about the possible benefits of any form of decarceration and called for the increased use of penal custody for young people in order to deter juvenile offenders during those periods in which they were most actively involved in crime (Boland, 1980; Boland and Wilson, 1978).

Despite continuous and at times vigorous objections, the period between 1960 and 1990 can be seen as an era in which decarceration in its various forms was pursued through a number of different channels. Within the juvenile justice literature it has become a convention to identify three general approaches – welfarism, back to justice and corporatism – as the dominant approaches through which the reduction in the number of juveniles in custody was attempted. An examination of the application of these three approaches allows an assessment to be made of the most appropriate and effective decarceration strategy. A review of the developments between 1960 and 1990 provides some salutary lessons about the difficulties in attempting to influence the scale of imprisonment, and the problems associated with reorganising the distribution of sanctions between custodial and non-custodial options.

The Welfare Approach (1965–72)

During the 1960s a number of critiques of the use of incarceration were forcibly expressed, particularly where it was used for young people. These critiques in many cases were far from new, but during the 1960s they gathered momentum and crystallised around three main themes. They were for the most part premised on the assumption that welfare-orientated, inclusive and community-based sanctions are in general preferable and that penal custody, whether it be in the form of prison, borstal, remand centre or detention centre, was either inappropriate or counterproductive. The three major themes which emerged in this period can be identified as debilitation; decriminalisation; and discrimination.

Debilitation
A significant impetus to the decarceration movement was given by Erving Goffman's (1968) critique of 'total institutions'. He argued that rather than reforming or rehabilitating offenders, the experience of institutionalisation was more likely to have a negative impact upon prisoners, resulting in a process of 'debilitation' through the combined

effects of alienation, institutionalisation and marginalisation. A few years later Norval Morris' (1974) critique of enforced forms of rehabilitation within prisons pointed out the ethical and practical issues associated with 'enforced cures'. These combined critiques placed considerable doubt upon the extent of reform and rehabilitation that could be achieved within the prison setting, since they suggested that short periods of incarceration did not allow for the possibility of rehabilitation, while longer periods of confinement always carried the danger of institutionalisation and further marginalisation. For a number of critics, arguments relating to the damaging effects of incarceration were combined with the long-standing assertion that, rather than reforming offenders, penal institutions serve as 'schools of crime', turning young and inexperienced offenders into hardened and committed criminals.

Decriminalisation

A second theme which gained prominence during the 1960s was a questioning of both the degree of criminal responsibility of young people and the significance of juvenile offending. For a number of commentators juvenile offending was seen as a symptom of an underlying personal or social problems which needed to be addressed. For this reason it was not enough simply to respond to a specific act or offence, but the aim should be to uncover the underlying processes that had led to the offending. In the more radical version of this argument it was suggested that juvenile misbehaviour was a normal part of growing up, and therefore juvenile offending should be tolerated as much as possible without implementing formal sanctions (Schur, 1973). Young people, it was suggested, would grow out of crime and there are very real dangers of entangling them unnecessarily in the criminal justice system, since this might serve to reinforce their delinquency through the process of stigmatisation and labelling (Lemert, 1970; Rutherford, 1986).

Closely related to the drive towards the decriminalisation of juvenile misbehaviour was the apparent inappropriateness of the juvenile court for identifying the underlying problems and needs of the child. The emphasis within the adversarial system on the determination of guilt or innocence was seen by many observers as largely irrelevant to the situation of the young person. As the authors of the Kilbrandon Committee of Inquiry Report (1964) pointed out, the vast majority of cases in the juvenile court are not contested. The aim of any court or panel, Kilbrandon argued, was to identify the needs of the young person within a context that allowed for the proper formulation of a suitable disposal.

Discrimination

A third theme which ran through much of the literature in the 1960s was that penal sanctions are largely reserved for working-class and poor people, while middle-class young people who may be troublesome tend to be dealt with in more informal and less stigmatising ways. Echoing the sentiments that had been expressed by the young Winston Churchill some 50 years earlier, the authors of the influential Longford Report, *Crime – A Challenge to Us All* (1964), wrote:

> Chronic or serious delinquency in a child is, in the main we believe, evidence of the lack of the care, guidance and the opportunities to which every child is entitled. There are few children who do not behave badly at times, but the children of parents with ample means rarely appear before the juvenile courts. The machinery of law is reserved mainly for working class children, who, more often than not, are also handicapped by being taught in too big classes in unsatisfactory school buildings with few amenities or opportunities for out of school activities. (Longford Committee, 1964: 21)

The fact that troublesome young people from middle-class and upper-class backgrounds were in practice excluded from the juvenile justice system and from penal institutions, and dealt with in more informal and less stigmatising ways, persuaded Longford that a similar approach could and ought to be employed in relation to working-class youth. Thus it was suggested that the age of criminal responsibility should be increased to the current school leaving age, and that 'children should receive the kind of treatment they need without any stigma or association with the penal system'. The accusation that the juvenile courts and penal institutions were highly selective in terms of class was extended during the 1970s and 1980s to include what was seen as the discriminatory treatment of young Afro-Caribbeans and young disadvantaged females.

In many respects these objections to the use of penal custody for young people are generally seen as applicable to other groups of offenders. The growing scepticism about the benefits of imprisonment which was expressed throughout the 1960s led to the development of a number of alternatives to custody, designed to reduce the reliance on the prison, the borstal and the detention centre. Much of this anti-custodial thinking was encapsulated in the White Paper *Children in Trouble* (Home Office, 1968) which set out to both decriminalise and deinstitutionalise juveniles. The White Paper included proposals to abandon the juvenile court and to replace it wherever possible with informal and voluntary agreements between the parties involved, in order to minimise the effects of stigma. Exhibiting a deep social work influence, *Children in Trouble* reinforced the view that delinquency was presenting a symptom of deeper maladjustment.

The proposals included in this White Paper formed the basis of the 1969 Children and Young Persons Act (CYPA), which is widely seen as a watershed in juvenile justice. This Act raised the age of criminal responsibility to 14 and proposed that young offenders should not have to go to court, but should be allowed to negotiate a suitable form of treatment in conjunction with their parents and social workers. At the same time the 1969 CYPA directed that considerable power was to be placed in the hands of local authorities through the provision of care orders, which were to replace the use of approved schools. Attendance centres and detention centres were also to be replaced by a new form of intermediate treatment which was to be run by local authorities. As a consequence decisions over the implementation of sanctions shifted away from magistrates and towards juvenile justice practitioners (Pitts, 1996).

It is interesting to note that the movement towards decriminalisation and deinstitutionalisation of juveniles took place against a background of rising juvenile crime (Bottoms, 1974). In 1961 the delinquency rate for males aged between 10 and 16 was around 28 per 1000 population, by 1966 it had increased to 30.5 per 1000 and by 1971 it was just over 42 per 1000. During this period there had been a 50 per cent increase in the number of young people aged 10–16 who had been cautioned or convicted for an indictable offence (Farrington, 1992). It should be noted, however, that, despite the growing emphasis upon the need to deal with young people in less stigmatising and more informal ways, the number of young people in borstals, detention centres and prisons continued to increase.

The aspirations of the 1969 CYPA were never fully realised. This was mainly because the Act was not implemented in its entirely because there were considerable objections to parts of the Act by the Magistrates Association and by members the Conservative government elected in 1972. Some commentators have, however, argued that even if the Act had been fully implemented, it would never have achieved its objectives, as it lacked consistency and because of its conceptual inadequacies. Andrew Rutherford (1983), for example, has argued that the 1969 CYPA failed to face up squarely to the issue of the role of penal custody in relation to young offenders and did not provide a clear indication of the allocation of responsibilities between central and local government.

The outcome of the 1969 CYPA was that elements of the new system – such as intermediate treatment – were brought in, but the existing system centred around the juvenile court and the use of penal custody for juveniles was not phased out. The result was an expansion of the welfare–justice continuum and the creation of a more complex and diverse system of juvenile justice, involving a mix of care and control, punishment and welfare, organised through a combination of local and central government systems of regulation. Detention centres, borstals and remand centres remained in place and the numbers incarcerated continued to increase (Pitts, 1988).

Closely related to the creation of this hybrid system was the development of a policy of bifurcation, which divides offenders into two relatively distinct groups – the normal and the dangerous. This is in part an outcome of social positivist thought, which sees offending behaviour mainly as a product of poverty, bad housing or poor childrearing. Though these explanations gained some prominence in the 1960s, they have, according to Anthony Bottoms:

> always tended to exclude two groups from this type of analysis – on the one hand the so-called 'psychiatric' offender, who offends because of individual pathology and on the other hand the straightforward, rational, calculating, entrepreneurial professional criminal – or in other words respectively the 'mad' and the 'bad'. The bifurcation tendency seems increasingly to be isolating selected groups of the 'mad' and the 'bad' as those against whom we really wish to take serious action while we are prepared to reduce penalties for the remainder. (Bottoms, 1977: 89)

The logic of a policy of bifurcation is to see offenders as polarised types – the salvageable and the unsalvageable, the serious and petty criminal, the corrupter and the corrupted. Penal detention is to be reserved for the more serious and persistent offenders, while the remainder are to be given non-custodial sentences. The flaw in the logic of the division of offenders into two distinct groups is that in practice a significant percentage of those in borstals and detention centres have also received non-custodial sentences at some point. In fact, of 5000 young offenders sent to borstal in 1967, just over a third had previously been in approved schools. Among the borstal population in that year about half were convicted of burglary, about a quarter for theft and less than 10 per cent for crimes of violence (Home Office, 1968).

The outcome of this policy of bifurcation and the operation of the expanded juvenile justice system was the growth throughout the 1970s of the number of young people detained both in penal custody and in institutions providing care and protection. Writing in the mid-1970s, Millham *et al.* (1978) found that there were some 6000 boys aged between 14 and 16 who had experienced the detention centre, and 1200 boys aged 15 and 16 who were sent to borstal in 1975. In the same year there were also 5400 juveniles remanded in adult prisons or remand centres. On the basis of these figures, they concluded that during this period more juveniles experienced a spell of penal custody than at any time since 1908.

The Justice Model (1973–82)

The realisation that the numbers of juveniles in penal custody was steadily increasing led a number of critics to blame the 'welfarism' of the 1960s for producing a system which was both more intensive and more punitive. The road to the expansion of penal custody, it was argued, was littered with well-meaning liberals with good intentions. The treatment orientation of 1960s 'welfarism' had over-pathologised the delinquent and encouraged the development of an extensive range of intrusive and ultimately counterproductive interventions. Rather than decarceration what had occurred, critics claimed, was a process of 'net widening' and a 'blurring of the boundaries' between care and control (Cohen, 1977).

By the term 'net widening' critics refer to the process by which more people are drawn into the control system and the simultaneous development of new agencies that creates a complex network of interventions. Although many of these interventions are ostensibly benign they construct a larger and more intricate 'web' of control in which a growing number of young people become entangled. As a consequence they are recycled through a network of different agencies and institutions, some of which are public and others are private (Lerman, 1982). Within the system the continual movement of individuals between different agencies and the shifting remits of the agencies themselves results in a blurring of the boundaries between those agencies that are formally charged with providing care and treatment and those that are involved in the administration of punishment. Consequently the demarcations between care and control, inclusion and exclusion, community-based and custodial forms of intervention begin to overlap and eventually become less clearly defined (Cohen, 1985).

The culmination of these explanations turned the optimism which was prevalent in the 1960s about the possibility of reducing the custodial population through the development of community-based sanctions into pessimism. It became widely believed that the proliferation of apparently benign agencies can, and often does, contribute to the expansion of a more punitive juvenile justice system (Morris and Giller, 1987). Consequently it was suggested that the purpose of intervention should be to do 'less harm' rather than 'more good'. In the words of Edwin Schur (1973), the aim should be 'to leave the kids alone whenever possible'.

Thus the 'back to justice' movement was premised on a reduction in the level of intervention. Welfarism, it was argued, had over-extended the range and depth of state intervention. The aim of penal policy should be to reduce the degree of intervention by focusing more on the act than on the actor. The failure of welfarism was that it subjected juveniles to forms of intervention which were overly intrusive while negating individual rights. In a reformulation of the tenets of classicism, the emphasis shifted from the welfare of the child to the protection of the offenders by the strict observation of due process and through the extension of formal legal representation. By moving the focus away from the care and welfare of the young person, the justice model shifted the locus of decision-making back to the magistrates and to the juvenile court.

The growing revelations about the abuses inflicted on young people in local authority care provided the necessary ammunition to close down a number of these institutions and to reduce the number of young people in residential homes (Thorpe *et al.*, 1980). Between 1977 and 1986 the use of the care order fell from 14 per cent of court disposals for all juveniles aged 14–17, to 4 per cent. Seeing the delinquent as a rational and largely responsible actor, the 'back to justice' lobby sought to impose the same 'safeguards' as the adult court, thereby reducing the distinction between the two (Morris *et al.*, 1980).

The 'back to justice' lobby had a strong punitive edge. It lent itself readily to the calls of the incoming Thatcher government to introduce a system of 'short, sharp shocks', through the implementation of tough military-style custodial regimes for juveniles. The rapid realisation that many of the young men subject to these regimes saw the military training as a perk rather than a punishment and were attracted to these activities led to the 'experiment' being abandoned and custodial institutions for juveniles reverted to their previous form (Shaw, 1985).

Although it was the aim of the justice model to ensure that juveniles were given the least restrictive sentence in each case, and that sentences should be determinate rather than indeterminate, the numbers given penal custody between 1973 and 1982 continued to increase. The number of males aged 14–16 who were sent to a detention centre increased from 4890 in 1976 to 5958 in 1981. Over the same period the number of males aged 14–16 held in this institution remained relatively stable at around 1500.

Much of the thinking associated with the 'back to justice' lobby was incorporated into the 1982 Criminal Justice Act which made provision for legal representation. This option was taken up in a significant number of cases (Burney, 1985). But probably the most important aspect of the 1982 Act was that it set limits on judicial discretion to make custodial orders. Before passing a custodial sentence the magistrate was required to justify his or her decision publicly in court. In order to pass a custodial sentence, three criteria had to be considered: that the offender is unable and unwilling to respond to non-custodial penalties; that a custodial sentence is necessary for the protection of the public; or that the offence is so serious that a non-custodial sentence cannot be justified. Although there was an increase in the number of custodial sentences given to juveniles in the period immediately after the passing of the Act, the number of juveniles in custody began to decrease in 1985–6 and the supporters of the Act claimed that the control of judicial discretion played a major role in achieving this decrease. Critics of the justice model did not agree. They claimed that the emphasis on legal processes and safeguards had undermined the juvenile justice system by increasingly treating juveniles like adults. The emphasis upon legality and formal equality masked, critics claimed, the underlying inequalities, social disadvantage and social problems experienced by many of the young people who appeared in the juvenile court (Hudson, 1987).

While academics were debating the advantages and disadvantages of 'welfare' and 'justice' or trying to find ways of reconciling these apparently oppositional approaches, practitioners and policy-makers were developing other strategies to reduce the numbers of juveniles in custody and to reorientate the juvenile justice system. Juvenile justice workers around the country were publicly claiming to establish 'custody free' zones, and different areas were being increasingly assessed by the numbers of juveniles given custody, with those areas with the highest juvenile custody rates being seen to be 'failing'.

In the mid-1980s the emphasis shifted away from the concerns about welfare and justice and towards the management and administration of delinquency. Through strategies of diversion and the introduction of effective 'gatekeepers', the aim was to prevent juveniles becoming entangled in the formal system of juvenile justice and to overcome blockages and bottlenecks within the system. During the latter half of the 1980s, as this 'delinquency management', or 'corporatist' approach became more widespread, the numbers of juveniles in custody decreased dramatically and the nature of juvenile penal institutions also changed significantly. The question which arises is the extent to which these emerging forms of managerialism were responsible for reducing the reliance on juvenile penal institutions and for fostering the eventual demise of the detention centre and the borstal in the late 1980s.

Corporatism (1984–95)

The term 'corporatism' is used as a generic term to cover a range of strategies which emerged in England and Wales during the 1980s. John Pratt (1989) has identified the key components of a 'corporatist' strategy as the increased use of administrative discretion, the extension of pre-court tribunals, and the increased use of cautioning and other forms of diversion. Corporatism in the 1980s also involved the increase of inter-agency co-operation, which served to blur the boundaries between public and private realms and between statutory and voluntary agencies. In many respects corporatism aims to side-step the controversies between welfare and justice, focusing instead on the management and increasing the cost-effectiveness of the system.

Between 1981 and 1987 the number of males aged 14–16 sent to detention centres and borstals almost halved, falling from 7473 to 3689. The decrease in the average daily population was even more dramatic, with the number of males aged 14–16 in custody falling from 1637 in 1981 to 547 in 1988. Apart from the possibly delayed impact of the 1982 Criminal Justice Act, there were significant demographic shifts in the 1980s which reduced the numbers of young people in the population. During this period delinquency became something of a 'scarce resource' and a number of agencies expressed difficulties in recruiting a suitable number of 'clients' (Pratt, 1985). These demographic changes have been identified as being responsible for up to 30 per cent of the decrease in the numbers of juveniles in custody over this period (Allen, 1991).

There was a significant increase in the use of cautioning. Between 1969 and 1986 the total number of juveniles given a police caution increased from 33 702 to 69 900. Changes in the use of cautioning have also been credited with reducing the numbers of juveniles appearing in court and being given a custodial sentence. Whereas in previous decades cautioning had merely been associated with 'net widening', during the 1980s it became widely viewed as an effective form of diversion. Although the number of juveniles cautioned increased significantly, it should be noted that the offences for which the majority of juveniles received a caution were not normally those which would have resulted in a custodial sentence.

Probably a more significant development in relation to the decreased number of juveniles appearing in court and receiving a custodial sentence was the introduction of multi-agency, pre-court diversion panels. These panels were designed to keep young people out of the juvenile court, and in particular to find a suitable disposal for those persistent petty offenders who had 'used up' their cautions. These Juvenile Liaison Bureaus (JLBs), as they became known, could make recommendations ranging from no further action to a caution or reparation, as well as other informal sanctions.

It is difficult to assess how effective these multi-agency panels were in reducing the custodial population, as the majority of serious offences were not referred to them. However, what was interesting was the ways in which these panels, which had no statutory role or formal constitution, could make critical decisions about juvenile disposals. These panels expressed a preference for administrative as opposed to judicial decision-making, which raised questions about the operation of the juvenile justice system:

> Some might think it paradoxical that a whole new agency (the JLB) has been created in order to divert young offenders from a system of justice and welfare created (very expensively) for their reception. It is certainly intriguing that the state, having organised a network of statutory services intended to cater for the needs of children, should support this new hybrid organisation which defines its brief in terms of keeping young offenders out of the clutches of those same agencies. (Davis, Boucherat and Watson, 1989: 232)

A related corporatist strategy which was designed to focus on those young offenders who were seen as at risk of receiving a custodial sentence was the development of 'intensive' intermediate treatment. This initiative, known as LAC 83(3), was funded by the DHSS. It was designed to develop over a two- or three-year period specialist projects specifically aimed at serious offenders. It involved the creation of more realistic non-custodial alternatives to custody for 'hardened' offenders which would involve inter-agency co-operation. This form of delinquency management was less concerned with the causes of crime or with the questions of 'just desserts'. Instead, it embraced elements of labelling theory and propounded a minimalism and anti-custodialism.

The effectiveness of 'intensive' intermediate treatment is again difficult to assess. Some of these projects were taken over and developed by local authorities after the initial pilot projects had run out of DHSS funding, and it seems probably that a certain percentage of serious offenders were dealt with in this period through non-custodial measures, and that the provision of competing and realistic alternatives did have some impact on reducing the custodial population. It should be noted, however, that the reduction in the use of custody for juveniles was subject to considerable regional variation, with some 70 per cent of those incarcerated being located in the North of England. It was also the case that although the number of juveniles coming before the courts decreased during this period, sentence lengths on average became longer. Finally, it is significant that the custody rates for young Afro-Caribbeans and for females did not decrease significantly during the 1980s (Matthews, 1995b).

Thus the combined effect of demographic changes and corporatist strategies does appear to have had a significant impact upon the custodial population. But equally significant in this period were the changes in the types of alternatives to custody being developed, as well as changes in the nature of juvenile incarceration itself. Three important developments took place during the 1980s in relation to the use of custodial and non-custodial options. These involved: firstly, a growing emphasis upon the use of time-based sanctions; secondly, a growing preoccupation with the monitoring of offenders; and thirdly, the demise of the borstal and the detention centre and their replacement by a new form of 'youth custody'.

Time in different forms has increasingly become the focus of criminal justice sanctions over the last decade or so. In relation to community-based interventions, greater emphasis is placed upon using up the spare time of offenders through the increased use of curfews sanctions such as community service orders. Although this sanction involves the use of a time-based punishment, it is not work time which is the focus but the offender's spare time: it involves placing a limit on the availability of leisure time. At the other end of the spectrum the use of custody for juveniles has become more time-orientated. The concerns about the cost-effectiveness of custody have given impetus to the claims that the period of incarceration should be as short as possible. Sentences have become determinate, with an emphasis on the offender serving the full length of the sentence. Thus in certain respects the use of custody for young people has reverted back to its nineteenth-century form as a punishment of measured time (Pratt, 1989).

The growing emphasis upon surveillance and the monitoring of offenders was evident in the development of 'intensive' intermediate treatment. Whereas intermediate treatment in the 1970s had been mainly concerned with counselling, face-to-face work and group work, in the 1980s it became increasingly directed towards to the monitoring of young people 'at risk'. The aim of the strategy was to monitor closely the daily activities of juveniles and provide forms of 'enhanced' supervision. The growing emphasis upon monitoring and supervision has been characterised by Stanley Cohen (1985) as the 'new behaviourism'. This strategy, he suggests, has developed out of the belief that 'solving problems by changing people is simply unproductive' and that, rather than engage in forms of treatment, counselling or supervision, 'we have to accept them as they are, modify their circumstances or deal with the consequences of their intractability'. The recent movement towards the imposition of curfews and night restriction orders can be seen as an extension of a strategy which is concerned with regulating behaviour rather than changing minds (Audit Commission, 1996).

The demise of the borstal in 1982 met with little comment or apparent regret. Its replacement by the new forms of youth custody, however, involved more than just a change of name. The new institutions were to be largely devoid of rehabilitative goals and were designed to be primarily punitive. They signalled a retreat from the notion of a therapeutic institution into something more restrictive. Corresponding changes in the internal nature of these regimes was reflected in the fact that the staff began to wear uniforms and there was a decreased emphasis upon the provision of training facilities and education. The recent interest in American-style 'boot camps', with their emphasis upon strict discipline and military-style training, indicate how far removed contemporary custodial thinking is from the pioneering ambitions which were associated with the introduction of the borstal as an alternative to the prison at the beginning of the century.

In the *Thematic Review of Young Prisoners* carried out in 1997 by the Prisons Inspectorate it was found that there was a noticeable absence of 'rigorous, purposeful and humane regimes' for young people. Instead bullying was found to be rife, accompanied by low levels of education and training and high levels of recidivism. A significant percentage of young people were found to be held in what the Inspectorate identified as 'unacceptable conditions'. Having made these observations, the report concludes that: 'There is no such thing as a neutral environment in custodial institutions. Young people are either helped or damaged by the experience'.

Thus, with a general shift from judicial to administrative forms of decision-making within the juvenile justice system, important changes have taken place in the nature of the penal institutions as well as community-based sanctions. These do not necessarily involve the process of 'net widening' and the 'blurring of boundaries'. Instead, as John Pratt (1989) has argued, it has produced a more rationalised and differentiated system of juvenile justice, in which the gulf between custodial and non-custodial sanctions has widened, while the gap between different forms of custody has narrowed.

In assessing these developments in England and Wales it is interesting to compare changes which have taken place in relation to the regulation of juveniles in other European countries, as it is evident that some other European countries also experienced substantial reductions in the number of juveniles incarcerated during the 1980s.

DECARCERATION IN EUROPE

Some brief comments on the use of custody for juveniles in Europe are necessary because there appear to be some parallel developments which occurred during the 1980s in a number of different countries. In Germany, for example, which also experienced a reduction in the number of 14–16-year-olds in the general population during this period, there was a considerable reduction in the number of young people who were subject to formal prosecution. Between 1982 and 1987 the number of 14–20-year-olds sentenced to imprisonment in West Germany fell by just under 40 per cent. It has been argued that it was a reduction of the number of young people appearing in court, as well as limiting the number held on remand, rather than a reduction in sentence lengths that caused the reduction of the juvenile custodial population (Feest, 1991; Graham, 1990). What is interesting about these developments is that both in West Germany and in England and Wales the policies of decarceration appear to have been mobilised primarily by practitioners rather than policy-makers and academics. These changing practices reflected a changing climate of opinion about how best to respond to juvenile crime and the appropriateness of custodial sentences for certain juvenile offenders.

In France, where the number of juveniles in custody also decreased during the 1980s, the juvenile justice system is focused much more towards forms of social crime prevention which aim to reduce young people's involvement in crime and limit the number of cases that come to the attention of the authorities. Within the French system there is a specialist children's judiciary in the form of the *juges des enfants*, who handle all child protection and juvenile delinquency cases which reach the courts. These judges can exercise a large degree of discretion and work closely with social workers and child care experts.

What is interesting, although a little perplexing, is that the decarceration of juveniles occurred in the 1980s in a number of different European countries through a different combination of strategies. Underpinning these different approaches appears to be a significant change in how juveniles were conceived in this period and in particular how responses to much juvenile misbehaviour appeared to take more tolerant forms. These shifts in social attitudes are even more remarkable when the extensive restructuring of Europe which occurred at this time is taken into consideration.

CONCLUSION

In many respects the history of juvenile justice has turned full circle. Although the numbers of young people currently in custody in England and Wales may be relatively low compared to the numbers incarcerated at the end of the 1970s, many of the progressive elements which were introduced at the beginning of the century have been gradually undermined or reversed. The emphasis on training, education and rehabilitation has been eroded in recent years and juvenile custodial institutions have come increasingly to resemble those adult prisons they were originally designed to replace. The introduction of the borstal marked an important development in the history of penal custody, by both diluting and extending the original penal processes. The development of juvenile penal institutions served to redefine the meaning and experience of imprisonment.

The reaffirmation and redistribution of time-based punishments can be seen as an attempt to reassert the notion of proportionality in relation to the use of both custodial and non-custodial sentences for juveniles. At the same time the growing emphasis on surveillance and the monitoring of behaviour has gradually shifted the emphasis away from responding to the perceived needs of offenders and providing care and support. The growing administrativisation of juvenile justice and the disdain for 'welfarism' has encouraged the development of new forms of managerialism which remain largely impervious to the links between social and economic disadvantage and patterns of offending. The unwillingness to explore and confront these 'deeper causes' means that the possibility of addressing the basis of offending becomes increasingly unlikely. The danger of managerialism, particularly during a period of growing inequality, unemployment and poverty, is that it can too easily turn into neglect and indifference. In this climate many young people who may be facing serious difficulties are simply left to their own devices and rather than being victims of 'net-widening' have an increased likelihood of falling through the net of social control altogether.

8 Women's Imprisonment

INTRODUCTION

The analysis of crime and punishment has suffered from a masculinist bias. Much of the literature on imprisonment has assumed the exist-ence of an undifferentiated system of incarceration and has paid little attention to the differences between the imprisonment of men and women. As a consequence many of the standard texts, such as those by Georg Rusche and Otto Kirchheimer (1968), David Rothman, (1971) and Michel Foucault (1977), which make only a passing reference to gender differences, require some qualification – if not fundamental rethinking. Adrian Howe (1994), for example, claims that: 'from a feminist perspective, conventional masculinist histories are simply scandalous', and although she acknowledges both the value of developing a political economy of women's imprisonment and of adapting Foucault's insights on power and discipline, she is critical of those accounts of the history of incarceration which have focused on 'master' patterns and which remain insensitive to gender issues. As Eileen Leonard (1982) demonstrated in her incisive critique of conventional criminological theory, gender cannot simply be added onto the existing analysis. Rather, she clearly demonstrates that by ignoring gender the major strands of criminological theory are at best partial, and at worst seriously deficient, and that a number of theories which present themselves as gender-neutral turn out on closer inspection to suffer from gender bias.

In a similar vein a review of the history of women's imprisonment reveals that the nature and pace of the development of the incarceration of women involved significant differences from that experienced by men. These differences were a function of the nature of the sexual division of labour, dominant conceptions of 'femininity' and popular theories of female criminality in different periods. The use of solitary confinement for women, for example, was not always enforced, while women were more likely to sleep in dormitories rather than single cells and work in association rather than separately. Because women were generally perceived as being more sociable and fragile than men, the imposition of a system of isolation and silence was seen as being both more difficult to enforce and possibly more damaging than imposing it on men (Zedner, 1991). On the other hand women's prisons tended to exercise a higher degree of surveillance and operate with more rigid disciplinary codes. The relatively small number of women prisoners, who were housed in most cases in buildings which had initially been designed for men, meant that women often experienced worse conditions of confinement than men convicted of similar offences (O'Brien, 1982). At the same time the introduction of mother and baby units served to create a unique space in the prison, within which the normal rules of association, communication and prison discipline were necessarily suspended.

The differences between the form of regulation practised in men's prisons and that practised in women's prisons was exemplified in the different spatial models which were developed by Jeremy Bentham and Elizabeth Fry:

> Whereas Bentham's scheme advocates uniform treatment, formal direction, rigid adherence to rules, and no industrial differentiation between prisoners, Fry went so far as to suggest that willing co-operation and cheerful submission to rules by women was a prerequisite to their reform. Her insistence on the need for individualisation became widely accepted as the most distinctive feature of the treatment of women. (Zedner, 1991: 119–20)

It became widely accepted by prison administrators in the Victorian era that women would benefit from close personal attention and that this was best provided by prison officers of their own sex. Women, Fry (1827) argued, should be held separately from men, not only to limit the corruption and exploitation of female prisoners, but also to facilitate the efforts of middle-class 'lady visitors' to provide an example of propriety and virtue for these 'fallen women'.

Women in the early nineteenth century were subject to the same principles of 'measured time' as men, and these were linked to classicist notions of proportionality. The major difference in terms of the use of time-based penalties was that the sentences imposed on female offenders were generally shorter. The length of prison sentences in general in the mid-nineteenth century were relatively short compared to today, but women in particular were subject to particularly short sentences, often for weeks rather than months.

Towards the end of the century the concept of time in relation to women's imprisonment had become redefined in two important ways, both of which were linked to the notion of proportionality. The growing realisation that many women were imprisoned for offences relating to prostitution, public order and drunkenness was seen as involving forms of moral transgression which carried different levels of stigmatisation and punishment for women from those they carried for men, since these activities contravened not only the law but, importantly, the idealised roles of women as wives and mothers. Moreover, these forms of drunkenness and promiscuity became increasingly viewed as a product of 'feeblemindedness', which had the effect of undermining conventional notions of culpability and responsibility. At this point the widely held belief that women were more reformable and impressionable than men was increasingly called into question (Zedner, 1991).

Although there were considerable spatial and organisational differences between women's and men's prisons, it is in relation to labour and labour discipline that the most marked differences occurred. Women's position in the labour market and their domestic role, which involved a different use of 'public' and 'private' space, created a distinctly different relation between labour and imprisonment for women. There was a broad consensus that women, like men, should be required to engage in work in prison in order to instil labour discipline, promote individual reform and maintain order. In their account of the female convict prison at Brixton in the mid-nineteenth century, Henry Mayhew and John Binny observed that:

> The work done by the women prisoners is, of course, of different character to that performed either at Pentonville or the hulks. The tailoring of the former establishment gives place to a more appropriate shirt-making, hemming flannels, and stitching stays, &c; while the hard labour of prisoners working in the arsenal and dockyard is here replaced by the more feminine occupation of the laundry. (Mayhew and Binny [1860], 1971: 194)

Besides laundry work and needlework, the women were mostly employed in oakum picking (retrieving the tar from old rope), ropemaking, cooking and cleaning. The possibilities of reform through labour discipline, however, was limited by the relatively short sentences, with approximately 50 per cent of female prisoners in the 1860s serving sentences of less than a month. Moreover, towards the end of the century the emphasis in women's prisons shifted to moral reformation through the use of psycho-medical treatment programmes.

An important indicator of the differences between men's and women's imprisonment in the Victorian era is exemplified by their respective relationship to the criteria of 'less eligibility'. While Rusche and Kirchheimer (1968) have argued that the criterion of 'less eligibility' has been an important point of reference in influencing penal reform, this criterion appears less applicable to women's imprisonment. The frequent reports that local prisons were used by destitute women as forms of asylum or as sanctuaries suggests that many women in the second half of the nineteenth century experienced conditions on the 'outside' which were significantly worse than those on the 'inside'. Compared to the working day of women who worked extremely long hours in workhouses, the working day in prison was often shorter and the conditions comparable. There were organisational limits to extending the working day in prisons and as a consequence the aims of deterrence and the principle of 'less eligibility' came into conflict with the more pragmatic concerns of security and economy. The principle of 'less eligibility' was also undermined by mothers with young children in prison, who may have found themselves in a preferable position to that of many 'honest mothers' living in the community, who were trying to earn enough to support their offspring. The provision for mothers and their children in prison was, however, never entirely philanthropic. The establishment of mother and baby units in women's prisons in the mid-nineteenth century was promoted by the Eugenics Movement and other campaigners who argued for the control of 'weak' and 'unfit' mothers, and who were concerned primarily with 'improving' the moral and physical constitution of the species.

Thus the material conditions of women, particularly among the poor and the destitute, the segmented nature of the labour market and the general emphasis on moral transgressions shaped the use of women's imprisonment in the nineteenth century. The combined impact of these developments influenced the nature of the prison regimes for women and profoundly affected the ways in which women experienced imprisonment. Firstly, since there were fewer penal institutions for women, they tended to accommodate a more diverse population in terms of age and the type of offence committed. Secondly, because they were generally smaller units they involved higher degrees of surveillance and monitoring. Thirdly, and relatedly, they tended to be more intrusive, with less capacity to tolerate non-conformity. As a consequence, female prisoners were more likely to be sanctioned for committing disciplinary offences while in prison. Fourthly, the existence of mother and baby units created a distinctive space within the prison which served as a reminder of women's domestic role and their child-rearing responsibilities.

Being in smaller and more intimate units, the regimes in women's prisons tended to involve a unique mixture of intimacy and support on one hand and extreme hostility and antagonism on the other. It was not that women's prisons were 'better' or 'worse' than men's prisons, stricter or more lenient, or simply more or less punitive: rather they embodied differences in the deployment of the power to punish. From the end of the century, however, the use of women's imprisonment changed in a number of important respects. One of the most significant developments was the proportionate decline in the female prison population, as well as a decrease in the actual number of women in prison during the first half of the twentieth century.

THE DEMISE OF WOMEN'S IMPRISONMENT?

Throughout the second half of the nineteenth century women consistently made up around one in five of those committed to local prisons, and between 1860 and 1890 the average daily population of women in local prisons increased slightly, from 4567 to 4840 (Zedner, 1991). The number of women in convict prisons, which accommodated those serving sentences in excess of two years, however, began to fall in this period. In 1860 there were just over 1000 women sent to convict prisons, and by 1890 this had fallen to 95. However, the decrease in the average daily population was less dramatic, falling from 1249 in 1860 to 302 in 1890, indicating that the lengths of sentences for those who were sent to convict prisons increased in general over this period.

Lucia Zedner (1991) has suggested that the changes in the scale of female incarceration was due to four main factors. Firstly, the number of women prosecuted for various public order offences such as 'soliciting for the purpose of prostitution' declined in this period. Secondly, the level of recidivism was increasing, such that the proportion of those in prison with 10 or more previous offences grew steadily. The third factor was the growing disillusionment concerning the possibility of individual reform within the prison setting. The growing emphasis on 'feeblemindedness' as an explanation of female offending made the prospects of reform less likely. Finally, a greater proportion of women who were prosecuted for offences such as drunkenness were sent to newly-established reformatories instead of local prisons.

The growing emphasis upon reduced culpability and what was seen as the reformability of some women stimulated the movement, both in England and America, towards the development of reformatory prisons for women, organised along similar lines to the existing juvenile reformatories. Reformatories were normally organised around small 'houses' or units run by a matron and each had its own 'family' of inmates (Freedman, 1984; Rafter, 1985b). The rationale behind these newly constituted prisons was to provide a more domesticated and familial environment which could promote individual reform, while providing a more suitable setting in which supervision could be exercised in a more regular and detailed fashion. As with juvenile reformatories, women's reformatories incorporated the notion of indeterminacy, and prisoners were to be detained until 'reformed' and deemed ready for release.

Nicole Holt Rafter (1983; 1985a) has argued that women's reformatories were the first form of incarceration designed specifically for women and provided a contrast to the more 'masculinist' local and convict prisons. These new women's reformatories embodied a different set of values and objectives:

> Reformatory designers adopted the late nineteenth century penology of rehabilitation, but they tailored it to fit what they understood as women's special nature. To instil vocational skills they used not prison industries but domestic training. Inmates were taught to cook, clean and wait on table; at parole they were sent to middle-class homes to work as servants. Whereas men's reformatories sought to inculcate 'manliness', women's reformatories encouraged femininity – sexual restraint, genteel demeanour and domesticity. When women were disciplined, they might be scolded and sent like children to their 'rooms'. Indeed, the whole regime was designed to induce a child-like submissiveness.
> (Rafter, 1985b: xxii)

By the 1930s, however, the reformatory movement itself had fallen into decline. Between 1913 and 1921 the population in women's prisons had also fallen from 33 000 to 11 000, and by the 1960s it had fallen to less than 2000. General changes in penal policy contributed to this decrease. Similar developments occurred in both America and France over this period. The growth of 'alternatives' to custody, particularly in the form of probation and the increased use of the fine, have been identified as contributing to these changes (O'Brien, 1982).

The relatively low numbers of female prisoners in the post-war period combined with a shift in penal policy towards the decarceration of certain groups of offenders paved the way for a changed attitude towards women's imprisonment. In one official report it was predicted that: 'It may well be that as the end of the century draws nearer, penological progress will result in even fewer or no women at all being given prison sentences.' (Home Office, 1970). However, despite various predictions of this type during this period, the number of women incarcerated did not decrease during the 1970s and 1980s and at the end of the 1990s the average daily populating in England and Wales stands at just over 3000 (Home Office 1999). Consequently, penologists have turned their attention away from explaining the reasons for the decrease in women's imprisonment and have instead addressed the question of why the anticipated reduction did not take place.

THE CHANGING SCALE OF WOMEN'S IMPRISONMENT

The fact that the expected decrease in the number of women in prison did not occur during the 1970s led to a cross-Atlantic debate on why the apparent re-expansion of women's imprisonment occurred. The initial foray in this debate came from Freda Adler (1975), who claimed that the increase in female criminality, and by implication women's imprisonment, was a function of the development of women's liberation. Whether the changing values and aspirations commonly associated with the Women's Liberation Movement served to produce a new generation of female offenders, or whether existing female offenders began turning to more 'masculine' forms of crime, is not clear in Adler's presentation. Carol Smart (1979) has challenged the empirical and methodological basis of Adler's thesis on the grounds that there are a number of factors which can influence the crime rate and imprisonment rate in any period and that the type of mono-causal analysis which reduces the complexity of crime and punishment to one single factor is at best extremely limited, and at worst seriously misguided. In a re-examination of the statistics on female crime in England and Wales, Smart argues that sudden and dramatic change in the recorded level of female crime is not a new phenomenon and examples can be found in the decades prior to the emergence of the 'first wave' of women's liberation in which substantial increases have taken place.

There remains, however, the contention forwarded by Adler and others that the changing nature of gender relations since the 1970s has had an effect on the type of crime committed by women, particularly as a result of the increased occupational opportunities open to women (Walklate, 1995). Smart (1979), however, argues that the major changes in the labour market have involved predominantly middle-class women and 'white-collar' workers. Thus changes in the labour market participation by women is unlikely, she argues, to have much effect on crimes such as violence or robbery. More specifically, there is evidence of a worsening occupational position of certain groups of women. Smart suggests that: '[T]here is no evidence available yet to indicate whether girls who become officially defined as delinquent or women who are defined as criminal, accept, reject or are indifferent to the values of women's liberation.' Further, she argues that if women's liberation has had an impact upon the recorded level of female crime, then it may well be a consequence of changing perceptions of women by the various criminal justice agencies and a consequent change of response.

Although Smart's reinterpretation of the figures indicates that the increase in female crime has been more rapid than that of male crime in different periods, Roy Austin (1981) has pointed out that Smart's own figures do indicate that the greatest percentage increase in female crime relative to male crime for the more serious offences did occur during the 'first wave' of women's liberation (1965–75). He also argues that it is precisely in relation to these more serious offences of violence against the person and sexual offences that changing forms of discretion on the part of the police, the judiciary and other key agencies are likely to be relevant.

A further contribution to this largely polemical debate is provided by Steven Box and Chris Hale (1983), who suggest that there are major methodological deficiencies on all sides, that the debate had become bogged down in empiricism, and that the various contributors have failed to demonstrate any clear causal links between women's liberation and the changing levels of crime and punishment. Box and Hale endorse Austin's findings that there had been a significant increase in recorded levels of female crime between 1950 and 1980, particularly for crimes of violence against the person. However, they note that: 'If the rate of female to male convictions is examined then the female contribution to violent crimes against the person remains static, whereas crimes against property reflect a slight convergence.' The methodological issue at stake here is whether the point of reference should be the absolute conviction rate or the female relative to male conviction rate. From their own analysis Box and Hale (1983) conclude that it is the social circumstances common to both men and women which account for changes in the recorded levels of both violent and property crime in this period, rather than factors such as women's liberation. Like Smart, they conclude that it is the reaction or labelling by criminal justice agencies and the mass media which has exaggerated the impact of changing gender roles on violent crime and created the myth of the 'new female criminal'.

Although there are important methodological and conceptual issues associated with the debate concerning the relationship between women's liberation and crime, these explanations in general fail to examine the mediating links between these two phenomena and consequently veer towards empiricism. Differences in this debate may also reflect different levels of female crime and imprisonment on either side of the Atlantic, with the consequence that the various contributors are referring to somewhat different empirical realities. While the number of women imprisoned per 100 000 in England and Wales between 1970 and 1990 remained roughly stable, the incarceration rate for women in America increased dramatically. Between 1980 and 1989 alone the number of women in prison in America increased by some 230 per cent, while the number of men increased by 120 per cent over the same period. Although the male incarceration rate in America is 530 per 100 000, compared to a female rate of 29 per 100 000 in 1990, the rate of increase in women's imprisonment has been greater than that of men for every year between 1981 and 1991. In 1970 women made up 3 per cent of the prison population but by 1987 they accounted for 5.7 per cent (Chesney-Lind, 1991). Reviewing the changes in America during the 1980s, Meda Chesney-Lind (1991) concludes that the increases in women's imprisonment cannot be explained by increases in women's crimes, at least as measured by arrests. The question remains, however, whether the increase in the use of incarceration for women is in part an outcome of women engaging in different types of crime. The available evidence suggests that whereas more women are imprisoned for drug-related offences and public order offences, the proportion imprisoned for violent offences has actually decreased. The implication of this finding is that there is a greater willingness to incarcerate women for certain offences, while there is also evidence that prison sentences for women in America have generally been getting longer (Pollock-Byrne, 1992).

The increased use of imprisonment for women in the United States has also been fostered, according to Chesney-Lind (1991), by the use of mandatory sentences for particular offences. This has increased sentence lengths in many cases. In contrast to the contention that the changing scale of imprisonment for women is a consequence of changing gender roles and the creation of the 'new female criminal', she argues that there is little evidence of the emergence of a new type of more serious female offender in recent years. Rather, what appears to be occurring in some states is that incarceration is increasingly being used in cases which in previous periods would have attracted a noncustodial response. She reminds us that during this period there has also been a series of backlashes against women's liberation in an attempt to reinstate the imagery of 'true womanhood'. As a result there has been a growing intolerance of those who are seen not to live up to this ideal.

In England and Wales the trajectory of change has been slightly different. The exact nature of the change is, however, difficult to determine with any precision, since one of the most glaring omissions from the criminal statistics is the absence of arrest data for women. The data on cautioning and sentencing indicates that cautioning rates for females, while increasing, have roughly paralleled the cautioning rates for men between 1985 and 1995. Significantly, the cautioning rate for violence against the person increased from 1900 in 1985 to 4900 in 1995. In the same period the number of females offenders found guilty of indictable offences has decreased from 3600 to 2800. The number of females given sentences of immediate imprisonment increased slightly for violence against the person, sexual offences and robbery between 1985 and 1995, during which time the average length of sentence for adult female offenders has increased by an average of 26 per cent for violence against the person, 50 per cent for burglary, 25 per cent for robbery, 50 per cent for criminal damage and 64 per cent for drug-related offences. The major changes in this period has taken place in Crown Courts, while sentencing practices in Magistrates Courts have remained fairly stable.

An important development in recent years has been the increase in the remand population which, it has been argued, accounts for a significant percentage of women held in custody (Dobash *et al.*, 1986). An equally important development which has affected the number of women held in custody is the growing number of foreign nationals incarcerated. In 1995 foreign nationals made up some 16 per cent of the female prison population. Over half of these non-nationals are imprisoned for drug-related offences. Since this offence carries a relatively long sentence, it means that drug offenders make up a disproportionate percentage of the female prison population (Maden *et al.*, 1992). The increased proportion of foreign nationals in women's prisons in recent years suggest that we need to qualify the presumed relationship between women's liberation and the use of imprisonment.

As with male prisoners, the profile of female prisoners in England and Wales in the 1990s involves a larger percentage of those who have been convicted of violent offences than in the previous decade, while the proportion of those in the prison population who have been convicted of burglary, theft and fraud has decreased by over 30 per cent over the same period. These changes have been associated with changes in sentencing practices and have brought into question assertions about the differential sentencing of men and women, particularly in relation to the supposed leniency with which female offenders are treated by the courts.

SENTENCING, LENIENCY AND EQUALITY

It has been widely assumed that women are treated more leniently by courts than their male counterparts. This assumption, however, although true for certain offences, is not a general or universal truth. The historical evidence indicates that over the last century women have been incarcerated, particularly in reformatories, for lesser crimes and for longer periods than men. The introduction of reformatories, which were designed to be more benign and more responsive to women's needs, resulted in more minor offenders being locked up for longer periods of time 'for their own good' in order to allow them time to 'reform'. This strategy has been described as involving a form of 'benevolent repression' (Heidensohn, 1986).

Those who question the claim that the criminal justice system treats women more leniently than men point out that women continue to be imprisoned for offences which are less serious than those committed by men, that women in prison have an average fewer previous convictions and tend to be held in remand more readily than men (Genders and Player, 1986). This differential treatment arises, according to Pat Carlen (1983), because women make not only a 'class deal' but also a 'gender deal'. The 'class deal' she argues, which operates in relation to

work, affords fewer rewards for women than for men. The implications of the 'gender deal', on the other hand, is that those who transgress conventional female roles are likely to be treated particularly
harshly. Thus:

> The majority of British women prisoners have not been gaoled
> because of the seriousness of their crimes but because of either
> their aberrant domestic circumstances or less than conventional
> lifestyles, the failure of the non-penal welfare or health institutions
> to cope with their problems, or their own refusal to comply with cul-
> turally conditioned female gender stereotype requirements. These
> sentencing practices combined with academic and popular theories
> that have repeatedly implied that women criminals and prisoners
> are either mad, masculine, menopausal or maladjusted (to conven-
> tional female roles) have resulted in it not only being claimed that
> they are not 'real' women, 'real' criminals and 'real' prisoners, but
> also the claim that women's prisons are not real prisons. (Dwyer,
> Wilson and Carlen, 1987: 177–8)

The evidence that a greater proportion of women are serving prison
sentences for less serious crimes than men, and that a significantly
higher percentage of women than men in prison have no previous convictions, does not mean, however, that the criminal justice system
consistently discriminates against women. Statistical research indicates
that on average women are less likely than men to receive a custodial
sentence for all indictable offences, with the exception of drug-related
offences. When women do receive prison sentences, these are on
average shorter than men's, although women tend to receive longer sentences for criminal damage and drugs offences. Carol Hedderman and
Mike Hough (1994), working with data drawn from the offenders index,
indicate that women first time offenders are half as likely to be given a
sentence of immediate imprisonment as male first time offenders –
4 per cent compared to 8 per cent. Women with one, two, three or
more convictions were all found to be less likely to receive custodial
sentences than the equivalent men (Hood, 1992; Walker, 1981).

Although the statistical data presents a strong indication that
female offenders on average are less likely to receive a custodial sentence than their male counterparts for most offence categories, some
of the limitations of these statistical comparisons become apparent
when we compare specific crimes and specific cases. If we take domestic homicide, for example, we find that:

An analysis of cases dealt with between 1984 and 1992 shows that 23% of females compared with only 4% of males indicted for homicide were acquitted on all charges. Of those found guilty 80% of the women compared with 61% of the men were found guilty of the lesser charge of manslaughter and more than two-thirds of men convicted of manslaughter received a prison sentence compared with less than half of the women. (Hedderman and Hough, 1994: 3–4)

This type of statistical comparison is weak, in as much as the cases are not clearly matched, and the greater acquittal rates of women can be read as evidence that they are more readily prosecuted on flimsier evidence than men; whereas the greater percentage of cases in which the charge is reduced to manslaughter may well be a consequence of greater provocation and systematic abuse suffered by women, which is often reported to be associated with these cases. It is also likely that there are significant differences in the circumstances in which these cases of domestic homicide have taken place, given the differences in physical and social resources of the two parties (Walklate, 1995). It is not an unreasonable assumption that those women who engage in domestic homicide do so for different reasons and employ different methods from those routinely employed by men in the commission of this offence, with the consequence that substantial differences of culpability are likely to be apportioned to males and females who commit domestic homicide. In short, reducing the charge or comparing the percentage of males and females given custodial sentences in these circumstances cannot be directly interpreted as evidence of 'leniency'.

The apparent leniency of the criminal justice process towards women is also confounded by the smaller number of women going through the system, which affects the probability of bail being granted to female offenders. Because there are only a few prisons which take women on remand in England and Wales, the provision of bail services is linked to a large number of courts, and because of the lack of availability of suitable hostel places, particularly for those with children and with serious drug problems, bail provision is limited (HM Inspectorate of Prisons 1997b). In a similar vein, there is a lack of availability of suitable non-custodial alternatives to incarceration for women, either because they do not provide appropriate activities, or they are unavailable in particular areas, or they do not accommodate women with children (Carlen, 1990).

A major issue which arises is the substantive inequalities and power differentials which operate in relation to men and women (Connell,

1987). Correspondingly the question is whether the aim should be the pursuit of formal equality, so that men and women are treated in the same way; or whether, given the substantively differences in power and resources, the aim should be to treat men and women differently. Thus the choice appears to be whether to aim for 'parity' or 'equality'. If the latter is the aim, then statistical comparisons of sentencing outcomes are of limited relevance. The focus on 'equality' is likely to require more detailed qualitative information that can incorporate details of the background and the circumstances in which the offences to be compared were carried out.

As Kathleen Daly (1994) has argued, most disparity studies do not readily address issues of domination and subordination between the sexes, and do not take account of how: 'constructs of masculinity and femininity shape what people think about themselves, how they act and how they make sense of the behaviour of others'. In many of these studies men are taken as the point of reference. The danger of taking men as *the* point of reference is clearly exemplified in those American states that have introduced greater parity in sentencing outcomes or mandatory sentencing policies, and as a consequence have increased the severity of the sentences imposed on women in order to bring them into line with men. It apparently never occurred to anyone to take women as *the* standard and thereby reduce average sentence lengths for certain offences (Pollock-Byrne, 1992). Daly (1994) suggests that an analysis of the gendered dimensions of sentencing should aim to identify causal relations through the analysis of 'pathways' by which researchers can trace through the backgrounds and life histories of the men and women concerned. Employing this form of detailed qualitative analysis, involving paired cases and incorporating detailed narrative material, Daly found that, in contrast to the statistical studies which claim considerable disparities in sentencing, gender differences in sentencing were often negligible.

A recent study by Carol Hedderman and Loraine Gelsthorpe (1997) on magistrates' attitudes towards female defendants provides a useful vantage point from which to examine this process. This study suggests that female offenders are more likely to be perceived by magistrates as 'troubled' rather than 'troublesome', and as being subject to different pressures from male defendants. The nature of the offender's motivation, her demeanour and the level of deference displayed in court are all likely to influence decision-making. 'Troubled' defendants are seen as more in need of help than punishment, and probation is widely seen as the most appropriate response for a large percentage of female offenders. At the same time magistrates were found to be more reluctant to impose fines on women if they thought it would adversely affect their children. Family circumstances were found to be an important consideration in passing sentence, particularly if the women had dependant children, while an effort was normally made to help those in employment.

Thus issues of parity, equality and leniency remain contested and unresolved. It has been suggested that there is a need to develop a feminist jurisprudence which can move beyond the 'masculinist' preoccupation with abstract universal principles and the 'rule of law' and replace it by a feminist perspective on justice which emphasise personal and informal processes grounded in relationships (Heidensohn, 1975; Worrall, 1990). It may well be, as Catherine MacKinnon (1987) put it, that real 'equality means the aspirations to eradicate not gender differentiation but gender hierarchy'. Other writers have claimed that the aim should be to argue for both equality *and* difference by demanding, for example, equality in terms of resources and expenditure, while recognising the differences of need between male and female prisoners and consequently the different ways in which available resources should be distributed (Naffine, 1997; Young, 1997).

THE CHARACTERISTICS OF THE FEMALE PRISON POPULATION

The profile of women prisoners presented by the *National Prison Survey* (1991) indicates that in broad terms it is generally similar to the male prison population in that the majority of prisoners are drawn from disadvantaged sections of society and inner city areas, and have poor education and employment records. The *Thematic Review: Women in Prison* (1997), which was carried out by the Prisons Inspectorate and was based on a survey of 234 women, found that 70 per cent of the women claimed to have had no previous employment, one in ten had 'no fixed abode', and the majority had problems of accommodation prior to imprisonment. Nearly half of the women reported that they had been abused, almost one-third sexually. About 40 per cent had misused at least one controlled drug. Among those who reported heavy abuse or addiction over half had used heroin, and about a quarter had used cocaine or crack. Approximately 40 per cent of the women interviewed reported that they had harmed themselves intentionally or had attempted suicide. Just over half had children under 16, and over a third had one child or more under 5 years old (HM Inspectorate of Prisons, 1997b). Other research has confirmed this picture. Allison Morris and Christine Wilkinson (1995) found that over 60 per cent of women in their survey had been living solely on benefits prior to their imprisonment, while one-third said they had been in debt. However, given this profile, it is surprising that about half of the women in prison have no previous convictions and just over 70 per cent had not been in prison before (Prison Reform Trust, 1993).

The conclusion which arises from these surveys of women prisoners is that, while they are similar in terms of a number of basic socio-economic characteristics to male prisoners, they have a different range of physical and psychological needs. Moreover, as the Prison Inspectorate (1997b) reported, 55 per cent of the women interviewed said that they had received little or no help in prison, while nearly 40 per cent thought that the prison had not improved them in any way at all, and only about one in ten had received any type of counselling. Significantly, when asked what they would need to help them to not re-offend, their replies were: a job and money, a home, counselling, help with drug and alcohol problems, and moving to a new area. It is indicative that 150 years after the establishment of women's prisons, such a fundamental review of the needs of women prisoners is considered necessary as a basis for providing an appropriate set of policies for healthcare, education, employment, tackling drug and alcohol misuse and for providing proper childcare and counselling services.

One of the most significant features of the female prison population is the disproportionate number drawn from ethnic minorities. Among the female prison population in England and Wales in 1995, 24 per cent were described as being members of an ethnic minority group, of whom the majority were categorised as 'black'. Some 16 per cent were identified as foreign nationals, with just over a third of this group being African, a quarter West Indian and 18 per cent of European nationality. Approximately 40 per cent of sentenced black female prisoners are foreign nationals imprisoned for drug-related offences. Those convicted of drug-related offences tend to receive relatively long sentences, often in excess of three years, while those women who have been convicted of importing illegal drugs – 'mules' – can receive even longer sentences, which may be accompanied by deportation on completion of the sentence (Green, 1991). Two direct implications follow from the particularly long sentences given to those convicted of the importation and distribution of illegal drugs. The first is that there is a pronounced imbalance in the profile of women sent to prison and the make up of the female prison population on any one day. The second is that there are growing problems managing the increased percentage of long-term prisoners in women's prisons, particularly non-nationals.

Thus, in relation to the average daily population in England and Wales, 30 per cent of the female population in 1995 were imprisoned for drug-related offences, 29 per cent for theft and fraud, and 21 per cent for violence against the person. Over the past decade the main changes which have occurred in the profile of women in prison is that there has been an increase in the number of women serving sentences for violent and drug-related offences and a decrease in the proportion serving sentences for theft and fraud (Home Office, 1996b). However, when considering these trends it should be noted that the proportion of offences not recorded has increased from less than 5 per cent in the mid-1980s to around 15 per cent by 1995.

WOMEN IN PRISON

The relatively small proportion of the prison population which is female has a number of more or less direct implications for the organisation and experience of incarceration among women prisoners. The most immediate consequence is that the number of units holding women are few in number. As a result female prisoners tend to be held some distance from home, making visits more difficult to organise. The second implication is that the available prisons will necessarily have to accommodate a wider range of offenders in terms of age and offence category than men's prisons. The third implication is that the availability of work, training, education and various other specialist programmes in prison is likely to be limited.

It is within these organisational parameters that women's experience of incarceration has been established historically. It is these material conditions of imprisonment which in part explain the apparent 'invisibility' of women in prison. But there is also, as Pat Carlen (1983) has argued, an important ideological dimension to this process. Based on her pioneering work in Cornton Vale prison in Scotland, she argues that female prisoners are defined as being without 'sociability, femininity and adulthood and as being beyond care or cure'. The impact of these ideological and stereotypical constructions is that female prisoners are seen as not being real women but as deviants who need to be disciplined, medicalised and feminised. Thus, typically, work and training programmes tend to be linked to traditional domestic roles and may have little relevance to the reality of the women's lives on the outside (Eaton, 1993). It may also be the case that the forms of domestic training which many female prisoners are given may paradoxically be designed to push them back into those domestic roles and situations from which they may be attempting to escape. By the same token, the ideals of femininity promoted by prison authorities are denied by the removal of the normal physical and psychological props through which the ideal of femininity is socially maintained. This fundamental contradiction, Carlen (1983) suggests, leads to both a celebration and a denial of the feminine myth and results in confusion and bitterness.

The 'invisibility' of female prisoners to outside observers stands in stark contrast to the intensive forms of discipline exercised in women's prisons, which result in greater levels of intrusiveness and surveillance than is normally experienced in men's prisons Devlin, 1998). What prisoners say, who they talk with, their movements and moods are all closely monitored. It is this detailed form of supervision which is seen to explain, in part, the relatively high number of disciplinary offences in women's prisons and the tendency for personal relations to oscillate between punitiveness and support (Dobash *et al.*, 1986).

In a number of ways women are held to experience the 'pains of imprisonment' more acutely than men. This is not because women prisoners are any less resilient than their male counterparts, but because the material, physical and social conditions of their confinement are significantly different. Differences in perceived domestic responsibilities, lesser experience of confinement, limited criminal careers, as well as histories of physical and sexual abuse, suggest that a considerable percentage of women are already socially and personally 'damaged' before entering this alien environment. Childcare and the frequency and quality of visits are a major concern among women in prison.

The culture within women's prisons is influenced by women's identities as mothers. The mothering role provides women with a sense of identity and serves as a means of shared experience and information within the prison. However, the dynamics of imprisonment generate dependence and infantilisation among inmates. These twin processes have paradoxical consequences for the well-being of mothers and the development of children, since:

Infantilization and the push toward conformity undermine women's efforts to take responsibility as adults, mothers and citizens. The deprivational and controlling character of prison gives rise to reactive, self-serving modes of adapting and reinforces punitive parenting models. The prison reproduces some of the same destructive relational dynamics that the mothers experienced within their own families. Treatment modalities, although diverse, operate within and draw authority from the coercive prison order. (Clark, 1995: 326)

HOLLOWAY: RECONSTRUCTING IDEOLOGY

The changing structural relation between the dominant conceptions of the typical female offender and the function of imprisonment is nowhere better reflected than in the reconstruction of Holloway Prison. The prison, which had originally been built in the nineteenth century with a classic radial design, and which was seen as the 'sister' prison to Pentonville, was transformed between 1965 and 1988. Originally it had the façade of a fortress, with imposing high walls that emphasised the boundary between the imprisoned population and the rest of society. However, in place of the old prison, which increasingly became seen as bleak and outdated, was the attempt to reconstruct Holloway as a secure hospital providing a therapeutic regime for its inmates. This change of design reflected the view that came to dominate during the 1960s, which held that women were more in need of treatment than punishment. Female offenders became widely seen not so much as criminals as disturbed and defective people in need of care and treatment. Consequently, the aim was to construct an institution which allowed the development of rehabilitative programmes tied to a medical model (Rotman, 1990). The old structure was seen as an obstacle to achieving this objective.

The 'new Holloway' was not so much the negation of the old prison, but its inversion. Whereas the traditional radial prison had a central control structure from which activities could be controlled, the 'new Holloway' was to have an open space at the centre, which would be used for association. There would be less emphasis on physical security and the boundaries between the prison and the community would be less rigid. Thus:

The design of the new Holloway was original. It was the attempt of experienced penal practitioners and architects versed in educational design to produce the very converse of the old radial prison. The new Holloway was a schematic repudiation of the old. The wings and their centre were turned inside out: where there had been a controlling hub, there would be an empty green; where there had been constraint and surveillance, there would be freedom; where there had been great, intimidating spaces, there would be small intimate areas; the high, forbidding boundary of the total institution was to become a mundane and reassuring perimeter; what had been separate would become integrated; and where there had been punishment, there would be healing. In short, the terrifying symbolism of the old was to be replaced by the comfortable ordinariness of the new. (Rock, 1996: 143)

Because of the delays and problems of construction, the new prison, which was to be built in 1970, was not completed until 1984. In the interim, changes in the perceived nature of female offenders, combined with an assault upon the rehabilitative ideal, shifted the emphasis back towards security and incapacitation. The penological climate changed dramatically during the 1970s and by the time of its construction the new Holloway had already begun to be considered obsolete and outdated. Changes in the design and construction occurred during this period, such that when the prison was eventually finished it was constructed neither as a secure hospital nor a conventional prison.

Repeated reports of discipline problems and disturbances within the newly constructed prison were attributed to the design, which was seen to generate too much distance between staff and inmates, and this was compounded by problems of surveillance. The new structure, with its hidden spaces and corners, generated fear; while the separation of inmates into small units dispersed staff and made communication difficult (Casale, 1989). There was a lack of well-defined boundaries and consequently formal and informal divisions were regularly transgressed.

The result was an impoverished regime beset with problems. The influential report produced by the Holloway Project Committee in 1985 concluded that a building which had been designed to foster a high level of care for prisoners was having the opposite effect. Towards the end of the 1980s various prison governors attempted to change the style of management, reduce levels of physical security and modify staff and inmate relations. Nevertheless, despite these various attempts to reorganise Holloway, the view among many contemporary observers was that it was an experiment which had failed. This sense of failure was underlined by an unannounced inspection of Holloway in December 1995 in which the conditions in the prison were felt to be so bad that the inspection was called off pending immediate improvements.

In the wake of the 'failed' experiment at Holloway and the attempt to develop a prison regime which is able to respond to the perceived needs of women prisoners, penal reformers have considered other options. The three most widely discussed options are: the construction of 'new design' woman-centred prisons; mixed prisons; and the abolition or reduction of women's imprisonment and the attempt to deal with female offenders in what are seen as more constructive and appropriate community-based facilities.

ALTERNATIVE MODELS OF WOMEN'S IMPRISONMENT

Woman-centred Prisons

The recurring problem with women's prisons, as we have seen, is that they are too remote, too diverse and generally lacking in facilities. For the most part they have not been developed around principles which relate to the reality of women prisoners' lived experience and needs, but rather regimes are organised around ideologies of femininity and domesticity.

What is required, critics argue, are more local prisons with lower levels of security, and which are designed to cater specifically for women's needs. (Hannah-Moffat, 1995; Shaw, 1992a). This approach draws on the writings of Carol Gilligan (1982), who stresses the 'politics of difference' and argues that men and women hold different moral codes: women stress moral integrity and care for the self and others through a commitment to personal relationships, rather than employing 'objective' criteria in order to arrive at 'just' solutions. This for Gilligan means an emphasis on listening to the voice of otherness rather than the masculinist approach, which she claims involves masking different voices under an abstract cloud of universality.

Recent developments in Canada exemplify this growing interest in developing 'woman-centred' approach. In the report *Creating Choices* (1990) it was proposed that five new facilities, to be situated close to the major centres of population, would replace the existing prison for women at Kingston. The strategy was based on five 'feminist' principles. These were: empowerment; the provision of meaningful choices; treating women with respect and dignity; providing a physically and emotionally supportive environment; and finally the sharing of the responsibility for women's welfare between institutional staff, community members, and the women themselves (Shaw, 1996). The aim was to construct new facilities in several acres of land with cottage-style houses accommodating six to ten women in each, as well as providing a 'healing lodge' for Aboriginal women. Programmes in these 'houses' were to be holistic, in that they were to deal with the interrelated nature of women's experience. The aim of the various programmes was to enable women to understand their situation better within a broader social context and to encourage them to take greater control over their lives.

Exactly how effective these new facilities have been in achieving their objectives and in providing a more constructive environment for female offenders has been subject to some debate. Problems of funding and developing appropriate rehabilitative programmes in a setting, which remains after all coercive and segregative, has resulted in a number of ongoing difficulties. Restrictions of movement and limited work and training opportunities have both been seen as the negative attributes of these small local units, despite the fact that the women prisoners appear to have gained more self-confidence and an improved understanding of their situation. On the other hand, the assumptions underlying this type of approach have been criticised for overemphasising the passive and victimised nature of women in prison, since it is argued that this tends to pathologise and depoliticise them (M. Shaw, 1992).

The thinking behind the development of small, woman-centred prisons has also been criticised for treating women as a homogeneous group and for not paying enough attention to issues of race and class (Hannah-Moffat, 1995). There is also a danger that, in failing to challenge the essential role of imprisonment and assuming that introducing a number of 'feminist' principles, incarceration can be made acceptable. Indeed, the language of 'empowerment' can serve to encourage women prisoners to take responsibility for their actions within a context where the ultimate objectives are not of their own making. Although woman-centred regimes may emphasise treatment over punishment, self-determination over passivity, vertical collaboration and decision-making over hierarchical and authoritarian structures, there is a danger that the social and political context in which women's offending takes place is ignored and the

oppressive nature of imprisonment is obscured. Thus, as one critic
has argued:

> The woman-centred prison and its capacity for empowerment is
> constructed as a challenge to the hegemony of punitive carceral
> regimes and oppressive technologies of surveillance and discipline.
> Woman-centred prisons and the ethics of empowerment have not
> significantly challenged this hegemony; rather they have softened
> some of the rough edges of incarceration. Despite the influx of
> 'empowerment discourse', woman-centred corrections is about
> responsibilising the prisoner and not empowerment as defined by
> some feminists. Corrections Canada's acknowledgement of the
> structural barriers facing women and their attempt to remove some
> of the 'pains of imprisonment' are compatible with the liberal
> notion of individual responsibility. The emphasis on responsibility
> decontextualises feminist constructions of women's resistance and it
> disregards feminist analysis of the social, economic, and political
> barriers experienced by women – and in particular, by marginalised
> women. (Hannah-Moffat, 1995: 159)

Hannah-Moffat concludes her critique by arguing that woman-centred
prisons tend to reproduce normative standards of 'femininity', and
although they appear to be a less intrusive and a less punitive form of
incarceration, the coercive qualities of incarceration 'are simply
obscured by feminized social control talk that tends to deny the legal
and material realities of imprisonment.' In a similar vein, Kathleen
Daly (1994) has challenged the suggestion put forward by Gilligan and
developed by others such as Francis Heidensohn (1986) that the criminal justice system currently embodies a masculinist notion of justice
centring around individualism, the rule of law and abstract notions of
equality, and that a feminist model of justice involves caring and the
use of informal networks of support. Daly (1994) argues that both
notions of justice are in fact present within the criminal justice system
and constantly compete for ascendancy. Inasmuch as one can talk
about a 'female voice', it is to emphasise that in practice notions of
culpability are conditioned by the *relation between the offender and the
victim*, rather than as a response to a specific act which takes the individual offender as the social unit of punishment. This mode of analysis
leads her, in turn, to a consideration of 'justice' in terms of power
differentials and the role of class and race among men and women
(Daly and Tonry, 1997).

Mixed Prisons

The growing interest in a number of countries in mixing male and female prisoners has been encouraged by both the desire to locate female prisoners closer to their homes and the desire to reduce the costs of imprisonment. Separate prisons for women are expensive, particularly if they have any pretensions to provide a comprehensive range of educational, training and recreational facilities. The degree and style of integration of males and females in prison varies considerably between different countries, but in England and Wales the debate has focused on the advantages and disadvantages of either creating more accommodation within men's prisons, so that women prisoners would be increasingly dispersed throughout the prison system but would be kept on separate wings or landings from men; or organising prisons so that male and female prisoners work together during the day and/or meet during association and recreational periods.

Apart from the arguments about the greater proximity to family and friends, the potential savings, and the possibility of providing women with a wider range of facilities in prison, there are two related arguments which have been mobilised in support of greater integration of the sexes. One set of arguments is associated with the concept of normalisation and the other with the notion of rehabilitation. The strategy of normalisation is based upon the premise that the aim of imprisonment is the deprivation of liberty and that apart from this sanction prisoners should be allowed to live as normally as possible within the constraints of confinement (King and Morgan, 1980). Thus all democratic and legal rights remain in place during the period of imprisonment and prisoners should be able to engage in all those activities which they would normally be involved in outside the prison. This would include mixing and engaging in relationships with people of the opposite sex. By segregating men and women in prisons, it is argued, an abnormal and distorted environment is created. Thus the strategy of normalisation is seen as being directly linked to that of rehabilitation, since one of the central rehabilitative aims of imprisonment is to prepare prisoners to manage in the outside world, and keeping men and women apart is seen as potentially undermining this objective (Shaw, 1992b). While certain countries such as Spain, Sweden and the USA have practised various degrees of integration between male and female prisoners in recent years, the interest in mixed prison in Britain is less to do with the development of fully integrated regimes and more focused on placing males and females in the same institutions in order that they can share facilities while being kept physically apart (Hayman, 1996; Leander, 1995).

There have, however, been a number of objections to men and women either sharing the same site or actually mixing together in prison. The objection to shared site detention is that it would result in women being subject to much higher levels of security than would otherwise be considered necessary, combined with a probable lack of appropriate facilities. The principle objection to the physical integration of male and female prisoners, on the other hand, is that a large percentage of female prisoners have been victims of violence and abuse at the hands of men, and that women's prisons provide, if nothing else, some respite from this abuse. For some of the more damaged women confronting men, and particularly violent men, could be a traumatic experience. Thus it is claimed that mixed prisons are likely to be more stressful for women than for men, and that the advantages of 'normalisation' would be outweighed by the negative effects upon many women. The gendered nature of power, combined with the numerical domination of men, it is suggested, would ensure that the resources would go mainly to the majority group and that the needs of female prisoners would become marginalised (Tchaikovsky, 1991). There could also be problems associated with relationships that might develop between male and female inmates, which might cause additional stress and anxiety within the enclosed world of the prison, while potentially creating further difficulties for already strained relationships with those outside the prison.

Partial Abolitionism and Reductionism

The third option available is the adoption of a strategy of partial abolitionism or reductionism whereby the sanction of imprisonment is removed for all or some female offenders. These strategies stand in opposition to the previous two 'reformist' approaches, which aim to improve and reorganise women's imprisonment (Fitzgerald and Sim, 1979). From an abolitionist perspective the danger of reformist strategies is 'incorporation' (Mathieson, 1974; Sim, 1994). As the critiques of woman-centred prisons indicate, the dilemma is that in the process of reforming these problematic institutions they become relegitimised and revitalised. The shared premise of partial abolitionism and reductionism is that prisons, for certain categories of prisoners at least, have lost their legitimacy, and rather than trying to reform them it is more constructive to find some other way of dealing with certain groups of female offenders. The difference between these two approaches as applied to female prisoners is that, whereas the abolitionists question the basic legitimacy of imprisonment for the vast majority of female offenders, the reductionists limit their focus to certain types of offenders and offences (Rutherford, 1984). Underlying these different penal reform strategies are different sets of assumptions and rationales and therefore it is not necessarily the case that those who support one type of reform will support the other.

The partial abolitionists point out that the majority of women in prison are there because they have been denied work, housing and educational opportunities, but they believe that the reduction of poverty and inequality will not in itself resolve the problems of imprisonment (Carlen, 1990). They argue that attempts to reduce the prison population through the development of more community-based 'alternatives' to custody or by simply altering sentencing policies are going to have at best a marginal impact and at worst, as the American experience demonstrates, it could result in women inadvertently serving longer sentences. Moreover, they claim that the level of imprisonment in general has little or no effect on the level of crime (Carlen, 1990; Mathieson, 1990). In developing this form of abolitionism, Pat Carlen (1990) argues that there is a need to abolish the 'tariff' system of punishments and to abandon the assumption that imprisonment is the inevitable back-up to non-custodial penalties. The abolitionists believe that imprisonment for the vast majority of women is unjustified, inappropriate and in many cases counterproductive. On the basis that a relatively small number of women are incarcerated, it is argued that there is the possibility for: 'an experimental period of five years imprisonment should be abolished as a "normal" punishment for women and that a maximum of only a hundred places should be retained for female offenders convicted or accused or abnormally serious crimes' (Carlen and Tchaikovsky, 1996).

The immediate problem which arises in relation to this form of partial abolitionism is that, while it is recognised that the needs and experiences of female prisoners are in certain respects different from those of men, it is difficult to argue, particularly in the present political climate, that in cases in which men and women suffer similar levels of disadvantage and have committed similar crimes in similar circumstances, one should be imprisoned while the other is exempted. The strategy of abolitionism applied only to women's prisons would appear to be particularly divisive if it means that a woman convicted of a relatively serious crime is given a non-custodial sentence while a man with a similar background who is convicted of a lesser crime receives a term of imprisonment. Even during the proposed 'experimental' period, these discrepancies would be extremely difficult to 'sell' to the general public and would undoubtedly undermine notions of fairness and justice. By the same token, it is not clear why it is suggested by some abolitionists that female drug-users should be dealt with outside the prison, while it is apparently acceptable that rehabilitation for male drug-users should continue to be carried out within the prison. Finally, the desire not to use prison as the back-up institution to non-custodial penalties overlooks the fact that prison is distinguished from all other penalties (except of course in countries with capital punishment) in that it is the ultimately coercive sanction employed when offenders do not comply with non-custodial penalties (de Haan, 1990; Matthews, 1992).

Reductionism, on the other hand, adopts a more limited approach, which focuses on the removal of certain categories of offenders from prison. In a recent report by the Howard League (1997) on the use of custody for girls under 18 years of age, for example, it is argued that; 'prison is a brutalising experience and it is ineffective in combating youth crime', while they point out that reoffending rates for young people following terms of imprisonment have been consistently between 80 and 90 per cent. On the basis of these observations it is argued that neither the offenders nor the community at large gains any real benefit from placing the 300 or so girls aged 18 and under in prison each year. Women's prisons have no specialist educational or rehabilitative programmes for teenagers, while many of these young girls, it is argued, are vulnerable and should not have to mix with adult female offenders. Despite the fact that some 50 per cent of girls under the age of 18 in prison were found to have been imprisoned for violent offences, the report concludes with the recommendation that prison for those under 18 should be prohibited by law. In line with the abolitionists they suggest that the few girls who require secure conditions should be placed in secure units, while the others should be dealt with through the promotion of non-custodial sentences. This form of reductionism, however, raises similar questions of fairness and justice if girls are to be given non-custodial sentences in situations in which boys committing the same offence would receive a prison sentence. Moreover, the proliferation of alternatives to custody, as Carlen and others have pointed out, may produce a 'net-widening' effect and ultimately serve to increase the prison population as the use of 'alternatives' for particular offenders is 'exhausted', or in cases in which community-based sanctions are breached (Carlen, 1990; Matthews, 1989).

An alternative reductionist strategy aims to abolish the use of imprisonment for specific offences. Two recent examples of this strategy in England and Wales are the attempt in 1983 to remove the sanction of imprisonment for those women convicted of 'soliciting for the purposes of prostitution', and more recently the abolition of imprisonment for those convicted of not paying fines. The removal of imprisonment as the formal sanction for women convicted of 'soliciting for the purposes of prostitution' had the initial effect of reducing the number of women sent to prison for this offence, but the inability or unwillingness of those arrested for this offence to pay the often frequently imposed fines meant that many were eventually imprisoned by the back door, as it were, due to the non-payment of fines.

A similar process occurred in respect to the attempt to reduce the considerable number of people who are sent to prison each year in default of payment of fines. In the mid-1990s policy-makers and the judiciary generated a number of directives and legal judgements which aimed at avoiding the imprisonment of the majority fine defaulters (Epstein, 1996). These interventions were spurred by the realisation on one hand that many people ended up in prison for offences which themselves were non-imprisonable and extremely minor, while on the other hand it was felt that these fine defaulters contributed to the general problems of overcrowding in prisons and to the soaring costs of imprisonment. Although no legislation was passed, a combination of more or less formal guidelines effected a decrease in the numbers sent to prison for non-payment of fines from a total of 20 157 in 1995 to 8555 in 1996 and to 6336 in 1997. Amongst the female population the number sent to prison in England and Wales in default of payment of fine decreased from 1370 to 372 over this period (Moxon and Whittaker, 1996).

The partial abolitionist strategy aimed at removing virtually all women from prison and the reductionist strategy of removing certain categories of female offenders from prison overlap at two critical points in that neither, in fact, really challenges the overall legitimacy of imprisonment as the dominant sanction and as a result raises issues about fairness and justice. Unless it can be demonstrated that the culpability of women is essentially different from that of men, both positions are left with the question of why imprisonment should remain appropriate for certain types of offenders rather than others. It would also seem that if abolitionism is to be consistent and to distance itself effectively from reductionism it needs to confront imprisonment as a totality. Paradoxically, however, abolitionism is at its most theoretically coherent when it is at its most far-reaching, but it is precisely at this point that it is politically least viable. Reductionism, on the other hand, while effecting the decarceration of specific groups of offenders or certain types of offences, leaves the central issues of legitimacy untouched and offers a selective strategy of reform working mainly at the margins (Matthews, 1992; Rutherford, 1984).

CONCLUSION

The development of women's imprisonment is in the process of transition. The old male-orientated institutions are seen as being increasingly unable to meet the needs of female prisoners and as creating a form of incarceration which imposes an unnecessary level of security on female prisoners and subjects them to over-classification. The attempts to 'medicalise' female offenders by 'treating' them in secure hospitals such as the 'new Holloway' provided an approach which now seems misdirected and unrealistic. In terms of reform strategies the choice appears to be between three different options – woman-centred prisons, mixed prisons and the reduction or abolition of women's prisons. The advantage of woman-centred prisons is that women can be accommodated in smaller, purpose-built prisons which are designed to accommodate their perceived needs better. The downside of these prisons from the prisoners' perspective is that they are normally very small intensive units which are closely monitored; while from the vantage point of the prison authorities they involve problems of security and control. The second option which appears to be gaining more support formally and informally in England and Wales is some form of mixed prison which allows women to be distributed amongst a greater number of prison establishments. The advantages gained from being nearer to family and friends for many women may, however, be outweighed by the disadvantages of power differentials which would operate in these establishments, and the allocation of resources to the male majority. The third and most radical option is selective abolitionism or reductionism which aims to remove sections of female offenders from prison. These strategies, however, raise issues of fairness and justice and face practical problems of implementation. If we are to move beyond the present situation, which is clearly unsatisfactory, however, there is a need to embrace one or a combination of these options.

9 Race and Imprisonment

INTRODUCTION

When the system of ethnic monitoring was first adopted by the Prisons Department in England in 1985, it was revealed that those who were identified as black constituted 8 per cent of the prison population although they only made up approximately 1 per cent of the general population. Since that time the proportion of both male and female black prisoners has grown steadily, such that by 1995 11 per cent of the male prison population and 20 per cent of the female population were classified as black. Ethnic minority groups currently make up approximately 5.5 per cent of the total population in England and Wales but constitute some 17 per cent of the male prison population and 24 per cent of the female prison population. The racial disproportionality among those incarcerated is particularly pronounced amongst the remand population (Home Office, 1996b).

A similar pattern of racial disproportionality is evident amongst the American prison population in which, according to the Bureau of Justice Statistics, there were 250 500 black males and 10 200 females in state and federal prisons in 1985. Over the last decade these numbers have more than doubled to 500 900 for black males and more than tripled for black females to 31 000. Another way of looking at these figures is that in 1995 there were 461 white males sentenced prisoners per 100 000 of the population compared to a staggering 3250 per 100 000 blacks. The impact of these developments is that within an overall framework of prison expansion in America, Afro-Americans currently make up just over half of the adult sentenced prison population although they constitute only 12 per cent of the general population (Mauer, 1994). What is surprising about this comparison of racial disproportionality in England and Wales and in America is that the probability of being imprisoned if you are black is slightly higher in England, which has a ratio of approximately 6.5:1 compared with 6:1 in the United States (Langan and Farrington, 1998; Tonry, 1995).

Recent research focusing on Western Europe has also shown that a number of different minority groups are arrested and imprisoned at a disproportionally higher rate than the indigenous population. In a number of European countries the proportion of foreign nationals exceeds 30 per cent of the prison population. In some urban centres the proportion is close to 50 per cent (Council of Europe, 1995). In fact, it has been suggested that the impact of the changing composition of prison populations across Western Europe has resulted in the emergence of a two-tier system of incarceration: one for nationals and one for non-nationals (Tomasevski, 1994; Tonry, 1997). These simultaneous developments on both sides of the Atlantic raise questions about the changing function of imprisonment in contemporary society and its role in relation to certain disadvantaged minority ethnic groups. The growing evidence of racial disproportionality in prisons has been taken by some observers as prima-facie evidence of the discriminatory nature of the criminal justice system and has been used to counteract the suggestions which were put forward by the police and sections of the media in the 1970s that the differential rate of involvement in the criminal justice system by Afro-Caribbeans was a function of their greater involvement in crime, particularly street crime (Holdaway, 1996).

The debate about whether racial disproportionality in prison is a consequence of the nature of offending by particular ethnic minority groups or the operation of a discriminatory criminal justice system remains the central point of reference. This ongoing debate has been underpinned by a somewhat less visible but no less acrimonious debate about whether or not ethnic monitoring should take place at all. On one side it is argued that collecting data of the involvement of different ethnic groups in crime and the criminal justice system is likely to reinforce racial prejudice; while others argue that ethnic monitoring is a necessary step in gathering the information which is required to combat racial prejudice and discrimination. Over the years the argument has been gradually won by those who favour the collection of ethnic data, although a number of critics continue to maintain that systems of data collection are never neutral, and that close attention needs to be paid to the classification schemes which are used in collecting, organising and presenting the data.

THE PROBLEM OF CATEGORISATION

Some reference has already been made (see Chapter 2) to the lack of consistency in the now familiar division in the criminal statistics in Britain between black, white and Asian to the extent that the first two categories distinguish subjects by skin colour whereas the third category identifies subjects in terms of country of origin. Categorising different ethnic groups in relation to country of origin raises the issue of nationality. Of those imprisoned in England in 1995, 8 per cent were known to be foreign nationals, while approximately 24 per cent of black prisoners and 42 per cent of South Asians were foreign nationals. Interestingly, the official statistics have recently introduced the category of 'black British' and 'black Afro-Caribbean' in order to make the distinction between race and nationality clearer, although there is no equivalent set of categories for Asians.

It is only when we begin to consider these variations that we begin to realise that the categories which are used in the official statistics are largely a product of common-sense distinctions. The fact that the same forms of categorisation are widely used for general systems of ethnic and equal opportunities monitoring does not make them any more objective or consistent.

A major obstacle to the examination of race and racism in the criminal justice system is that each of the different agencies use different types of classification. The police, for example, normally use six ethnic categories – white, black, European, Asian, Chinese and Other – while the Prisons Department up to 1992 used four main categories – white, black, South Asian and Other – which have subsequently been subdivided into black (African, Caribbean and Other), South Asian (Indian, Bangladeshi, Pakistani) and Chinese (Other Asian and Other). Interestingly, white remains an undifferentiated category in this system of classification, although the category 'whiteness' is no less problematic.

Probation statistics, in contrast, divide clients into four slightly different groups – white, black, South Asian and a general category, 'all ethnic minority groups'. Although the annual probation statistics take the trouble in the footnotes to point out that the category South Asian includes Indian, Pakistanis and Bangladeshis, separate figures for these sub-groups are not actually given. The categories of white and black, however, remain undifferentiated and significantly in the 1996 probation statistics some 10 per cent of probationers had no ethnic origin recorded, while 40 per cent of those given community service orders had not been given an ethnic identity code (FitzGerald, 1995; Home Office, 1996c). These omissions, changes and inconsistencies make the task of examining the process of discrimination a difficult and uncertain business. This problem is compounded by the fact that the classification of ethnic minorities in the 1991 Census and in the

Labour Force Survey are again different, not only from those employed by criminal justice agencies, but also from each other.

There has been considerable criticism of criminal justice agencies imposing rigid categorical distinctions on suspects and offenders, and increasingly it has been seen to be preferable to allow individuals to identify their own ethnic group. However, this approach still leaves open the problem that the framework for identifying ethnic differences is pre-given, and therefore the range of choice is structured in advance. Moreover, significant differences may arise between the ways in which individuals classify themselves and those forms of classification which are imposed by criminal justice agencies.

To some extent the type of ethnic classification adopted in official circles and by researchers is conditioned by the desire to construct large enough sample sizes to carry out statistical analysis and to run significance tests. Since Afro-Caribbeans make up 1 per cent of those aged between 15 and 64, while South Asians account for 3 per cent and a further 1 per cent were classified as Chinese or Others in the 1995 *Criminal Statistics*, it can be seen that dealing with sub-categories will produce relatively small data sets. Consequently in much of the literature various ethnic groups whose geographical, linguistic or cultural interests may be entirely different are lumped together into one undifferentiated category in the course of analysis. The more regularly this is done, the more ethnic differences are overlooked, and what may in reality be diverse and in some cases oppositional groupings are treated as if they were homogenous.

RACE AND RACISM

In the various forms of classification which are adopted in different countries there is a tendency, as we have seen, to equate race with skin colour. It is small step from this point to associate race with certain essential biological characteristics or to generate differences which are held to define racial 'types'. The fact that there is no scientific basis on which the world's population can be legitimately categorised in this way does not prevent popular commentators talking as if there were. Notions of racial 'types' are often used to attribute (usually negative) characteristics to certain groups, and to establish claims of superiority and thereby legitimate forms of domination and exploitation (Jones, 1993; Miles, 1993).

Despite the lack of a real object, the idea of race remains a common-sense construct, or an ideology, which is sustained by the everyday reality of semantic and cultural differences between people. Ethnologists, however, rather than seeing race as a taken-for-granted category, have turned their attention to the social and historical conditions under which notions of 'race' have emerged, and in particular to the role of colonialism and imperialism in fostering the conditions for the creation of modern racist ideologies (Gilroy, 1987). The dilemma for ethnologists is that, although it has become convention to place terms such as 'race' or 'black' (but not normally 'white') in parenthesis in order to draw attention to the problematic, and at times racist, ways in which these terms are used, it is necessary constantly to employ these key terms in order to engage in the debate on race.

Thus, the immediate problem is how to engage in academic, social and political debates about 'race and imprisonment' without uncritically adopting common-sense categories or alternatively assuming that certain groups have a natural propensity towards anti-social behaviour which is based on an assumed transhistorical essence. The claim, for example, by Richard Herrnstein and Charles Murray (1994) in *The Bell Curve* that blacks have a lower IQ than other races and that this accounts for their low socioeconomic status and their subsequent involvement in illegitimate opportunity structures is spurious because it reduces social to biological processes. The fact that this assertion has been confounded by research which shows considerable variation in the IQ levels of blacks and which has pointed to the culturally and socially biased nature of IQ tests has largely discredited these assertions (Cullen *et al.*, 1997; Jones, 1993).

In an attempt to see race as a changing socially constructed concept, a number of writers have shifted their attention towards the analysis of racism and racialist discourses in order to de-reify and critically deconstruct the key terms. Such a strategy is seen as necessary in order to engage critically in the issue of race, and embodies a number of key elements. Firstly, there is a focus on the historical evolution of racial ideologies in order to uncover the conditions of their emergence and to asses their effects. Secondly, critics have turned their attention to the examination of racist stereotypes in order to question their validity. Thirdly, since race itself is a contested issue, attention has shifted to an examination of the process of cultural identification and identity formation among different ethnic groups (Back, 1996). Fourthly, researchers have deconstructed race into its component parts, rather than treating blacks, for example, as an homogeneous group with fixed characteristics. Fifthly, attempts have made to counter those over-racialised conceptions which circulate widely in the sphere of criminal justice which tend to see crime, victimisation and the operation of the criminal justice process primarily in terms of race rather than as a function of other variables (Miles, 1993: Solomos and Back, 1996).

These considerations will remain an ongoing point of reference in our examination of the relation between race, crime and imprisonment and also in relation to the charges of racial discrimination which have been levelled against the operation of the criminal justice system. The charge of discrimination has been made in a number of different forms, including that of systematic and institutionalised racism. Institutionalised racism is normally seen to operate in both direct and indirect forms. In its direct form it is consciously aimed towards ethnic minorities, while indirect discrimination is seen to operate in those situations in which certain policies, although not specifically designed to disadvantage particular ethnic minority groups, operate in such a way that they work consistently to their disadvantage. A related concern is whether the operation of racism within the criminal justice system is largely attributable to one or two particular agencies, or whether discrimination works in a cumulative way with different degrees of discrimination operating at each stage of the criminal justice process (Smith, 1997a; Waters, 1990).

RACE AND CRIME

Do blacks commit more crime than whites? This is the question which dominates contemporary criminological thinking on both sides of the Atlantic. Putting the question in this stark form, however, is not only seriously misdirected but it is also likely to produce racist conclusions and reinforce racist ideologies. This is principally because the question invites a false comparison (Lea and Young, 1984).

One of the major problems in engaging in the debate on 'race and crime' is comparing like with like. We know that crime is not evenly distributed across the social spectrum and that the best indicators of both offending and victimisation are socioeconomic position, age, location, and gender. Endless volumes of criminological research demonstrate that most forms of recorded crime and victimisation are concentrated among the poor and disadvantaged, the young, and those living in certain parts of the inner city (Bottoms and Wiles, 1997). The experience of crime and victimisation is, of course, also

highly gendered. For a number of social and political reasons the
immigrants who came to Britain from the West Indies in the post-war
period have been mainly involved in manual and unskilled work and
have experienced high levels of unemployment, poor housing and
education, and tend to be concentrated in those parts of the inner city
which have historically been high crime areas. Thus to compare the
black population in Britain with the general population of whites is
not only sociologically and criminologically meaningless, it is also
politically disingenuous. Every apprentice criminologist could predict
on the basis of socio-demographic data alone that an unqualified comparison between black and white populations will demonstrate that
blacks are proportionately responsible for more crimes than whites.

    The corollary of the claim that blacks commit more crime than
whites is that Asians, although a minority group, tend to have a generally lower level of criminal involvement than whites (Smith, 1997a;
Tonry, 1997). This is because, it is intimated, Asians are 'naturally'
more law-abiding than either blacks or whites. This second assertion,
although no less spurious than the first, has the added appeal to many
criminologists that it demonstrates not only their own even-handed-
ness in relation to this issue, but also that the relatively low proportion
of Asians involved in the criminal justice system shows that at worst
racial discrimination is selective or at best it is minimal, since they
argue that if racism were endemic in the system all racial minorities
would receive the same discriminatory treatment. This is an exercise
in wishful thinking, not sociological analysis. It is not their natural pre-
disposition towards law-abiding behaviour which distinguishes Asian
involvement in crime and the criminal justice system. Instead their
limited involvement in these processes can be largely explained
through an analysis involving the four key variables: class, age, gender,
and location.

    In one of the few British studies which has attempted to incorporate
some consideration of socio-economic grouping, age and location into
a study of different ethnic groups, Stevens and Willis (1979) showed
that there is good evidence of an association between deprivation,
location and arrests. Although the kind of deprivation which is
significant varies between the different ethnic groups. Moreover, they
argue that when demographic differences are taken into account the
level of arrests between whites, blacks and Asians is roughly similar.
Thus it is suggested that if we are to determine the 'race effect', some
account of socioeconomic status, age distribution, gender relations
and location must be taken into account. The conspicuous lack of

attention in the literature to the socioeconomic characteristics of offenders has resulted in a disproportionate amount of crime being attributed to race. Whereas in the past many criminologists were accused of 'colour-blindness', they now appear to suffer from 'class-blindness'.

(Decontextualised comparisons between blacks and whites are not only sociologically bankrupt, but can lead to the over-racialisation of offending. It is therefore necessary, as Stuart Hall and his colleagues argued in *Policing the Crisis* (1978), to confront the stereotypical images of black youth presented by the mass media and the disproportionate amount of attention which they pay to certain forms of crime. In a similar vein the riots of the 1980s which occurred in a number of urban centres were presented as overwhelmingly black riots, despite the fact that they involved different ethnic groups in different parts of the country (Campbell, 1993; Gilroy, 1987).

However, recognising that the media tend to racialise, dramatise and decontextualise crime, is not to deny or romanticise the significant involvement of young black people in certain forms of crime. Nor is this involvement adequately conceptualised as a process of labelling or criminalisation (Keith, 1993). The overwhelming evidence is that the victims of crimes committed by black offenders are also generally disadvantaged and live in the same area. This means that, given the nature of racial concentration in the inner city, a significant percentage of the victims are also going to be drawn from the same racial group (Burney, 1990). This should, however, not be read simply as 'black on black' crime, since it is not only intra-racial but also intra-class. It is neighbour on neighbour, youth on youth, and poor on poor.

The lack of a distinctive black middle class in Britain means that it is difficult to make accurate class comparisons, but the probability is that the involvement of middle-class blacks in crime in Britain is roughly similar to middle-class whites. As John Pitts (1993) has suggested, the level of street crime among black middle-class accountants is probably the same as that of white middle-class accountants. Indicatively, in William Julius Wilson's (1987) study, delinquency rates among non-underclass African Americans were very similar to those of white youths living in similar areas.

In many respects the nature, level and intensity of black crime is much as might be expected given the socioeconomic characteristics, age distribution and social location of black people living in Britain. Thus in terms of the different levels of recorded crime between blacks and Asians the real issue is not so much how do we explain the apparently high level of black crime, but conversely how we explain the relatively low level of Asian criminality. Although this question remains, as yet, relatively under-researched, there are a number of factors which might help to account for the difference. The first involves the very different experience of colonisation experienced by Asians and Afro-Caribbean, and in particular the effects of slavery and other forms of degradation and dislocation suffered by Africans which did not form part of Asian experience. As Edward Said (1993) has argued, the experience of colonisation and imperialism not only played a critical role in shaping forms of exploitation and subordination but also deeply influenced the ways in which different races are viewed by the imperialist powers.

Secondly, the sequence of immigration in the post-war period was important in that second-generation Afro-Caribbeans fell victims of the fiscal crisis which developed in Britain in the 1970s and to the shift from full employment to structural unemployment. Thirdly, the largest group of Asians were the more entrepreneurial and middle-class Indians, who were more easily assimilated into British society. Although the Pakistanis and Bangladeshis were less well qualified and experienced greater levels of unemployment, the presence of a large group of Indians gave these other minority groups a lower political profile and lower 'specific weight'. Fourthly, as a result of cultural and religious differences, the Asian community operated with different forms of informal control, greater privatisation and better opportunity structures within their own community. In a sense it was the greater distance between Asian and British culture than that which existed between West Indian and British culture that facilitated assimilation. Although the assimilation of West Indian youth has been more rapid, opportunity structures for this group has been more restricted, and particularly since the late 1970s they have experienced a greater level of relative deprivation, which in turn has fostered a different form of subcultural adaption (Lea and Young, 1984).

Thus, if proper comparisons are to made between different ethnic minority groups, and if blacks, Asians and whites are to be compared, it is essential to compare like with like. This means that it is necessary to at least begin by allowing for socioeconomic variations, demographic characteristics, and geographical location. Different patterns of offending between different groups are not simply a function of absolute deprivation, however: they are also linked to forms of relative deprivation and styles of subcultural adaption. Once these processes are examined, the variations in offence levels and patterns become less surprising and it is possible to begin to identify the 'race effect' in terms of both crime and victimisation.

ARRESTS, CAUTIONING AND PROSECUTION

A great deal has been written about racist attitudes among the police, but the question is to what extent these attitudes are translated into discriminatory practices (Holdaway, 1996). In the aftermath of the 1980s riots the consensus was that these disturbances were caused by antagonistic and unmediated relationships between ethnic minorities and the police, which were a function of what was seen as heavy-handed and selective law enforcement practices adopted by the police (Scarman, 1982). One of the first major studies which examined the relationship between the police and ethnic minorities was carried out by the Policy Studies Institute in the mid-1980s. They found that: 'racialist language and racial prejudice were prominent and pervasive and many individual officers and also whole groups were preoccupied with ethnic differences' (Smith, 1983). Thus the problem of racism in the police went far beyond a few 'bad apples' and appeared to be an endemic part of police culture at that time (Lea, 1986).

One indication of the translation of racist attitude into racist prac-tices has been the use of stop and search strategies. Although the available evidence confirms the suspicion that Afro-Caribbeans are more likely to be stopped and searched than other groups, there is some doubt about how many prosecutions of a serious nature result from stop and search, and therefore ultimately what impact this policy has on the prison population. David Smith (1997a), for example, claims that only 3 per cent of stop and searches result in a prosecu-tion, while Roger Hood (1992) in his study found a significant number of Afro-Caribbeans appearing in Crown Court on quite serious charges – particularly those involving drugs – who had come to police attention through stop and search.

It is certainly the case, however, that the primary definers of 'crime' are the victims who make the critical decision of whether or not to report incidents to the police. It is clear, that this decision is not only a function of the nature and severity of the offence, but is also condi-tioned by the victim's belief that the police will take the report seri-ously and will be willing and able to do something about it. For this reason there is a symbiotic relationship between the police and the public, in which the police response will itself influence the decision to report. Therefore, it is not possible to maintain a clear distinction between 'crime' and the response, since the construction of 'crime' itself is a product of a dynamic process of action and reaction (Matthews, 1994; Matthews and Young, 1992). The implication of this process is that the question of whether it is the involvement of certain ethnic minorities in crime or the discriminatory practices of the criminal justice system which results in racial disproportionately among the prison population is never a clear-cut issue.

There are two potentially counteracting implications of this analysis. The first is that the decision of the police to prosecute will also be influenced by their assessment of the likelihood of a case being acted upon by the Crown Prosecution Service and the possibility of conviction. This decision, again, is not taken purely on the basis of the available evidence, but will also be conditioned by the quality of the defence and the demeanour of the defendant. On the other hand, if the police are generally racist, there may be a tendency to devalue reports in cases where victims are drawn from ethnic minorities and they may be less motivated to process these cases.

There is no national data available on arrests among different ethnic groups in England and Wales, but the reports from the Metropolitan Police indicate a high arrest rate among Afro-Caribbeans. Just over 50 per cent of those arrested for street robbery, 21 per cent of assault, 21 per cent for fraud, and 17 per cent for burglary were described as black. Although the evidence is fragmented, it suggests that black people are more likely to be prosecuted than white people and less likely to receive a caution (FitzGerald, 1993; Landau and Nathan, 1983; Smith, 1983).

COURTS AND SENTENCING

The decision-making process in the courts has been identified as a pivotal stage in the criminal justice process, since it is at this point that previous decisions can effectively be modified or reversed and critical decisions in relation to the use of custody are made. The sentencing process, however, involves wider issues of justice and public safety. It is therefore not just a 'tap' for regulating the flow of offenders into prison or community-based sanctions, but it is also a point at which justice must be seen to be done (Ashworth, 1983).

The Race Relations Act (1968) and subsequent legislation has made it unlawful to discriminate on the grounds of race, colour or nationality and consequently the courts themselves must be seen to act in non-discriminatory ways. Since the make-up of the judiciary is overwhelmingly white, middle-class and conservative, it might be assumed that sentencing decisions would tend to work systematically against ethnic minorities. In 1994 there were only four judges in England and Wales who were either Afro-Caribbean or Asian. However, although the research on this issue has found a number of specific examples of racist bias in sentencing, in general it has been found that if the seriousness of the case and the defendant's previous history is taken into account, there is a rough parity in the sentences handed out to offenders from different ethnic minority groups. (Blumstein, 1982; Hood, 1992). By the time offenders from different ethnic groups appear in court they appear to be roughly similar in terms of socio-economic characteristics, although some discrepancies remain which may have an impact upon sentencing decisions. For example, in the study carried out by Imogen Brown and Roy Hullin (1992) which examined the decision-making process in relation to over 3000 defendants, they noted that over 50 per cent of the Afro-Caribbean defendants were unemployed and that this was almost twice that of the white and Asian defendants (Crow and Cove, 1984; Moxon, 1988).

Much of the research which has attempted to examine judicial decision-making process in relation to ethnic minorities has encountered the problem of devising a large enough sample in order to construct meaningful comparisons. For this reason most investigations operate with the three main categories, namely black, white and Asian, which are treated for the purposes of analysis as if they were homogeneous and exclusive groups. One imaginative piece of research which attempted to come to terms with the considerable methodological difficulties involved in developing comparisons between different ethnic groups is a study based on a sample of 2884 defendants who appeared in Crown Courts in the West Midlands. This piece of research, carried out by Roger Hood (1992), employed multivariate analysis. By developing a 'risk of custody' score, which was designed to calculate the probability of custody for different groups, the aim was to identify the 'race effect' of sentencing. That is, on the basis of 15 selected variables, excluding race, the study was designed to identify the variation in the use of custody for each ethnic group.

In line with previous research, Hood (1992) found that the racial disparity in sentencing is less than might have been assumed, with blacks on average being about 5 per cent more likely than whites to be given a custodial sentence; while the Asian group were about 5 per cent less likely to receive a custodial sentence than the white group. Criminal histories, it was found, and the severity of the offence accounted for approximately 80 per cent of the over-representation of black male offenders in prison and the remaining 20 per cent was largely accounted for by the fact that a significant percentage of black offenders opted for Crown Court and pleaded not guilty, with the consequence that if they were convicted they were more likely to receive a prison sentence and probably a longer prison sentence.

Hood also noted that black offenders were more likely to have been remanded in custody by magistrates. Being already in custody, pleading not guilty and consequently not having a Social Inquiry Report written on them, they were more likely to receive a custodial sentence if convicted. A higher proportion of black and Asian defendants received sentences of over three years, and there were significant differences in the deployment of non-custodial options, with black offenders receiving generally higher tariff alternatives than whites. Other research has shown that blacks were also less likely to be given a probation order or a community service order than whites (Mair, 1986).

Although Hood's study (1992) addresses some of the methodological issues involved in making comparisons of this type, there are a number of problems which remain and which tend to limit the validity of his overall research findings. Despite the fact that Hood is critical of earlier studies which lump together different ethnic groups under two or three general headings, he adopts a similar strategy and divides his sample into the familiar categories of black, Asian and white. Relatedly, there are issues about the choice of location and the representativeness of the sample, as well as the ability to generalise from these specific findings to the whole country.

In relation to the representativeness of the survey, it should be noted that there were significant differences in the sentencing practices of the five different Crown Courts which Hood investigated, with the Dudley Courts, in particular, generating much higher rates of racial disparity. Whereas in Birmingham Crown Court, which involved the largest percentage of the total sample, a black offender had a 1 in 3 probability of receiving a custodial sentence, in Dudley a black offender had a 1 in 2 chance. Thus, if the distribution of cases had been different, with more cases taken from Dudley, the study would have shown a much greater racial bias. Consequently, the conclusion that there were only a few percentage points difference in the sentencing of different ethnic groups would have to be revised. Hood's conclusion that the decision to plead not guilty and the lack of Social Inquiry Reports suggests that the question of disparity is largely a procedural and technical issue, on the one hand, and a consequence of adopting the high-risk strategy of choosing to be tried in the Crown Court by black defendants, on the other. The question of why so many choose Crown Court and decided to plead guilty is not, however, addressed.

There are fundamental methodological issues related to the use of a prediction scale which is only accurate in 75 per cent of cases, while the 'risk of custody' score is limited to legally 'relevant' factors and excludes factors such as unemployment. The exclusion of this particular factor is surprising, to the extent that Hood himself in the course of his analysis of the operation of different Crown Courts makes repeated reference to the significance of unemployment, but nevertheless treats it as an extraneous independent variable. At the same time he refers to the higher use of fines for Asians and implies that this might be a function of a generally higher level of employment among this group.

A major difference between the black and white offenders who appeared before the Dudley Courts, according to Hood (1992), was that: 'the proportion of black offenders given a custodial sentence was significantly higher for those who were employed' (p. 64). He points out that at Birmingham Court, where the disparities in sentencing were at a minimum, there were no significant difference between the proportion of blacks and whites who were known to be unemployed or in receipt of welfare. In his explanation for ethnic variation in sentencing patterns in Coventry, Hood states that: 'The reason for their different practice appeared to be the much greater use of custody at Coventry for offenders who were unemployed' (p. 93), and he notes in another passage that: 'Being unemployed was a factor significantly correlated with receiving a custodial sentence if the defendant was black but not if he was white or Asian' (p. 86).

This is not to argue that unemployment is necessarily one of the main factors influencing the use of custody, or that it operates in some direct and unmediated way to affect rates of imprisonment. Rather, it is to suggest that there are causal links between unemployment and imprisonment, and therefore there is good reason for including it among the key variables (Halevy, 1995; Hood, 1995; see Chapter 5 above). The point is that not all variables that might possibly affect sentencing can be included in the analysis; while the influence of excluded variables that do have a racial correlation may be mistakenly attributed to those variables which are included. As Hood (1995) himself admits, his study does not aim to provide a causal explanation but operates at the level of aggregates and concludes by stating that the reasons for the disparities in the treatment of black and white males must remain open to speculation. The main weakness, however, of Hood's study is the assumption that factors such as previous offending or convictions are themselves racially neutral (Bowling and Philips, 1999).

Although the percentages are not very large, Hood's study does provide evidence of both 'direct' and 'indirect' discrimination in Crown Courts. Direct discrimination was evident in terms of bail decisions, the rate at which blacks were sentenced to custody and the length of custodial sentence imposed. Indirect discrimination is seen to occur in relation to the decision to plead not guilty and the use of Social Inquiry Reports. However, Hood's general argument is that discrimination in relation to sentencing in Crown Courts is neither systematic nor universal (FitzGerald, 1993).

Hood's (1992) conclusion that 80 per cent of custodial decisions among the black group of offenders is accounted for by the nature and severity of the offence is similar to that presented in Alfred Blumstein's influential American study on sentencing and racial disproportionality in prisons. Blumstein (1982) arrives at a similar conclusion to Hood, but adopts a different mode of analysis. He compares arrest and imprisonment patterns using a four-stage model. Having divided the prison population into eleven categories, he then proceeded to examine what percentage of each category of sentenced prisoners was black. Using FBI data on arrests he then proceeded to find out what proportion of persons arrested for the same eleven categories of offence were black. His analysis is based upon the assumption that in a non-biased system the racial proportions in arrests would be mirrored in the racial proportions imprisoned. Thus, for example, he found that 52.3 per cent of those imprisoned for homicide were black and that 51.6 per cent of those arrested for homicide were black. He thereby concluded that 97.2 per cent of the racial disproportionality for that offence could be accounted for by the black homicide arrest rates. Interestingly, like Hood, Blumstein found that there was evidence of discrimination among the less serious offences and in those cases in which there was room for judicial discretion. Thus the implication of both Blumstein and Hood's analysis is that reducing racism in the criminal justice system is unlikely to have much effect on the size or the racial composition of the prison population and that the only way to change the present level of racial disproportionality in prison would be to reduce the involvement of black people in serious crime.

Blumstein (1988), however, does raise an important point about the possibility of comparing like with like in relation to different categories of offence, particularly if institutional racism is prevalent:

> If, for example, a prosecutor was systematically favouring whites by dropping less serious cases for them, then the whites convicted of a particular offence would have committed more serious crimes than non-whites; judges who were perfectly race blind in their sentencing would impose harsher sentences on white offenders than non-white offenders. This apparently harsher treatment of whites (as it might be seen by people who did not understand the prosecutor's screening policies) would camouflage a systematic bias against non-whites. This is merely one of the ways by which discrimination that did exist could be masked. (Blumstein, 1988: 249)

This problem of masking discrimination can also be affected by the possibility of 'victim discounting' if the victim is black. This process has implications for the validity of statistical inferences which Hood presents. Given the evidence of racist attitudes among the police, the differential use of cautioning and bail for certain ethnic minority groups appears to be the product of precisely the process which Blumstein identifies, such that discrimination is not only masked but compounded by an apparently 'neutral' judiciary. This problem arises in part from the attempt to investigate racial discrimination in the criminal justice system through a series of snap-shots, rather than attempting to examine it as part of a process which is both subtle and opaque. There is a complex interaction between the social characteristics of different groups of offenders, their offending histories, the type of offence they commit, the decision to remand offenders in custody and ultimately the deployment of custodial and non-custodial sentences. As Marian FitzGerald and Peter Marshall point out in relation to Hood's study:

> [So] the factors which drive up the remand rate for black defendants go beyond their offending histories and the characteristics of the offences with which they have been charged; they appear to include evidence of both direct and indirect discrimination. What is particularly striking is that the amount of unexplained difference in

the bail/remand decision was at least twice as large as the difference found at the point of sentencing. That is, there is a strong
inference of discrimination in the decision to bail or remand. Yet
this decision is one of the apparently 'race neutral' or strictly legal
factors which 'explains' ethnic disparities at the sentencing stage,
minimizing any possible inference of discrimination at this point.
(FitzGerald and Marshall, 1996: 153)

Thus, given that socioeconomic variables such as unemployment, home-
lessness and single-parent households have all been held to influence
the remand/bail decision, removing these considerations from the
analysis may provide a more sanitised form of analysis which allow the
construction of a more comfortable set of conclusions, but does not do
justice to the complex interplay of socioeconomic and decision-making
processes at the various stages of the criminal justice process.

RACE AND THE EXPERIENCE OF INCARCERATION

There has been considerable debate about whether black and white
offenders experience imprisonment in different ways (see Chapter 3
above). The experience of confinement will be conditioned by the
levels of solidarity among different ethnic groups, their subcultural
backgrounds and the power relations within the prison itself, involving
not only interpersonal relations and systems of control but also the
design and management of the prison. The internal power relations
among prisoners will affect the distribution of work, the forms of interpersonal support, and the experience of bullying and intimidation.

   The pains of imprisonment are felt most acutely by non-nationals.
The intensification of the problems of imprisonment among this group
are often a result of problems of language and communication, the
lack of information, isolation from family and friends, and in particular the uncertainty which is associated with knowing little about the
operation of the criminal justice system and as a consequence being
unsure about procedures and the length of time involved for cases to
be heard and decided. There are related problems of organising good
legal representation and following through the developments of the
case. Foreign nationals are less likely to be given bail and may not be
eligible for home release or benefit from early release policies. For
these reasons foreign prisoners tend to become marginalised in the
world of the marginalised. Foreign prisoners on remand experience

specific difficulties in relation to the initial notification to their families, the general lack of outside contact and in particular not knowing how long they will remain in custody (Cheney, 1993; Matthews, 1994).

In England and Wales the geographical concentration of ethnic minority populations in the inner city areas of London and the West Midlands means that prisoners from these groups are not evenly distributed across the country but tend to be located mainly in the South East, where they make up between a quarter and half of the prison population (Genders and Player, 1989). Relations between rank-and- file prison staff and ethnic minority prisoners is mediated by certain widely held stereotypes, in which Afro-Caribbean prisoners are described as being aggressive, difficult, lazy and as having a 'chip on their shoulder'. Probably, not surprisingly, black prisoners tend to keep their distance from white prison officers and are suspicious of them. In contrast, Asian prisoners are portrayed by prison officers as 'model prisoners'. Consequently, whereas prison officers are reported to be generally hostile and unsympathetic towards black prisoners, they are more sympathetic towards Asian prisoners, who are frequently described as 'scapegoats', and are seen as suffering from bullying and intimidation. Asian prisoners are also seen to suffer from a lack of adequate facilities in prison to meet their dietary needs and to enable them to practice their religion.

Elaine Genders and Elaine Player (1989) found evidence of different degrees of solidarity between both black and Asian groups which provided some degree of support. However, the type of organised political groupings of black prisoners which has been reported in some American prisons was not evident in the prisons they visited. According to the *National Prison Survey* (1991), there are significant differences between different ethnic groups in prison terms of the offences they have committed. Black inmates tend to have a much higher rate of conviction for robbery than whites or Asians but a lower rate for burglary. Over 40 per cent of the adult black prison population had been convicted of drug offences, although black prisoners are less likely to have either very short or long sentences.

RACE AND IMPRISONMENT IN AMERICA

The debates around race and imprisonment in Britain have been influenced to a large extent by developments in America. This is partly because this issue has been more widely discussed and partly because statistics on the ethnicity of offenders and prisoners have been collected over a much longer period of time. Also, the politicisation of race and imprisonment during the 1960s and 1970s through the writings of black activists like George Jackson (1970) and Eldridge Cleaver (1968) brought attention to the plight of black people within the American prison system.

Although the debate on race and imprisonment in America has been extensive, and at times heated, it has in some respects been peculiarly narrow, in the sense that ethnic and racial differences are condensed within much of the academic and official literature into a direct 'black–white' or 'white–non-white' opposition. As a consequence the experiences of other ethnic groups tends to be marginalised or ignored, which in turn has consequences not only for the way in which the race and incarceration issue is conceived and discussed, but also that the differences between different minority groups remains largely unexamined.

Of particular significance are Hispanics, who currently constitute the second largest ethnic minority group in the United States, making up 9 per cent of the population – compared to blacks, who make up approximately 12 per cent at present. In the next decade or so, however, Hispanics are destined to become the largest ethnic minority group in America. Hispanics currently constitute the largest ethnic minority group in some of America's largest cities, including Detroit, Chicago and Los Angeles. Moreover Hispanics have been the fastest growing ethnic minority group among the prison population in recent years, increasing from 163 per 100 000 in 1980 to 622 per 100 000 in 1995 (Bureau of Justice, 1996).

Despite these trends, the predominant focus among American criminologists in relation to race is on black offenders and prisoners. Indicatively, Hispanics can be classified as either 'black' or 'white', and in some of the literature and statistical presentations they are divided into blacks and whites, although the basis of this decision if rarely clear. In some studies they are classified as 'non-white', which is often read as 'black'. Although Hispanics are identified as an ethnic group with a common language, they are seen to be made up of different 'races' (Irwin and Austin, 1994). In the attempt to explain the apparently arbitrary and inconsistent nature of racial classification, Robert Sampson and Janet Lauritsen (1997) inform us that:

Not sharing a common culture, the myriad groups classified as Hispanics thus fail to meet the criteria we typically think of as constituting an ethnic group. For these and other reasons the construction of Hispanics has been criticised as a political definition which has little meaning, with many preferring the label 'Latino' instead. (Sampson and Lauritsen, 1997: 315)

It is strange that whereas the term 'Hispanic' is seen to be politically loaded, it is apparently less problematic than 'Latino'. However, the authors use the term 'black' as if it were neither politically loaded nor problematic. To some extent there is a rationale for adopting the term 'black' less critically than other ethnic designations, because of the nature of social and spatial segregation in America, but it evident that the notion of 'black' too needs to be critically deconstructed and treated with caution if it is to have any real policy relevance.

The attitudes towards Hispanics and the methods of classification say a great deal about how the issue of race is seen in America. Clearly for many writers 'race' is synonymous with 'black'. This form of racialisation is no doubt a function of the social and geographical concentration of large segments of the black population in inner city ghettos. For many Americans the issue of crime and the fear of crime is translated into a fear of black crime (Skogan, 1995). As Andrew Hacker (1992) has pointed out: 'The dread whites feel of black crime goes beyond actual risks and probabilities.' The predominant focus on black crime is, however, not presented only in terms of white fears but also, it is argued, because the victims of black crime are disproportionately black.

For many conservative critics the translation of the problem of crime into the problem of race is politically convenient. Punitive interventions are justified against blacks in general, since criminality is seen to be endemic in this group. Getting tough on black crime is rationalised not only in terms of the extent and seriousness of the transgression but also in terms of protecting the public (Dilulio, 1994). Liberals, on the other hand, although they largely agree that black crime is a major problem, argue that blacks are subject to processes of criminalisation whereby the types of activities they are involved in receive undue attention from crime control agencies. Michael Tonry (1995), for example, in his book *Malign Neglect*, argues that the rapid growth of the prison population in America in recent years has been largely a consequence of the 'War on Drugs' and that this war has been largely waged against inner city blacks.

He produces evidence to show that drug use during the 1980s was widespread among different sections of the population, but that the 'War on Drugs' was aimed at crack cocaine users, who were overwhelmingly young and black. The implementation of this selective policy was not accidental and its consequences were predictable. According to Tonry:

> The 'War on Drugs' foreseeably and unnecessarily blighted the lives of hundreds of thousands of young disadvantaged black Americans and undermined decades of effort to improve life chances of members of the urban black underclass. The war was fought largely from partisan political motives to show that the Bush and Reagan administrations were concerned about public safety, crime prevention, and the needs of victims (as if Democrats or any responsible mainstream figures were not). The bodies counted in this war, as they lay in their prison beds, however, are even more disproportionately black than prisoners already were. War or no war, most people are saddened to learn that for many years 30 to 40 per cent of those admitted to prison were black. The War on Drugs was a calculated effort foreordained to increase those percentages and this is what happened. (Tonry, 1995: 82)

Tonry makes the important point that the effects of crime control policies during the 1980s have made a major contribution to declining levels of lawful employment among young black males. It is estimated that 1 in 12 young black males are incarcerated in America at any one time, while 1 in 4 are under the control or supervision of the criminal justice system (see Figure 9.1). The stigmatising and marginalising

Figure 9.1   US adult population in State and Federal prisons or in local jails, by race and sex, 1984–95

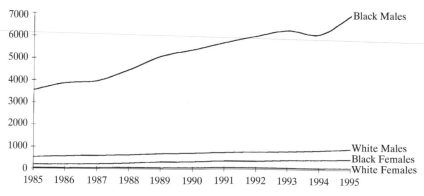

Source: Correctional Populations in the United States 1996, (Washington, DC: Bureau of Justice Statistics).

effects of imprisonment, combined with the probabilities of recidivism, means that the possibilities of legitimate employment for a significant number of black males is greatly reduced, while their dependants and partners are destined to a life of welfare dependency. At the same time, of course, it means that the experience of imprisonment and of prison subcultures is 'exported' back into the urban ghetto. Thus the conclusion of Tonry's study is that, however ineffectual the 'War on Drugs' might have been in reducing drug use, it was very effective in increasing the level of black incarceration. Through selective intervention the police were able to target blacks and thereby be seen to be effectively fighting the 'War on Drugs' by maintaining a high rate of arrest. Tonry's work can therefore be seen as both a critique and an elaboration of Blumstein's (1982) account of the dynamics of racial disproportionality in prisons. Tonry (1995) draws attention to the ways in which arrest figures can be constructed through selective enforcement and how subsequent arrest rates for drug offences help to turn this into a predominantly 'black' issue.

Tonry (1995), however, is critical of Blumstein's (1982) focus on murder, rape and assault and his lack of consideration of the role of drug-related arrests, although Blumstein in a re-examination issue does acknowledge the significance of drugs in this process (Blumstein, 1993). Tonry is also critical of Blumstein's use of aggregate data which may well hide important differences in the forms of discrimination experienced by different groups in different locations. There are also, Tonry reminds us, a number of different processes which occur between the point of arrest and prosecution, and Blumstein's analysis suffers from the problem of 'slippage', as the time gap between arrest and prosecution means that the data relating to arrests is from 1978, while the data on the prison population is based on the 1979 figures. Blumstein's analysis also conflates the data on prison admissions with the length of sentence. Blumstein can also be criticised for discounting the considerable degree of discrimination exercised in relation to minor offenders. Given the propensity for offenders to reappear in the criminal justice at a later date this discrimination can have a considerable long-term cumulative effect (Bowling and Philips, 1999).

Thus Tonry's (1995) analysis can be seen to add an important dimension to the relation between race and imprisonment. However, as an examination of race and crime and race and imprisonment it has a number of limitations. Firstly, like the conservative criminologists, Tonry tends to over-racialise crime by presenting the material predominantly in 'black' and 'white' terms, largely leaving out Hispanics and other ethnic minorities, and by presenting his findings in terms of race rather than class. Although he acknowledges the socioeconomic position of the black 'underclass', the issue is largely translated into one of race rather than one of poverty or deprivation. This point is best exemplified by Tonry's focus on the discriminatory way in which anti-drugs policies were implemented in the 1980s. He gives a number of reasons to explain why the police focused mainly on black communities. These include vulnerability, visibility, accessibility and the probability of successfully prosecuting those arrested. All these factors relate primarily to the socioeconomic nature of the population rather than their race. That is, Tonry does not clearly demonstrate a 'race effect'. Interestingly, poor Hispanics were also targets of the 'War on Drugs' and their incarceration rate also increased – not one suspects, primarily because they were Hispanics but because like poor blacks they were subject to selective enforcement because of their accessibility and vulnerability.

The predominant focus on race and on the issue of drugs serves to blinker Tonry's (1995) analysis and produces a series of unresolved tensions. On one side, if the criminal justice agencies are racist and are prone to target blacks (and other ethnic minorities), then why should they just do this only in relation to drugs? Why do they not adopt the same policies for all offences? On the other hand, if this is really a class issue, then it suggests that criminal justice agencies tend to routinely enforce policies in a selective manner and concentrate on those targets which are most accessible and most vulnerable. If it is the case that Tonry is arguing that the poor and the powerless are normally at the receiving end of discriminatory practices, then the implications for both his own and for Blumstein's analysis are far-reaching since it suggests that patterns of arrest for the majority of offences are a function of differential crime control strategies whereby the socially disadvantaged are more likely to be the targets of intervention.

CONFINING ETHNIC MINORITIES IN FORTRESS EUROPE

Just as the prison systems in Britain and America have undergone profound changes in relation to their ethnic composition, prisons across Western Europe experienced parallel developments. The major and immediate difference, however, is that although there have been profound changes in recent years in relation to the ethnic composition of those incarcerated in Western Europe, the majority of these ethnic groups are 'white'. In many cases they are immigrants, transient workers and refugees from Eastern Europe who have become caught up in the criminal justice systems of their country of residence.

In the majority of Western European countries the percentage of foreign nationals has grown steadily over the last decade and in a number of countries over 30 per cent of the prison population is made up of non-nationals. In certain prisons, particularly those located in industrial centres, foreigners make up over half of the prison population. The increased number of foreign nationals in prison across Western Europe has been widely attributed to their growing involvement in crime. However, an examination of prison statistics indicates that a significant percentage of foreigners are detained on migration-related, rather than criminal grounds (Tomasevski, 1994). The growing proportion of foreigners held in Western European prisons, particularly where overcrowding is already present, has raised a number of human rights issues since the conditions under which foreign prisoners are held and the abuses which they suffer have been reported by organisations such as Amnesty International and by the Council of the European Committee for the Prevention of Torture and Inhuman or Degrading Treatment or Punishment (Morgan and Evans, 1994; Spinellis *et al.*, 1996).

The principal reasons given for the increase in the proportion of foreign nationals in prisons throughout Western Europe is migration and the attempts to control it, on one hand and the internationalisation of crime – particularly drugs and fraud – on the other. Many migrants living in Western Europe live under conditions which are depressingly familiar:

> The large concentrations of migrants in urban ghettos makes their presence – and also their problems – particularly visible: levels of unemployment are regularly higher than amongst citizens, and the prevalence of low skilled workers diminishes prospects of employment. Migrant communities inhabit the worst housing in the poorest areas of inner cities. Mutual accusations between the native and migrant populations abound; the former object that migrants reject integration by transferring their own lifestyle to the host country; the latter object that they are rejected, stigmatised and discriminated against, often because of their race, colour, ethnicity, or religion, or all of these. Nationals often equate migrants with increased criminality, while migrants see themselves as targets of racist violence, harassment, or at least prejudice. (Tomasevski, 1994: 36)

As with the black–white dichotomy which informs so much of the British and American literature, the distinction national–foreigner has been found to be inadequate and unable to account for variations in status between, for example, visitors, residents, asylum seekers, and tourists. There are now a number of emerging groups in Western Europe who are not foreigners and are not citizens, and are variously referred to as the 'new minorities' or as 'non-native ethnic groups'.

Interestingly, the recording of race has been discontinued in a number of Western European countries, both outside and inside the prison system, in order to overcome the ideological separation of diverse populations into races. However, the abolition of these categories of race has not, it would appear, had the effect of reducing racism. Racism has been flourishing throughout Western Europe in recent years, and foreigners and the 'new minorities' are not subject to the same legal protections and safeguards as the indigenous population; rights and freedoms are normally only accorded to citizens. Thus the general prohibitions against discrimination, which are designed to protect the human rights of minorities seldom apply to foreigners.

Foreign nationals detained in prisons have the familiar problems of isolation and lower levels of legal and personal support. The growing proportion of non-nationals in prisons is also creating new problems for prison administrators in different countries. The aims of reintegration into society do not readily apply to foreigners and the lack of rehabilitative purpose tends towards warehousing in prisons which are often overcrowded. The net effect of the growing racial disproportionality in prisons is that there appears to be developing a two-tier system of imprisonment in Western Europe: one for citizens and one for foreign nationals. These two systems of imprisonment, although occurring in the same building, mean that the experiences, the purposes and the effects of incarceration are likely to be very different for the two groups.

Thus a review of recent developments in Britain, America and Western Europe reveals that in each location there is a growing racial disproportionality among the prison population and that prisons are filling up with members of different minority groups who tend to be socially and economically disadvantaged, and are drawn mainly from deprived inner city areas. There is also an indication that the prison system itself is becoming divided, and reconstructed along racial lines and may well be undergoing a change of function (Faugeron, 1996).

CONCLUSION

In the attempt to explain the growing racial disproportionality in prisons in different countries it has been necessary to trace the process back to its source. As always, it is a case of thinking backwards and writing forwards. In this process of reflection it has been necessary to problematise the very terms 'race', 'black', 'white' and the like and to treat them as if they were always in parentheses. At the same time it has also been necessary to explore critically the methods of classification adopted, since they provide the conceptual grids through which the debate is structured.

At the core of the debate on race, crime and imprisonment the three recent contributions, by Alfred Blumstein (1982), Roger Hood (1992) and Michael Tonry (1995), provide accounts which are complementary on one level and contradictory on another. Whereas Blumstein's study, which focuses on the relation between arrests and convictions, concludes that approximately 80 per cent of the racial disproportionality in prisons can be accounted for by differential arrest rates between ethnic groups for serious crime, Tonry's analysis qualifies Blumstein's approach by emphasising the ways in which crime control policies can be selectively enforced, with the result that 'indirect racism' is a contributory component of arrest data. But Tonry agrees with Blumstein and Hood that the sentencing process is much less discriminatory than is often assumed, and that although racism is not totally absent the 'race effect' in sentencing is probably less than 10 per cent. The implications of this conclusion for Blumstein is that reducing racism among criminal justice agencies will make little real difference to the numbers of people in prison or to the level of racial disproportionality. To make any real difference to the composition of the prison population the socioeconomic basis of offending would have to be addressed. Hood, on the other hand, suggests a number of largely administrative strategies which would minimise the adverse consequence of pleading not guilty, as well as calling for a reconsideration of the sanctions for trading in cannabis. All three authors, however, would probably agree with Marian FitzGerald and Peter Marshall (1996), who point out that the construction of crime is a process of action and reaction and that it is difficult to operate in the real world with a clear-cut distinction between recorded patterns of offending and strategies of law enforcement. It is not always easy in specific cases to disentangle the offender from the offence, or the offence from the response.

Michael Tonry (1995) takes the issue further by arguing that sentencing policy, rather than simply endorsing discriminatory practices which have occurred at an earlier stage in the process, should attempt to compensate in some form for social adversity. If it is the case, he argues, that the reason for the disproportionate involvement in serious crime is a consequence of the socioeconomic pressures which different groups experience and the range of temptations and disincentives to which different groups of people are subject, then rather than treat all offenders as if they were alike, greater recognition should be paid to their circumstances and the context in which the offending takes place. In essence, Tonry's argument raises the classicist dilemma of whether it is correct to treat people who are unequal as if they were equal, since this tends to compound inequality. Interestingly, Hood's (1992) analysis demonstrated how in Dudley Crown Court it was the lack of consideration given to mitigating circumstances which resulted in more black offenders being given a custodial sentence (Zatz, 1984). However, as Andrew von Hirsch and Julian Roberts (1997) point out, Tonry's suggestion that black people who are unemployed should be given some consideration in relation to the severity of their sentence could serve by implication to penalise those black offenders who are employed. Thus the extent to which we should take mitigating factors into account rather than focus on 'just desserts' needs to be seriously considered. The implications of Tonry's own analysis, however, is that it is discretionary law enforcement which should be the primary object of intervention rather than decision-making at the sentencing stage.

Despite these differences and controversies, the debate around the racial disproportionality in prison has, however, taken on a strangely reassuring quality in which virtually all parties can claim some degree of correctness. There is considerable evidence of both direct and indirect racism at different stages of the criminal justice process. There is also evidence of cumulative racism operating at different points of the process; of stereotyping and scapegoating; and of specific forms of racism operating in the major criminal justice agencies, particularly among the police and sections of the judiciary. On the other hand, evidence can also be mobilised to show a disproportionate involvement of certain ethnic minority groups in particular forms of offending, and that whatever the material and social basis of these patterns of offending it has real effects and consequences on individual victims and communities. At the same time, however, it is a debate which operates with restrictive and inconsistent categories. At one moment processes are over-racialised, while at other times racial factors are played down or ignored altogether. It is a debate which both conflates and confuses ethnic and national differences and in which the major criminal justice agencies appear equally culpable and equally neutral in processing offenders from different ethnic groups.

What is left unresolved in this debate is the 'race effect'. The tendency to talk in terms of race rather than class not only over-racialises offending and victimisation, but also lends weight to the notion that the problem is 'black crime' and is therefore primarily or exclusively a race issue. It is a short step from this point to the identification of all blacks, or another minority group, with crime, and once having 'demonstrated' this relation to use it as a basis for directing 'get tough' crime control policies at this group. If we are to overcome the current mixture of complacency and uncertainty there is a need to identify more clearly how race fits into the equation and thereby to begin to uncover the forms which racism takes in different contexts.

10 The Future of Imprisonment

INTRODUCTION

The modern prison, which emerged at the beginning of the nineteenth century, has been closely linked by social historians to modernism. As a form of punishment it embodied the central tenets of Enlightenment thought with its emphasis on the application of rational and scientific principles to social problems such as crime and disorder. In this way, the prison was conceived of as a social laboratory in which individuals could be transformed and social progress could be achieved. Embracing the guiding notions of proportionality and penal economy, Enlightenment thinkers sought to provide a mode of punishment which would remove errant individuals from the corrupting influences of their environment. By placing them in segregative institutions and subjecting them to the rigours of labour discipline, it was believed that it would be possible to instil the habits of industry, thereby turning unproductive and recalcitrant individuals into useful law-abiding subjects.

The modern prison was an institution which embodied the coercive powers of the developing democratic state in ways which accommodated classicist notions of justice, emphasising due process and equality before the law. This new social experiment differed from previous forms of confinement in that its objective was to punish individuals by removing that commodity which all free citizens held in equal amounts – time. But critics like Karl Marx began to argue in the mid-nineteenth century that underneath the appearance of freedom and equality was a system of exploitation, inequality and wage slavery (Berman, 1983). The modernist project was, according to Marx, deeply flawed because underlying the sphere of formal equality there were substantive inequalities. The social revolutions, civil wars and other forms of class struggle which occurred across Europe in the mid-nineteenth century called into question the legitimacy of the social system and its ability to realise the ideals of individual freedom and social justice.

The mounting critiques of the modernist project in this revolutionary period were specifically applied to those newly fashioned regula-

236

tory state institutions such as the prison. As a mechanism for controlling or transforming the 'dangerous classes' and 'criminal classes' into docile and useful citizens it appeared to be of limited utility. The evidence which emerged during the second half of the nineteenth century of growing levels of recidivism, violent disturbances, strikes against prison workshops, disagreements over wages and rewards for prison work, as well as the increasing costs of running penal institutions, strongly suggested that either the penal project was failing or that it needed considerable rethinking to make it work. There were also growing problems of overcrowding and the spread of disease in prisons, as well as disturbing and frequent reports of suicide and insanity among prisoners. Rather than produce a steady stream of reformed offenders, the prison succeeded in producing, as Foucault (1977) has argued, a manageable population of recidivists, as well as the 'delinquent' as an individual existing before and outside the criminal act. By providing a social laboratory for the study of the delinquent the prison succeeded in producing a new science: the science of criminology. 'Delinquency', as Foucault put it, 'is the vengeance of the prison on justice'.

The various strands of criticism which began to appear towards the end of the nineteenth century tended to oscillate between the question of the effectiveness of the prison in reforming individuals and concerns about its economic and social cost. Thus:

> It should be noted that this monotonous critique of the prison always takes one of two directions; either that the prison was insufficiently corrective, and that the penitentiary critique was still at the rudimentary stage; or that in attempting to be corrective it lost its power as punishment, that the true penitentiary technique was rigour, and the prison was a double economic error; directly by its intrinsic cost and indirectly by the cost of the delinquency that it did not abolish. (Foucault, 1977: 268)

The ostensible 'failure' of the prison to achieve its various objectives promoted a range of penal reforms and led to the decreasing scale of imprisonment across Europe and America from the end of the nineteenth century to the first half of the twentieth century. These developments were complex and diverse and took different forms in different countries, but they can be broadly summarised as being conditioned by three central determinants. The first involved changes in the nature of the capitalist state which had taken on responsibility for financing and running the prison system. The development of the welfare state towards the end of the nineteenth century marks a major shift in the mode of regulation (Garland, 1985). The second development of some consequence was the introduction of a system of mass production based on assembly line principles known as 'Fordism' (after the famous car manufacturer Henry Ford). This changed the nature of labour discipline by building factory discipline into the assembly line itself (Lea, 1979). Also, by the end of the nineteenth century the habits of work were widely established and class struggle had become increasingly mediated by national trade union organisations. Thirdly, the emerging discipline of criminology encouraged and attracted a growing range of experts – psychiatrists, doctors, lawyers, criminologists – who aimed to develop a more scientific system through which the rehabilitation of offenders could be achieved (Ignatieff, 1978). These approaches relied less on the punitive strategies of arduous prison labour and more on medical and psychological techniques which could identify and reform offenders who were considered salvageable. This form of intervention was more likely to succeed if special reformatory institutions were established and if the 'experts' were given enough time to allow deviants to benefit from their expertise. The possibility of the prison exacting a 'just measure of pain' was increasingly called into question as more details about offenders became known and as systems of punishment were seen to require more flexibility in the period of time served. The adoption of indeterminate sentencing and parole provided prison administrators with powers which were more intensive and wide-ranging.

Thus, during the period which might be referred to as 'high modernity' at the end of the nineteenth-century, a marked shift in emphasis took place involving a decreasing precoccupation with the problems of production and labour discipline and an increasing focus on issues associated with biological and social reproduction and the 'quality' of labour power. Through the development of the 'welfare sanction' the prison increasingly became a punishment of last resort, acting as a back-up sanction to the emerging range of community-based punishments. The decline in the use of the prison in various countries during the first half of the twentieth century encouraged Rusche and Kirschheimer (1968), who were writing in the 1930s, to conclude that the modern prison had initially been the product of industrial capitalism and post-Enlightenment thought and that the contradictory developments of modernity had rendered the prison an increasingly anachronistic institution such that in advanced capitalist societies it became a subordinate sanction in relation to other penalties such as the fine.

However, the expected demise of the prison has not occurred in the post-war period. On the contrary, the prison has maintained its central role within the penal system and in many countries the number of those imprisoned has increased. This development has occurred against a backdrop of what are widely seen as major changes in the nature of work, culture and social organisation. Increasingly, references are made to terms such as post-industrialisation, postmodernism and post-Fordism and these terms are deployed to suggest that we are currently undergoing a major transformation in social and economic relations. Since it has been suggested that the development of the modern prison was closely associated with modernity and modernism then it might be expected that the shift towards postmodernism would have profound implications for the future of imprisonment.

MODERNISM AND POSTMODERNISM

If modernism is associated with the rational control of society through the application of scientific principles aimed at achieving individual and social transformation in the pursuit of progress, justice and equality, postmodernism emphasises the opposite. Thus the postmodernists question the rationality of science and the possibility of achieving progress through the application of scientific techniques. Rather than serving as an instrument for illumination and clarification, science is seen to operate as a tool of oppression and control. The evidence of the gulags and the Holocaust is presented as a damning critique of the modernist project and of its ability to realise the ideals of freedom and justice. Postmodernists are suspicious of 'grand narratives' and their emphasis on the totality. Instead they argue for recognition of difference, autonomy and for local and specific interventions rather than aiming for all-encompassing forms of change (Harvey, 1989; Lyotard, 1986; Smart, 1992).

In the review of the supposed transformation from penal modernism to postmodernism David Garland (1990) notes that there have been changes in recent years in relation to be the rehabilitative ideal, the rise of the 'back to justice' movement, the growth of community-based corrections, as well as an emphasis upon new forms of managerialism which reflect a growing concern with aggregate groups rather than with individual offenders. He concludes, however, that the description of penality as being 'post-rehabilitative', 'post-disciplinary', or 'post-institutional' and ultimately postmodern is not supported by the evidence. The experience of the gulags, Garland argues, does not signal the collapse of the modernist project but rather exposes the dangers or the 'dark side' of modernism. Moreover, contradiction and critique are essential and indispensable features of the modernist project. Although the development of modernity is uneven and there had been various shifts of emphasis as well as ongoing conflicts concerning the meaning and significance of imprisonment, Garland argues that neither the prison apparatus nor penal practice is currently undergoing major change. In addition, he points out that the professional groups that staff the penal apparatus have remained essentially the same throughout the twentieth century. Thus, in opposition to the claims of postmodernists he argues that:

> The age of penal modernism is not yet over. Nor is penal modernity about to fade. Instead, what we have been witnessing since the late 1960s is that transformation of penal modernism from being a critical, reforming program to being itself but part of the fabric of modern penality, and hence a target for other critical, reforming movements. With this shift, one sees the closing of a long period of a naïve enthusiasm and optimism regarding the modernist project and the emergence of a more mature, more informed, more ambivalent understanding of what it entails. Modernism has come to understand itself better and to appreciate the program of modernist penality has serious limitations and is riven with deep moral ambiguity. (Garland, 1995: 203)

Thus, despite the postmodernist critiques and a series of internal rumblings within the penal system itself, Garland argues that the modernist project remains intact, although he concedes that it is becoming increasingly pragmatic, managerialist and directionless. Although Garland claims that changes occurring in the penal sphere may be more to do with the rhetoric than changes in material practices, there is an abiding feeling among those working both inside and outside the penal system that significant changes are under way. It has been suggested in the various chapters of this book that there are a number of important development taking place in the penal sphere which require an explanation.

The most notable change in recent years has been the development of 'mass incarceration' in America and the repositioning of the prison as a punishment of first rather that last resort. The second most prominent development has been a marked change in the composition of the prison population on both sides of the Atlantic, involving an increased level of racial disproportionality. There has been growing expansion of the correctional complex with a growth of both community-based sanctions and the prison population in a number of different countries. There is some evidence, in Britain at least, of growing regional disparities in the use of incarceration. The demise of the rehabilitative ideal of the 1970s and the growing preoccupation with deterrence and the warehousing of prisoners. The growing involvement of the private sector in the running of prisons has raised questions of the role and responsibility of the national state in administering coercive forms of punishment. The introduction of 'new design' prisons suggests that changes both in the conception of criminality and management of prisons is taking place. There is evidence of the entrenchement of a strategy of 'bifurcation' by which certain types of offenders are receiving more punitive responses resulting in longer periods of imprisonment, while others who are considered to be more reformable are diverted into community-based sanctions.

Among those commentators who recognise all or some of these developments there are contrasting predictions on the direction which future social control strategies will take and by implication the future of imprisonment. On one hand there are those who predict the development of more inclusive control strategies with the existing social and political institutions being replaced by a 'fluid, pluralistic and contingent informalism' (Lea, 1998). On the other side there are those who see future developments as entailing more exclusive strategies, with the implication that it is towards segregative forms of control such as imprisonment that society is moving (Young, 1998b). Therefore, whereas one set of predictions sees a reduced reliance on the prison, the other forecasts its expansion.

Rather than examine these options directly in terms of claims and counter-claims by modernists and postmodernists, with the danger of becoming enmeshed in this unresolved polemic, it may be more useful to examine current developments in terms of what have been identified as the three essential elements which have shaped the development of the modern prison – space, time and labour. Examining changes in the nature of penality from this vantage point might allow us to develop a more nuanced understanding of current developments.

Analysing recent developments through the three-way lens of space, time and labour is, however, not to move that far away from the modernism/postmodernism debate since, as Anthony Giddens (1984) has suggested, the separation and commodification of time and space was one of the defining features of modernity while David Harvey (1989) depicts the shift towards the postmodern condition as involving the 'annihilation of space through time' which he sees as resulting in greater 'time–space compression' in Western capitalism since the 1960s. The processes which Harvey (1994) outlines also involve a changing relation between time and labour. He suggests that the processes of globalisation and consequent changes in the international division of labour are connected to the development of the 'information society', involving the speeding up of communications, changing forms of individual and national identity and, importantly, the changing role of the state, as well as other regulatory institutions of modern society such as the family and the prison. Most critically, the shifting emphasis from Fordism to flexible accumulation, which Harvey and others see as one of the most significant developments in the last three decades, involves not only profound changes in the organisation of the production process but also has implications for the process of socialisation and the deployment of discipline.

FORDISM AND POST-FORDISM

The perceived shift in the balance in recent years from industrial production based on Fordist principles towards more flexible forms of accumulation has a number of import consequences both in relation to participation in the production process and also in relation to the organisation of the labour market itself (Amim, 1994; Lea, 1997). These changes have been well-documented and can be briefly summarised as having three general characteristics: a general decline in manufacturing and a consequent shift of personnel from the industrial to the service sector; the restructuring of the workforce leading to mass unemployment and greater job insecurity, not only for the young but also for the older sections of the community who may have worked for a number of years previously; and the 'feminisation' of the labour force, with a greater proportion of women engaging in paid work, although often involving low paid, temporary, short-term contracts.

The two most immediate consequences of these changes is an increase in structural unemployment among certain groups and a simultaneous increase in inequality. Alongside these developments has been the demise of the Keynsian welfare state which sought to provide a comprehensive system of welfare extending 'from the cradle to the grave' and its replacement by a 'workfare state' designed to respond to and promote forms of flexible accumulation (Jessop, 1994). One feature of the 'workfare state' is its growing 'privatisation' and the consequent adoption of the management practices and forms of organisation which are characteristic of the private sector.

How do these changes impact upon the process of imprisonment? These developments may be seen to influence the scale of imprisonment both by increasing the level of crime and victimisation, on one hand, and by simultaneously affecting the penal climate in which judges make their decisions, on the other. Much criminological literature has mistakenly separated the analysis of the changing levels of crime from the nature of punishment, on the misguided reasoning, often attributed to Rusche and Kirchheimer (1968) and Michel Foucault (1977), that because the *form* of punishment is not given by the nature and level of crime, there is no need to include crime in the equation. Although it may be the case that the form of punishment may be a function of forms of productive relations or the changing nature of power relations, this does not mean that the level of serious crime (however defined) will not affect the scale of the imprisonment. At the most general level umemployment, as we have seen in Chapter 5 above, can have a number of consequences for the use of imprisonment – ranging from the differential deployment of custodial and non-custodial sanctions by sentencers, to the changing levels of property guardianship; as well as an increased exposure to victimisation as a consequence of more women entering the workforce on a more regular basis (Braithwaite *et al.*, 1995; Crow *et al.*, 1989). Growing inequalities, Steven Box (1987) has argued, stimulate relative as well as absolute deprivation and serve to increase the level of offending not only among the poorest sections of the community but also among those who consider that they are not receiving their fair share of the available goods and rewards.

Most significantly, the effects of mass unemployment tend to impact upon the young and the less well-qualified sectors of society. The net result of growing unemployment among the younger sections of the workforce is that the period of 'youth' is extended, since the transition to adulthood takes place, if at all, at a later age. One immediate consequence of this period of extended youth is that many young people do not 'grow out of crime' as they might have done in the past (Rutherford, 1986). Research has consistently shown that the process of engaging in work and taking on domestic responsibilities is critical in encouraging people to desist from involvement in criminal activities (Graham and Bowling, 1995). There are in the current period, however, two formally contradictory assessments of the growing problem of crime. On the one hand there is a powerful lobby that claims that the bulk of crime is committed by a relatively small hardcore of persistent criminals. On the other hand, there is an equally vocal group of social commentators who, by invoking notions of the underclass, assert that criminal activities, rather than being concentrated in a small identifiable group are rampant among large swathes of the poor, the marginalised and the socially excluded.

The decrease in the availability of secure, well-paid work and consequent forms of personal and social instability have, in turn, undermined the viability of the two-parent household. The delay in entering marriage, the preference for short-term, less-structured relationships, and the increased levels of divorce can be seen as a consequence of growing economic instability. The decreasing numbers of men involved in paid employment, particularly in the industrial sector, has resulted in what has been referred to as the 'crisis of masculinity'. Beatrix Campbell's (1993) assessment of the riots and disturbances which took place at the beginning of the 1990s in various inner-city areas identified them as an attempt by unemployed young men to reassert their identity by capturing certain social spaces and by exercising highly visible, if fleeting, forms of control.

As William Julius Wilson (1996) has pointed out, widespread poverty in certain neighbourhoods creates serious problems, but where poverty is aligned to the lack of work or the lack of the prospect of work these problems take on an even more serious and invidious character. This is not only because work is a way of making a living or supporting one's dependants, but also because it constitutes a framework for organising everyday patterns of interaction by imposing certain routines and disciplines. As Wilson puts it: 'regular employment provides an anchor for the spatial and temporal aspects of daily life'. In America the absence of regular employment is disproportionately concentrated among a black 'underclass', who are marginalised both economically and spatially (Simon, 1993). The growing involvement of ethnic minorities in the criminal justice system and the development of what appears to be a two-tier system of incarceration across Western Europe has been linked to the changing forms of employment and changes in the nature of labour mobility. A significant percentage of non-national prisoners in European prisons are migrant workers or refugees. A number are imprisoned for offences relating to illegal immigration, while others are imprisoned for not having the required securities which might have allowed bail, or because they do not have the resources to pay for good quality legal representation (Tomasevski, 1994).

In many respects the rapid increase in the levels of serious crime and disorder which were recorded in America between 1970 and 1990 have been explained in terms of a number of related processes, including widespread unemployment, declining levels of welfare, growing marginality, increasing spatial and social divisions and greater social instability (Currie, 1998; Skogan, 1990). It was during this period that America adopted the policy of mass incarceration and shifted the emphasis away from rehabilitation towards deterrence and incapacitation (Irwin and Austin, 1994). At the same time sentence lengths increased and the growing punitiveness culminated in the 'Three Strikes and You're Out' policy which was designed to take serious and persistent offenders out of circulation altogether. It was felt during this period that an increase in the use of imprisonment was the only way to stem the rapid increase in crime in the absence of other effective regulatory mechanisms (Murray, 1997). Whatever the validity of these claims may have been, a large percentage of the increase in the prison population in America involved those convicted of drug related offences as well as offences involving violence. There can be little doubt that the fragmentation of communities, the decline of informal control, the demise of the two-parent family, and limited state welfare facilities served to fuel the rapid expansion of the penal system between 1970 and 1990. It is this multi-faced process of decline which James Q. Wilson and George Kelling (1982) captured so well in their classic article 'Broken Windows'. The phenomenal impact which the article had on the criminological community was not so much due to its theoretical sophistication or practical utility, but arose from its description of the breakdown in community relations, which clearly resonated with a wide-ranging audience (Kelling and Coles, 1996; Matthews, 1992).

In the same way, the emphasis on rehabilitation in prisons has continued to wane despite the fact that the claims that rehabilitation does not work have been refuted (Martinson, 1979; Palmer, 1992). In this context what needs to be explained is why these unfounded critiques have gained so much support among academics and policy-makers. The demise of rehabilitation may therefore have been less to do with the incisiveness of the critiques directed against it and more to do with the material shifts associated with transition to a post-Fordist culture, in which the promise of secure employment is largely absent, and in which the established socialising mechanisms by which the young are inculcated into the world of work are in decline. By the some token the ability of communities to absorb ex-prisoners is more circumscribed, while the better-off sections of society – who are also experiencing increasing uncertainties – express an apparently contradictory desire for greater protection from crime and simultaneously an increased reluctance to meet the mounting costs of incarceration (Currie, 1998; Simon, 1993).

The modernist tendency towards globalism and the development of international systems of production has led to the emergence of supra-national bodies whose function is to co-ordinate the processes of production and distribution of commodities around the world. As a result these bodies have come to dominate critical aspects of the policy-making process. At the same time state powers have tended to devolve down to the local or regional level in order to defend and promote local economies in the wake of a global restructuring. The term 'glocalism' has been coined to capture the twin movements of globalism and localism (Swyngedouw, 1992). The net effect of the horizontal and vertical shift in decision-making processes has been what Bob Jessop (1994) has referred to as the 'hollowing out' of the national state. This process is exemplified by the development of international bodies dealing with the general issues of human rights, on the one hand, and the cultivation of more informal neighbourhood systems of dispute resolution on the other (Matthews, 1988). There appears to be a tendency towards the creation of a greater plurality of sites for resolving conflicts and disputes, ranging from local mediation schemes through to small claims courts and criminal courts, as well as bodies such as the European Court of Human Rights, which is able to influence sentencing decisions across Europe and provides guidelines for the treatment of prisoners in different member states (Neale, 1991). At the same time there have developed in recent years international bodies to monitor prison conditions in various countries (Morgan and Evans, 1994; Santos, 1987).

In this process of restructuring, the long-held assumption that the sovereign state is capable of providing security and law and order is being called into question (Garland, 1996). Increasingly, it is evident that the state alone is not and cannot effectively be responsible for preventing and controlling crime. In this context it is probable that the state and the state-sponsored institutions such as the prison will more readily be identified as being in 'crisis' and become increasingly enmeshed in problems of legitimacy. It is thus one of the paradoxes of the current situation that while trends towards mass unemployment and growing inequality are creating the preconditions for a more crimogenic society, the national institutions of criminal justice are experiencing growing legitimacy deficits. Faced with these difficulties, it is probably not surprising that the main criminal justice agencies appear to be adopting a more pragmatic approach, geared to managerialist principles, and have become preoccupied with the development of measurable outcomes. The growing interest in risk assessment in relation to crime control and penality can be seen to arise from the promise of rationalising resources by targeting potentially difficult and dangerous populations, while providing struggling agencies with a new set of pseudo-scientific rationales (Feeley and Simon, 1992; Jones, 1996).

Another favoured option of the reconstituted state is privatisation. This involves not only the handing over of the management of prisons but also the development of inter-agency alliances involving the private and voluntary sectors (Beyens and Snacken, 1996; Matthews, 1989). The management of prisons by private agencies has become an established practice over the past decade, although the actual savings to the taxpayer of this option remains uncertain. Privatised prisons have raised issues about accountability and the role of imprisonment (Harding, 1997). Privatisation in its various forms has rendered the conventional divisions between 'public' and 'private' problematic and in turn has invited a re-examination of the adequacy of state-centred approaches for the management of crime control. At the same time the attempt to devolve responsibility for crime control onto local communities is undermined by the fact that it is precisely in those communities in which the level of crime and disorder are highest that neighbourhoods are fragmented and where informal controls are at their weakest, and therefore are more difficult to mobilise. The consequence in the majority of cases is that victims either have to 'lump it' or alternatively they are increasingly forced to refer incidents directly to overburdened state agencies.

Within the context of this increasingly blurred relation between 'public' and 'private' agencieis and the 'hollowing out' of the national state, Hirst and Thompson (1992) have suggested that the national state is likely to take on more symbolic and ideological role. At the same time there is increased pressure to develop effective responses to crime and to find a new 'technological fix' whether it be in the form of CCTV or electronic monitoring. The aim is to extend the range and certainty of social control while reducing the cost. In fact, the aspiration of increasing the effectiveness and range of social control while reducing costs has become one of the collective fantasies of state administrators. Another way of reading recent developments is that in the wake of an increase in crime and disorder and the simultaneous demise of various regulatory mechanisms, traditional institutions such as the prison are being re-mobilised to absorb these problems and to provide a semblance of stability. The re-mobilisation of the prison becomes the preferred option in a climate of growing punitiveness and provides policy-makers with a convenient way in which to respond to public demands for greater security and protection in a world which is increasingly uncertain and unpredictable – even if it recognised that as a mechanism of discipline and reform it has limited utility.

One of the most disturbing paradoxes of post-Fordism is that in some areas where the legitimate economic livelihoods of communities have declined there is the tendency, particularly in America, to lobby for the construction of a prison in the locality in order to provide some form of employment for local population. As Nils Christie (1993) has argued, there is a real danger of crime control becoming an industry which serves to replace industries which have declined or disappeared. Thus, in as much as there are causal links between unemployment, crime and imprisonment, it is possible to conceive of a scenario in which, as structural unemployment occurs in certain areas, the level of crime and imprisonment increases and as a consequence more prisons are built. Thus the prison becomes both a product of and a solution to the problem of increasing unemployment. In this context the distinction between the 'respectable' and the 'disorganised' working class is likely to become more pronounced (Platek, 1996).

The growing concern with recidivism is widely seen as a consequence of the failure of prisons to instil labour discipline. The statement by the Home Office (1990) that 'prison is an expensive way of making bad people worse' appears to acknowledge this limitation, while strategically decreasing public expectations. The perennial problem of organising meaningful work and training programmes in prison and the continued decline of prison industries in part reflect the problems of production in the outside world, despite the repeated attempts to increase the profitability of work in prison. The issue of 'less eligibility' also appears be becoming less relevant as the conditions of the poorest sections of the general population decline, while the standards of civilised society demand that prisons are maintained to prescribed standards of comfort and hygiene.

Thus the shift to post-Fordism – which should not be over-exaggerated, since manufacturing remains a major part of the production process in many Western countries – has a contradictory impact on the development of incarceration. On one hand the creation of structural unemployment and the shift towards short-term contracts have created greated uncertainty, the fragmentation of communities, the breakdown of informal controls and changes in the nature and role of the national state. These developments have stimulated an increase in crime and encouraged greater punitiveness. On the other hand the cost-effectiveness of imprisonment is increasingly called into question and changes in the nature of the labour market, employment opportunities and the nature of work have increasingly undermined the role of the prison as a disciplining and reforming institution.

SPACE AND SPACISM

One of the major effects of post-Fordist forms of flexible accumulation and the associated decline in manufacturing is that they have a different impact on different regions and particularly on different urban areas. Urban sociologists tend to distinguish between three types of urban area: the deindustrialised city, characterised by a decline in manufacturing, rising unemploymnet and growing levels of deprivation; the reconstructed city, characterised by the introduction of new forms of maufacturing, such as chemical plants or computer companies, which have been introduced to replace the declining traditional industries; and the global city, which has become more service-orientated and linked more directly to international financial markets (Lasch and Urry, 1994).

In each of these three urban areas there are differences in the nature and availability of work as well as in lifestyle and in the pace of life. The feminisation of the labour market and the rise of the women's movement has also significantly changed the face of cities through the transformation of households and through the domestic division of labour, as well as through the use of public space. Women are increasingly becoming involved in disputes over the use of space between business, commercial and residential interests (Massey, 1997).

Disputes over the 'ownership' of urban space are also played out along racial lines (Webster, 1996). Alternatively, minority groups are managed through forms of spatial control by which work, leisure and shopping activities are re-located into suburban areas which are inaccessible to the poorer ethnic minority communities. Alternatively, ethnic segregation is managed through forms of ghettoisation or hyper-ghettoisation (Wilson, 1987). Although the strategy of ethnic segregation and exclusion by design – spacism – is widely used, particularly in America, the limits of this strategy as a mechanism of social control are reflected in the fact that it is from this population that a disproportionate percentage of the prison population is drawn. This is largely because spacism serves not to solve the problems of poverty and deprivation but rather to intensify and compound them.

Social and geographical space within the city is restructured in relation to growing social divisions, together with new demands for autonomy, privacy and the recognition of difference (Sennett, 1991; Soja, 1989; Young, 1990). This reorganisation of urban space allows for the development of new strategies of spatial regulation which are able to target more accurately selected problems and particular populations. Forms of regulation which embrace technological and informational systems are able to permeate the concrete structures of modernity. Within this mileu, private security police are able to operate alongside the proliferation of the glittering array of technology which has been made available by this growing body of private providers. Crime prevention through environmental design together with increasingly privatised forms of policing, has displaced crime and helped to construct what Mike Davis (1990) calls 'fortress cities'. As he suggests, these tendencies are nowhere more evident than in the 'the city of the future' – Los Angeles, where designer prisons are currently being constructed by celebrity architects:

> An extraordinary example, the flagship of the emergent genre, is Welton Becket Associates, new Metropolitan Detention Centre in Downtown Los Angeles. Although this ten-story Federal Bureau of Prisons facility is one of the most visible new structures in the city, few of the hundreds of thousands of commuters who pass by every day have even an inkling of its function as a holding center for what has officially been described as the 'managerial elite of narco-terrorism'. This postmodern Bastille – the largest prison built in a

major US urban centre in decades – looks instead like a futuristic hotel or office block, with artistic flourishes (for example, the high-tech trellises on its bridge-balconies) that are comparable to Downtown's best designed recent architecture. In contrast to the human inferno of the desperately overcrowded County Jail a few blocks away, the Becket structure appears less of a detention center than a convention centre for federal felons – a distinguished addition to Downtown's continuum of security and design. (Davis 1992: 176)

The creation of a number of smaller local prisons in urban centres where they may take the form of high-rise tower blocks or purpose-built constructions designed to mesh in with the wider environment appears to be gaining considerable support among prison administrators and penal reformers alike. There is also a growing interest in 'community prisons', which is linked to the growing preoccupation with localism. Community prisons are also rationalised in terms of the need for greater accessibility of prisoners' friends and families, as well as in relation to the calls for the construction of a number different types of prison that can accommodate the interests, needs and demands of different populations (Tumim, 1996).

Another major contribution to the theorisation of spatial control is Stanley Cohen's *Visions of Social Control* (1985), which provides a reconceptualisation of the relation between inclusive and exclusive strategies. In essence, Cohen argues that all societies involve a mixture of inclusive and exclusive strategies in which inclusion means integration, assimilation, accommodation, toleration, absorption and incorporation, while exclusion means banishment, expulsion, segregation and isolation. Importantly, although we tend to think of exclusion in negative terms and inclusion as something positive, there is no necessary reason why inclusive or informal strategies of control are necessarily any more benign or just than exclusive ones. This mistaken assumption was always too uncritically embraced by the first-generation abolitionists, who saw informal or non-state forms of control as intrinsically beign and progressive and were always faced with the problem of how to deal with vigilante groups and 'citizen patrols' (de Haan, 1990). Moreover, Cohen points out that the destructuring impulses which surfaced in the 1960s and which were designed to promote inclusionary strategies ultimately fed back into exclusionary processes. Drawing on Cohen's analysis, it is evident that it is not sufficient to think solely in terms of inclusion versus exclusion and that there are a number of different cross-cutting axes along which control strategies operate.

The prison, along with social control strategies in general, can be located along the various dimensions shown in Figure 10.1. At the same time these different options can combine in a number of different ways. Control can be state-sponsored but decentralised; informal and punitive; or can operate in ways which are visible and accountable but privatised; and so on. Currently it would seem that the prison system is becoming increasingly decentralised, but more punitive and less protective. The degree of segregation has also been reduced through the development of links with community organisations, while forms of accountability are becoming less trasparent as a result of privatisation (Harding, 1997).

John Braithwaite (1989) takes issue with Cohen's (1985) scepticism about the viability of inclusionary modes of control, and particularly with Cohen's contention that: 'inclusionary controls are ill-equipped to foster social integration' and that since 'rituals of blaming are difficult to sustain, they lose their moral edge'. Braithwaite claims that informal rituals of shaming can be effective as long as they aim to be reintegrative rather that stigmatising. Although at first sight

Figure 10.1   The dimensions of social control strategies

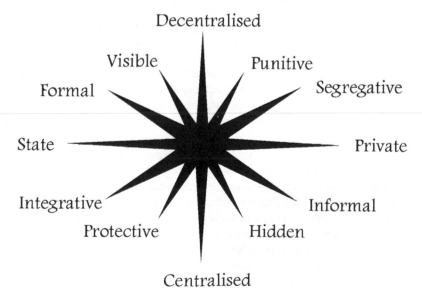

Braithwaite's response appears as a useful corrective to the excesses of labelling theory, it is ultimately unconvincing, since a great deal of crime is contested or denied. The rational, coherent, honest world which Braithwaite (1993) describes is far removed from the urban realities of modern life. Significantly, he cites Japan as a society which widely employs reintegrative shaming and consequently has 'safe streets and empty jails'. However, Braithwaite admits that; 'as much as I admire the crime control achievement of Japan, I would not want to live there because I think I would find the informal pressures of conformity oppressive'. This statement seems to confirm the point made by Cohen about the limits and disadvantages of 'inclusive' forms of control. It is also evident that Braithwaite's theory of reintegrative shaming avoids facing the central issue of the mutual relationship and interdependence of inclusive and exclusive strategies and that threat of exclusion is an ever present dimension of reintegrative strategies. Thus reintegrative shaming does not stand in opposition to segregative and exclusionary sanctions but forms part of an interdependent relation. Indeed, Braithwaite's call for a shift in the moral balance towards more informal forms of regulation was written at a time when the capacities of neighbourhoods to engage in such moralising practices was becoming progressively more limited. In short, Braithwaite's plea for reintegrative shaming appears to have occurred precisely at the point at which changing economic and social relations were making such choices increasingly untenable.

There is a sense, therefore, in which those arguing for inclusion in the form of developing more expansive forms of informal control and those who see the drift in the present period towards exclusionary strategies are both wide of the target. Although it is the case that in the current period both prisons and community based sanctions are expanding for certain categories of offenders, what also appears to be happening as Cohen (1985) has intimated, is the development of strategies of social control which are neither genuinely inclusive, in that they do not involve forms of incorporation or reintegration back into the community, and at the same time are not properly exclusive in that they do not involve segregation or expulsion. Thus the bulk of deviants and offenders are not 'swallowed up' or 'spewed out' to use Lévi-Strauss' (1992) analogy. Instead, they are subject to forms of intervention which are organised through a changing combination of state and non-state agencies and are subject to penalties which have little relation to the mores of the community in which they live. Indeed, they may involve a minimum degree of interpersonal contact and are more likely to be administrative. Forms of intervention tend increasingly to be directed towards the control of behaviour or involve low-level monitoring. Alternatively the aim is to deter prospective offenders through the increased use of surveillance, the deployment of private security police, or simply to prevent crime through environmental design.

A further spatial dimension of Stanley Cohen's (1985) analysis is his presentation of the 'dispersal of discipline' thesis which is adapted from Foucault's depiction of the spread of those disciplinary practices which were first developed in the prison and which at a later date were dispersed 'over the walls' into the community. That is, the scientific knowledge and the forms of treatment and evaluation, as well as systems of classification, which had originally been developed in the closed fortress of the prison were taken up and adapted by the growing body of professionals who organise community-based sanctions. Through the widespread adoption of these procedures, either in the name of science, progress or humanitarianism, the state is seen to engage in the more subtle, systematic and ultimately more invidious control of everyday life. The Orwellian nightmare of the totally controlled society is closely associated with this vision of discipline, gradually but relentlessly spreading through the social body (Cohen, 1979).

But this vision, at best, catches only part of the picture. As Anthony Bottoms (1983) has argued there are both conceptual and empirical limitations to this thesis. First, he suggests that Cohen and others have conflated corporal, judicial and carceral systems of punishment and consequently have assumed that all dispersed forms of social control are 'disciplinary' in the Foucaultian sense. Second, there are a range of penalties including the fine, compensation orders and community service orders which are becoming more widely used but which are not 'disciplinary' techniques as such. Third, that the 'dispersal of discipline' thesis tends to refer to discipline in an undifferentiated way with the consequence that the specificity of particular disciplinary practices, as well as the way in which they are used in relation to different groups, is overlooked. Finally that Cohen and others tend to equate social control with 'state control' which they see as being exercised as a negative 'top down' strategy; rather than seeing it, in some instances at least, as incorporating a series of defensive and adaptive measures.

The important point which Bottoms is making here is that some of the more prominent current crime control strategies do not involve 'discipline' in the sense that Foucault outlines it, but low-level monitoring and supervision, often accompanied by forms of non-intervention, neglect and indifference. Cohen (1983) in a rejoinder to his critique has referred to these developments as constituting what he calls the 'new behavioursism' which aims not to reform, rehabilitate or to confront the values of offenders but more simply aims to monitor their movements and regulate their activities. This strategy Cohen suggests is associated with a 'minimal statism' which is also less concerned with changing people than with limiting the range and costs of state intervention to particular types of offences or offenders. Alongside these modalities of action and inaction there are other developing control strategies which involve the expansion of bureaucratic and administrative measures, a shift away from the purely offender orientated approaches towards a greater consideration of the victim and their claims for compensation and support, as well as a growing emphasis on both restitutive and restorative sanctions (Dutton, 1992; Pratt, 1990).

The most significant and probably the most neglected feature of contemporary control systems, Bottoms (1983) points out, is the decrease in the proportionate use of imprisonment. He emphasises that successive governments in Britain and other European countries, whatever they may have said publily about 'getting tough', have been practically committed to a policy of decarceration over the past 30 years or so by developing 'alternatives to imprisonment' or expanding the use of existing non-custodial sanctions, such that the proportion of convicted defendants sentenced to imprisonment has fallen consistently over this period.

The main reason why this development has been neglected is because criminologists have tended either to examine crime and imprisonment as separate entities or to engage in the versions of crude empiricism which have correlated levels of crime with imprisonment rates in order to use the movement of one to explain the change in the other (Matthews, 1987). Without an appreciation of the nature and extent of the increase in victimisation, arrests, prosecutions and convictions in recent years and the extent to which the sheer volume of cases being processed through the criminal justice system has increased, the relationship between the use of incarceration and other penalties is obscured. To talk of increases in the prison population in isolation, whether reference is made to average daily populations, or receptions into custody, or increases per 100 000 of the population, provides a limited perspective if arrest and conviction rates are not taken into consideration. A further deficiency in forms of inquiry which separate crime from punishment is that they fail to recognise that the conditions which act to push up crime rates are not altogether unrelated to those which stimulate calls for more punitive sanctions, including the greater use of imprisonment (Young, 1997). It may be the case, as was discussed in Chapter 4, that although America (for example) has a higher rate of imprisonment per 100 000 than England and Wales, in relation to the number of cases roughly the same proportion of those convicted for different offences are given a prison sentence in both countries. Thus it is not the case that America is more 'punitive' – although it does tend to hand out comparatively longer sentences for most crimes – it is that it has a significantly higher number of people convicted of serious crime (Langan, 1991).

IT'S ABOUT TIME

Reference has already been made to the time–space compression which has been a feature of modernity but which has become more intensified in recent decades. David Harvey (1989) has outlined some of the implications of this process. Just as notions of space have been transformed through the creation of the 'global village', notions of 'hyperspace', 'cyberspace' and the use of new forms of electronic communication, so time has accelerated such that contemporary life is generally experienced as speeding up. The impact of time – space compression is nowhere more evident than in the operation of international finance markets. Seven days may be a long time in politics but, as they say, it is a lifetime on the stock exchange.

Alongside the acceleration of time and the consequent speeding up of decision-making processes, there is a simultaneous propensity to 'freeze' and repackage time through films and videos as well as by means of television and computer link-ups. Regular exposure to these forms of media reorganises the time–space relation and creates a constant interplay between fantasy and reality. Thus throughout the average day time is accelerated, suspended, frozen and then re-spent. Not surprisingly, the mass media itself is fascinated by this changing sense of time and various popular programmes and films have explored this theme in different ways.

Time also appears to be taking on an increasingly cyclical quality, with a tendency to oscillate continuously between the present and the past. Fashions, ideas and cultural artefacts are continuously recycled, and as the past fuses with the present even nostalgia is no longer available in the way in which it once was. This oscillation between the past and the present is in part a consequence of the fact that politically the future has been suspended. The prospect of a qualitative social transformation in the form of socialism has dissolved with the gradual collapse of Russian communism. The future appears only to offer more of the same and, as many post-modernists argue, global change appears less possible and only local political change is realistic. Utopia has been abolished and we appear to have been sentenced to an ever-recurring present. The demise of utopian thinking has implications for penology, in that the notions of individual reform and social progress through rehabilitation become less tenable (Young, 1992). In this context the functions of imprisonment are likely to shift towards deterrence and incapacitation. Moreover, the growing preocupation of risk analysis is a strategy for distilling the future into the present.

What impact, if any, do these changes in the conception of time have on the use of imprisonment as a 'punishment of measured time'? It will be recalled that the critical element in the formation of the modern prison was the commodification of time and space which was fundamental to commodity production. It was the nexus of this combination of forces which was signified in Rusche and Kirchheimer's (1968) phrase that the 'form' of punishment *corresponds* to the nature of production *relationships*. Rusche and Kirchheimer, like Marx, were clearly aware that production is always *social* production. Being linked to commodity production, however, creates an instability in the temporal and spatial principles through which social life is organised. Similarly, Foucault (1977) suggests that discipline can proceed only via the manipulation of time and space, and the significance of institutions such as the hospital and the prison is that they provide an 'analytic space' in which individuals can be watched, ordered and assessed.

The second implication of the separation of time and space is that time becomes conceived in spatial terms. In this way it assumes a linearity as it moves from point to point and takes on an evolutionary capacity which, in turn, fosters notions of progress and of individual and social transformation. Thus the goal of individual reform became a key feature of modernity and the forms of social production which it sustained. If, however, time itself is undergoing a fundamental transformation such that the established sense of linearity is being undermined or modified to accommodate a more diverse sense of time, then one of the conceptual pillars on which the modern prison is based and which in part accounts for its 'naturalness' maybe dissolving. In a similar vein, it is the case that as social time accelerates and time itself becomes a more valuable commodity, the experience of 'doing time' also lengthens.

Time, however, is not accelerating at the same rate for all sections of the population. Though among the informational elite there are never enough hours in the day, among those who live in declining deindustrialised urban areas, or in the segregated urban ghettos the experience of time is very different (Massey, 1997). Days are long and individuals are likely to find themselves with a great deal of time on their hands. Since it is from this population that the prison population is disproportionately drawn, it may be the case paradoxically that if a time-based punishment is to have a deterrent value it needs to be of a considerable duration. It may be this sense of the timelessness of the life-style of the unemployed, the marginalised and the ghettoised which lies behind the lengthening of prison sentences and particularly the 'Three Strikes and You're Out' policy in America. By the same token the decline of indeterminate sentencing and the movement towards determinate, mandatory and so called 'honest' sentencing, can all be seen as attempts to reinstate some degree of consistency in time-based punishments against a background in which the notion of time itself appears more differentiated and uncertain. This has, in turn, destabilised the notion of proportionality in sentencing. Moreover, where time-based punishments continue to be used they are increasingly concerned with the curtailment of 'spare' time and 'leisure' time.

Thus time itself appears to be losing its universality. It has different meanings for different individuals and groups as a consequence of variations in relation to work, life expectancy and life-styles. To be sure, time was always a less universal measure than is often assumed, and was in fact always a commodity upon which different groups had a different purchase. But over the last few decades these differences have become more pronounced and as a consequence time is becoming an increasingly uncertain measure. Thus changes in the experience and meaning of time, like the changing nature of space and labour, are likely to have a mixed impact upon imprisonment. There are movements to reassert time-based punishments, while the denial of utopias seem to both assure us that the prison will always be with us: However, by the same token, the denial of the possibility of social progress serves to undermine the basis upon which the 'naturalness' of the modern prison rests.

CONCLUSION

This chapter has analysed the changing nature and prospects for imprisonment in relation to a range of social developments and the changing nature of social control. The discussion could have taken a less speculative course by focusing on the official projections of the prison population or by reviewing sentencing trends and their likely impact upon the scale of imprisonment over the next few years. There are serious limitations, however, in relying on official projections of the prison population. Alternatively there are difficulties in presenting critiques of these projections and simply trying to demonstrate their inaccuracies, since they are produced primarily for policy purposes and are specifically designed to stimulate intervention which may itself change the scale of imprisonment (Austin *et al.*, 1992). As for sentencing trends, a number of developments have been identified in previous chapters. In England and Wales these include certain 'serious' offenders being given increasingly long sentences while those involved in more 'minor' offences such as theft and burglary are being given shorter prison sentences or non-custodial sentences. Demarcations between types of offences and offenders are becoming more clearly defined and the systems of classification are being modified accordingly. The available figures indicate growing racial disproportionality in prison and increases in the number of women incarcerated, which appears to be turning the prediction made 30 years ago that women's imprisonment would be abolished by the end of the century on its head. There is also evidence of an increase in the use of remand for certain groups of prisoners as well as a decrease in the proportionate use of imprisonment for those convicted of offences and the consequent expansion of non-custodial sanctions.

Among these non-custodial options it is the so called 'intermediate sanctions' which involve some form of monitoring, supervision, surveillance, 'intensive' probation, electronic monitoring and house arrest which are becoming more pronounced (Byrne *et al.*, 1992). Support for these forms of regulation is to be found in many quarters, including practitioners, politicians and members of the general public. Thus as Francis Cullen *et al.* point out:

[In summary] the community control movement is not the only correctional response that might have been made to the prevailing crisis in the system. Rather, this movement might be seen as a product of a particular social and political context that limited permissible options, making some potential reforms seem foolish and others sensible. Intermediate sanctions shared the rhetoric of punishment but offered to accomplish crime control at a reduced cost. It would do all this, moreover, in a way that neither incited public furore nor threatened the occupational and organisational interests of those who would implement the programs in the criminal justice system. No wonder it was a reform whose time had come. (Cullen, Wright and Applegate, 1996: 73)

Intermediate sanctions and community control appeals to conservatives, liberals and radicals alike, and in America some 70 per cent of state authorities use intensive forms of supervision, while about 50 per cent have electronic monitoring. The number of people on probation has increased from around 1 million in 1980 to just over 3 million in 1995, while the number on parole has increased from 220 000 to 700 000 over the same period (Bureau of Justice, 1996). In England and Wales the adoption of these measures has been more modest, but there is considerable official support for electronic monitoring and house arrest despite the repeated 'failure' of trials, while the number of people supervised in the community by the probation service has increased by over 30 per cent between 1992 and 1997, rising from just over 100 000 to 133 000 (Home Office, 1998; Mair and Nee, 1990). The question of whether or not these forms of community controls 'work' may be less relevant than the question of whether they fit, or as Rusche and Kirchheimer (1968) would say, 'correspond', to the prevailing social and productive relations in society.

As Stanley Cohen (1985) has suggested, social regulation incorporates a number of different dimensions and an awareness of these dimensions can help us to move beyond the inclusion/ exclusion dichotomy. The changing capacity, functions and composition of the prison population needs to be examined along a number of inter-related axes. In Britain and America trends can be identified towards decentralisation and privatisation, with a greater emphasis upon deterrence and incapacitation rather than rehabilitation. Forms of legitimacy and accountability are also changing in response to the recurring 'crises' of imprisonment. The examination of these developments through the three-way lens of space, time and labour has made it possible to identify a number of competing lines of force that are currently creating different pressures on the use of imprisonment, of which some involve expansion, while others involve contraction. Thus, there is no inevitability about the increase in the use of imprisonment. As was evident in England and Wales during the 1980s, there are periods in which the numbers sent to prison and even the numbers in prison may decrease. In fact, between 1970 and 1990 the prison population in England and Wales remained relatively stable. Few people however, attempted to explain this relative stability. Instead, they set about explaining an assumed increase. Over the same period, the decarceration of young people in a number of European countries indicates how social attitudes can change on the appropriateness of the use of imprisonment for certain groups of offenders.

Some of the wider social processes which can influence the nature and scale of imprisonment have been identified and discussed. There are, as we have seen, a number of pressures operating in different directions and with different degrees of intensity. Within a rapidly changing framework of social and economic conditions the prison is undergoing some significant changes in its design, its function and its organisation. These structural changes, however, are both a product of and a basis for different forms of intervention.

Bibliography

Adam, B. (1990) *Time and Social Theory* (Cambridge: Polity Press).

Adams, R. (1992) *Prison Riots in Britain and the USA* (London: Macmillan).

Adler, F. (1975) *Sisters in Crime: The Rise of the New Female Criminal* (New York: McGraw Hill).

Allen, H. (1989) 'Fines For Women: Paradoxes and Paradigms', in P. Carlen and D. Cook (eds), *Paying For Crime* (Milton Keynes: Open University Press).

Allen, R. (1991) 'Custody for Juveniles – From Elimination to Abolition?', *Youth and Policy*, **32** (March): 10–18.

All Party Parliamentary Penal Affairs Group (1980) *Too Many Prisoners: An Examination of Ways of Reducing the Prison Population* (London: HMSO).

Amim, A. (1994) *Post-Fordism: A Reader* (Oxford: Blackwell).

Ashworth, A. (1983) *Sentencing and Penal Policy* (London: Weidenfeld & Nicolson).

Audit Commission (1996) *Misspent Youth: Young People and Crime* (London).

Austin, J., S. Cuvelier and A. McVey (1992) 'Projecting the Future of Corrections: The State of the Art', *Crime and Delinquency*, **38** (2): 285–309.

Austin, J. and B. Krisberg (1981) 'Wider, Stronger and Different Nets: The Dialectics of Criminal Justice Reform', *Journal of Research in Crime and Delinquency*, **18**: 132–96.

Austin, R. (1981) 'Liberation and Female Criminality in England and Wales', *British Journal of Criminology*, **31** (4): 371–4.

Back, L. (1996) *New Ethnicities and Urban Culture* (London: UCL Press).

Bailey, V. (1987) *Delinquency and Citizenship* (Oxford: Clarendon Press).

Barak-Glantz, I. (1981) 'Toward a Conceptual Schema of Prison Management Styles', *Prison Journal*, **61**: (2): 42–60.

Barclay, G. (1995) *Digest 3: Information on the Criminal Justice System in England and Wales* (London: HMSO).

Barrett, N. (1991) *The Politics of Truth* (Cambridge: Polity Press).

Bauman, Z. (1989) *Modernity and the Holocaust* (Oxford: Blackwell).

Beccaria, C. (1764) *An Essay on Crimes and Punishments* (reprinted Indianapolis: Bobbs Merrill, 1963).

Beetham, D. (1991) *The Legitimation of Power* (London: Macmillan).

Bentham, J. (1791) *Panoptican* (London).

Berman, M. (1983) *All That Is Solid Melts Into Air: The Experience of Modernity* (London: Verso).

Bettelheim, B. (1960) *The Informed Heart* (New York: Free Press).

Beyens, K. and S. Snacken (1996) 'Prison Privatisation: An International Perspective', in R. Matthews and P. Francis (eds), *Prisons 2000* (London: Macmillan).

Blau, R. and W. Scott (1963) *Formal Organisations: A Comparative Approach* (London: Routledge & Kegan Paul).

Blumstein, A. (1982) 'On the Racial Disproportionality of the United States Prison Population', *Journal of Criminal Law and Criminology*, **73**: 1259–81.

Blumstein, A. (1988) 'Prison Populations: A System Out of Control', in M. Tonry and N. Morris (eds), *Crime and Justice: A Review of Research*, vol. 10 (University of Chicago Press).

Blumstein, A. (1993) 'Racial Disproportionality of the US Prison Population Revisited', *University of Colorado Law Review*, **64**: 743–60.

Blumstein, A. and J. Cohen (1973) 'A Theory of Stability of Punishment', *Journal of Criminal Law and Criminology*, **64**: 198–207.

Blumstein, A., Cohen, J. and D. Nagin (1976) 'The Dynamics of a Homeostatic Punishment Process', *Journal of Criminal Law and Criminology*, **67**: 317–34.

Boland, B. (1980) 'Fighting Crime: The Problem of Adolescents', *Journal of Criminal Law and Criminology*, **71** (2): 94–7.

Boland, B. and J. Q. Wilson (1978) 'Age, Crime and Punishment', *Public Interest*, **51**: 22–34.

Booth, W. (1890) *In Darkest England and the Way Out* (London: Salvation Army).

Bottomley, K. (1984) 'Dilemmas of Parole in a Penal Crisis', *Howard Journal*, **23** (1): 24–40.

Bottomley, K. and K. Pease (1986) *Crime and Punishment: Interpreting the Data* (Milton Keynes: Open University Press).

Bottoms, A. (1974) 'On the Decriminalisation of the English Juvenile Courts', in R. Hood (ed.), *Crime, Criminology and Policy* (London: Heinemann).

Bottoms, A. (1977) 'Reflections on the Renaissance of Dangerousness', *Howard Journal*, **16**: 70–96.

Bottoms, A. (1980) 'An Introduction to the Coming Crisis', in A. Bottoms and R. Preston (eds), *The Coming Penal Crisis* (Edinburgh: Scottish Academic Press).

Bottoms, A. (1983) 'Neglected Features of Contemporary Penal Systems', in D. Garland and P. Young (eds), *The Power to Punish* (London: Heinemann).

Bottoms, A. (1987) 'Limiting Prison Use: Experience in England and Wales', *Howard Journal*, **26** (3): 177–202.

Bottoms, A. (1995) 'The Philosophy and Politics of Punishment and Sentencing', in C. Clarkson and R. Morgan (eds), *The Politics of Sentencing Reform* (Oxford: Clarendon Press).

Bottoms, A. and R. Preston (1980) *The Coming Penal Crisis* (Edinburgh: Scottish Academic Press Press).

Bottoms, A. and P. Wiles (1992) 'Housing Markets and Residential Community Care Careers', in D. Evans, R. Fyfe and D. Herbert (eds), *Crime, Policing and Place* (London: Routledge).

Bottoms, A. and P. Wiles (1997) 'Environmental Criminology', in M. Maguire, R. Morgan and R. Reiner (eds), *The Oxford Handbook of Criminology*, 2nd edn (Oxford: Clarendon Press).

Bowker, L. (1977) *Prisoner Subcultures* (Mass.: Lexington Books).

Bowling, B. and C. Philips (1999) *'Race' and Criminal Justice* (London: Longman).

Box, S. (1987) *Recession, Crime and Punishment* (London: Macmillan).

Box, S. and C. Hale (1983) 'Liberation and Female Criminality in England and Wales', *British Journal of Criminology*, **23** (1): 35–49.

Box, S. and C. Hale (1986) 'Unemployment, Crime and Imprisonment and the Enduring Problems of Prison Overcrowding', in R. Matthews and J. Young (eds), *Confronting Crime* (London: Sage).

Braithwaite, J. (1989) *Crime, Shame and Reintegration* (Cambridge University Press).

Braithwaite, J. (1993) 'Shame and Modernity', *British Journal of Criminology*, **33** (1): 1–18.

Braithwaite, J., B. Chapman and C. Kapuscinski (1995) 'Unemployment and Crime: Resolving the Paradox', *American Bar Foundation*, Working Paper Series no. 9201.

Brown, I. and R. Hullin (1992) 'A Study of Sentencing in Leeds Magistrates Courts: The Treatment of Ethnic Minority and White Offenders', *British Journal of Criminology*, **32** (1): 41–54.

Bureau of Justice (1996) *Correctional Populations in the United States 1995* (Washington: US Department of Justice).

Burney, E. (1985) *Sentencing Young People* (Aldershot: Gower).

Burney, E. (1990) *Putting Street Crime in its Place*, Report for the Police Consultative Group for Lambeth (London Borough of Lambeth).

Byrne, J., A. Lurigio and J. Petersilia (1992) *Smart Sentencing: The Emergence of Intermediate Sanctions* (California: Sage).

Byrne, R. (1992) *Prisons and Punishments of London* (London: Grafton).

Caddle, D. and D. Crisp (1996) *Imprisoned Women and Mothers*, Home Office Research Study no. 162 (London: HMSO).

Campbell, B. (1993) *Goliath: Britain's Dangerous Places* (London: Methuen).

Canter, D. (1987) 'Implications for "New Generation" Prisons of Existing Psychological Research into Prison Design and Use', in A. Bottoms and R. Light (eds), *Problems of Long Term Imprisonment* (Aldershot: Gower).

Cantor, D. and K. Land (1985) 'Unemployment and Crime Rates in the Post World War II United States', *American Sociological Review*, **50**: 317–32.

Carlen, P. (1983) *Women's Imprisonment* (London: Routledge & Kegan Paul).

Carlen, P. (1988) *Women, Crime and Poverty* (Milton Keynes: Open University Press).

Carlen, P. (1990) *Alternatives to Women's Imprisonment* (Milton Keynes: Open University Press).

Carlen, P. and C. Tchaikovsky (1996) 'Women's Imprisonment in England at the End of the Twentieth Century; Legitimacy, Realities and Utopias' in R. Matthews and P. Francis (eds), *Prisons 2000* (London: Macmillan).

Carpenter, M. (1851) *Reformatory Schools for the Children of the Perishing and Dangerous Classes and for Juvenile Offenders* (London: Gilpin).

Casale, S. (1989) *Woman Inside: The Experience of Women Remand Prisoners in Holloway* (London: The Civil Liberties Trust).

Castells, M. (1994) 'European Cities, the International Society and the Global Economy', *New Left Review*, (204): 18–32.

Cheney, D. (1993) *Into the Dark Tunnel* (London: Prison Reform Trust).

Chesney-Lind, M. (1991) 'Patriachy, Prisons and Jails: A Critical Look at Trends in Women's Incarceration', *Prison Journal*, (71): 51–67.

Christie, N. (1993) *Crime Control as Industry: Toward Gulags Western Style* (London: Routledge).

Clark, J. (1995) 'The Impact of Prison Environment on Mothers', *Prison Journal*, **75** (3): 306–29.

Clarke, J. *et al.* (1975) 'Subcultures, Cultures and Class', *Working Papers in Cultural Studies* **7 and 8** (Summer): 9–75.

Clarke, R. (1992) *Situational Crime Prevention: Successful Case Studies* (New York: Harrow & Heston).

Clarke-Hall, W. (1926) *Children's Courts* (London: George Allen & Unwin).

Cleaver, E. (1968) *Soul on Ice* (New York: McGraw-Hill).

Clegg, S. (1990) *Modern Organisations: Organisation Studies in the Postmodern World* (London: Sage).

Clemmer, D. (1940) *The Prison Community* (New York: Holt, Rinehart & Winston).

Cohen, S. (1977) 'Prisons and the Future of Control Systems', in M. Fitzgerald *et al.* (eds), *Welfare in Action* (London: Routledge & Kegan Paul).

Cohen, S. (1983) 'Social Control Talk: Telling Stories of Correctional Change', in D. Garland and P. Young (eds), *The Power to Punish* (London: Heinemann).

Cohen, S. (1985) *Visions of Social Control* (Cambridge: Polity Press).

Cohen, S. (1979) 'The Punitive City: notes on the Dispersal of Social Control', *Contemporary Crisis*, **3**:339–63.

Cohen, S. (1992) *The Evolution of Women's Asylums Since 1500* (Oxford University Press).

Cohen, S. and L. Taylor (1972) *Psychological Survival* (Harmondsworth: Penguin).

Coleman, C. and J. Moynihan (1996) *Understanding Crime Data* (Buckingham: Open University Press).

Connell, R. (1987) *Gender and Power* (Cambridge: Polity Press).

Cooke, D. (1989) 'Containing Violent Prisoners: An Analysis of the Barlinnie Special Unit', *British Journal of Criminology*, **29** (2): 129–43.

Cooper, M. and R. King (1965) 'Social and Economic Problems of Prisoners Work', *Sociological Review Monograph* no. 9: 145–73.

Copas, J., J. Ditchfield and P. Marshall (1994) 'Development of a New Reconviction Prediction Score' Research Bulletin no. 36, Home Office Research and Statistics Department (London: HMSO).

Correctional Services Canada (1990) *Creating Choices: Report of the Task Force on Federally Sentenced Women* (Ottawa).

Council of Europe (1995) *European Sourcebook of Crime and Criminal Justice Statistics* (Strasbourg).

Crow, I. and J. Cove (1984) 'Ethnic Minorities and the Courts', *Criminal Law Review*: 413–17.

Crow, I., P. Richardson, C. Riddington and F. Simon (1989) *Unemployment, Crime and Offenders* (London: Routledge).

Cullen, F. (1994) 'Social Support as an Organising Concept for Criminology', *Justice Quarterly*, **11** (4): 527–59.

Cullen, F., P. Gendreau, R. Jarjoural and J. Wright (1997) 'Crime and the Bell Curve: Lessons From Intelligent Criminology', *Crime and Delinquency*, **43** (4): 387–411.

Cullen, F. and K. Gilbert (1982) *Reaffirming Rehabilitation* (Cincinnati: Anderson).

Cullen, F., P. Voorhis and J. Sundt (1996) 'Prisons in Crisis: The American Experience in R. Matthews and P. Francis (eds), *Prisons 2000* (London: Macmillan).

Cullen, F., P. Wright and B. Applegate (1996) 'Control in the Community: The Limits of Reform', in A. Harland (ed.), *Choosing Correctional Options That Work* (California: Sage).

Currie, E. (1998) *Crime and Punishment in America* (New York: Metropolitan Books).

Daly, K. (1994) *Gender, Crime and Punishment* (New Haven, Conn.: Yale University Press).

Daly, K. and M. Tonry (1997) 'Gender, Race and Sentencing', in M. Tonry (ed.), *Crime and Justice: A Review of Research*, vol. 22 (University of Chicago Press).

Dandeker, C. (1990) *Surveillance, Power and Modernity* (Oxford: Polity Press).

Davis, G., J. Boucherat and D. Watson (1989) 'Pre-Court Decision-Making in Juvenile Justice', *British Journal of Criminology*, 29 (3): 219–36.

Davis, M. (1990) *City of Quartz: Excavating The Future in Los Angeles* (London: Vintage).

Davis, M. (1992) 'Fortress Los Angeles: The Militarisation of Urban Space', in M. Sorokin (ed.), *Variations on a Theme Park* (New York: Hill & Wang).

Defoe, D. (1728) *Street Robberies Considered* (London).

de Haan, W. (1990) *The Politics of Redress: Crime, Punishment and Penal Abolition* (London: Unwin Hyman).

de Mandeville, B. (1725) *An Enquiry into the Causes of the Frequent Executions at Tyburn* (London).

Devlin, A. (1998) *Invisible Women: What's Wrong With Women's Prisons?* (Winchester: Waterside Press).

Dews, P. (1979) 'The Nouvelle Philosophie of Foucault', *Economy and Society*, 8 (2).

Dickenson, D. (1993) *Crime and Unemployment*, mimeo, Department of Applied Economics, University of Cambridge.

DiIulio, J. (1987) *Governing Prisons* (New York: Free Press).

DiIulio, J. (1994) 'The Question of Black Crime', *Public Interest* (Fall): 3–32.

Ditchfield, J. (1990) *Control in Prisons: A Review of the Literature*, Home Office Research Study no. 118 (London: HMSO).

Dobash, R. P., R. E. Dobash and S. Gutteridge (1986) *The Imprisonment of Women* (Oxford: Blackwell).

Dodd, A. and J. Roberts (1988) 'Public Punitiveness and Public Knowledge of the Facts: Some Canadian Surveys', in N. Walker and M. Hough (eds), *Public Attitudes to Sentencing* (Aldershot: Gower).

Dodd, T. and P. Hunter (1992) *The National Prison Survey 1991*, Office of Population Census and Surveys (London: HMSO).

Donzelot, J. (1979) *The Policing of Families* (London: Hutchinson).

Downes, D. (1966) *The Delinquent Solution* (London: Routledge & Kegan Paul).

Downes, D. (1988) *Contrasts in Tolerance: Post War Penal Policy in The Netherlands and England and Wales* (Oxford: Clarendon Press).

Downes, D. (1993) *Employment Opportunities for Offenders* (London: HMSO).

Dreyfus, H. and P. Rabinow (1982) *Michel Foucault: Beyond Structuralism and Hermeneutics* (Brighton: Harvester Press).

Dunlop, A. (1974) *The Approved School Experience*, Home Office Research Unit Report (London: HMSO).

Durkheim, E. (1952) *Suicide: A Study in Sociology* (London: Routledge & Kegan Paul).

Dutton, M. (1992) 'Disciplinary Projects and Carceral Spread: Foucauldian Theory and Chinese Practice', *Economy and Society*, 21 (3): 274–94.

Dwyer, J., J. Wilson and P. Carlen (1987) 'Women's Imprisonment in England and Wales and Scotland: Recurring Issues', in P. Carlen and A. Worral (eds), *Gender, Crime and Justice* (Milton Keynes: Open University Press).

Eaton, M. (1993) *Women After Prison* (Milton Keynes: Open University Press).

Elias, N. (1982) *The Civilising Process: State Formation and Civilisation* (originally publ. 1939) (Oxford University Press).

Epstein, R. (1996) 'Imprisonment For Non-Payment of Fines', *Justice of the Peace and Local Government Law*, 3 August: 160–2.

Evans, R. (1982) *The Fabrication of Virtue: English Prison Architecture 1750–1840* (Cambridge University Press).

Farrell, G. and K. Pease (1993) *Once Bitten, Twice Bitten: Repeat Victimisation and Its Implications For Crime Prevention*, Crime Prevention Unit Paper no. 46 (London: Home Office).

Farrington, D. (1992) 'Trends in English Juvenile Delinquency and Their Explanation', *International Journal of Comparative and Applied Criminal Justice*, 16 (2): 151–63.

Farrington, D. Gallagher, B. Morley, L. St. Ledger, R and West, D. (1986) 'Unemployment, School Leaving and Crime', *British Journal of Criminology*, 26 (4): 335–56.

Farrington, D. and P. Langan (1992) 'Changes in Crime and Punishment in England and America in the 1980s', *Justice Quarterly* (9): 5–46.

Farrington, D., P. Langan and P. Wikstrom (1994a) 'Changes in Crime and Punishment in England, America and Sweden in the 1980s and 1990s', *Studies in Crime and Crime Prevention*, 104–31.

Farrington, D., P. Langan and P. Wikstrom (1994b) 'Changes in Crime and Punishment in England and America in the 1980s', *Justice Quarterly*, 9 (1): 5–31.

Faugeron, C. (1996) 'The Changing Functions of Imprisonment', in R. Matthews and P. Francis (eds), *Prisons 2000* (London: Macmillan).

Feeley, M. and J. Simon (1992) 'The New Penology: Notes on the Emerging Strategy of Corrections and its Implications', *Criminology*, 30: 449–74.

Feeley, M. and J. Simon (1994) 'Actuarial Justice: The Emerging New Criminal Law', in D. Nelken (ed.), *The Futures of Criminology* (London: Sage).

Feest, J. (1991) 'Reducing the Prison Population: Lessons from the West German Experience', in J. Muncie and R. Sparks (eds), *Imprisonment: European Perspectives* (London: Harvester/Wheatsheaf).

Felson, M. (1986) 'Linking Criminal Choices, Routine Activities, Informal Control and Criminal Outcomes', in D. Cornish and R. Clarke (eds), *The Reasoning Criminal* (New York: Springer Verlag).

Ferdinand, T. (1989) 'Juvenile Delinquency and Juvenile Justice: Which Came First?', *Criminology*, 27 (1): 79–106.

Field, S. (1990) *Trends in Crime and Their Interpretation*, Home Office Research Study no. 119 (London: HMSO).

Fielding, H. (1751) *An Enquiry into the Causes of the Late Increase of Robbers*, 2nd edn (London).

Fitzgerald, M. (1977) *Prisoners in Revolt* (Harmondsworth: Penguin).

FitzGerald, M. (1993) 'Racial Discrimination in the Criminal Justice System', Home Office Research and Statistics Department Research Bulletin, no. 34: 43–8 (London: Home Office).

FitzGerald, M. (1995) 'Ethnic Differences', in M. Walker (ed.), *Interpreting Crime Statistics* (Oxford Science Publications).

FitzGerald, M. and P. Marshall (1996) 'Ethnic Minorities in British Prisons', in R. Matthews and P. Francis (eds), *Prisons 2000* (London: Macmillan).

Fitzgerald, M. and J. Sim (1979) *British Prisons* (Oxford: Blackwell).

Flanagan, T. (1995) *Long Term Imprisonment* (London: Sage).

Forsythe, W. (1990) *Penal Discipline, Reformatory Projects and the English Prison Commission 1985–1939* (University of Exeter Press).

Foucault, M. (1971) *Madness and Civilisation* (London: Tavistock).

Foucault, M. (1977) *Discipline and Punish: The Birth of the Prison* (London: Allen Lane).

Foucault, M. (1979) *The History of Sexuality Volume 1: An Introduction* (London: Allen Lane).

Foucault, M. (1982) 'The Subject of Power', in H. Dreyfus and P. Rabinow (eds), *Michel Foucault: Beyond Structuralism and Hermeneutics* (Brighton: Harvester).

Franke, H. (1990) 'Dutch Tolerance: Facts and Fables,' *British Journal of Criminology*, **30** (1):81–94.

Franke, H. (1992) 'The Rise and Decline of Solitary Confinement: Social History Explorations of Long Term Penal Changes', *British Journal of Criminology*, **32** (2): 125–43.

Freedman, E. (1984) *Their Sisters' Keepers: Women's Prison Reform in America 1830–1930* (Ann Arbor: University of Michigan Press).

Fry, E. (1827) *Observations on Visiting, Superintending and Government of Female Prisons* (London: John & Arthur).

Fyfe, N. (1997) 'Crime', in M. Pacione (ed.), *Britain's Cities: Geographies of Division in Urban Britain* (London: Routledge).

Galstar, G. and L. Scaturo (1985) 'The US Criminal Justice System: Unemployment and the Severity of Punishment', *Journal of Research in Crime and Delinquency*, **22** (2): 163–89.

Garland, D. (1981) 'The Birth of the Welfare Sanction', *British Journal of Law and Society*, **8** (Summer): 29–45.

Garland, D. (1983) 'Towards a Social Analysis of Penalty', in D. Garland and P. Young (eds), *The Power to Punish* (London: Heinemann).

Garland, D. (1985) *Punishment and Welfare* (Aldershot: Gower).

Garland, D. (1990) *Punishment and Modern Society* (Oxford University Press).

Garland, D. (1995) 'Penal Modernism and Postmodernism', in T. Blomberg and S. Cohen (eds), *Punishment and Social Control* (New York: Aldine de Gruyter).

Garland, D. (1996) 'The Limits of the Sovereign State: Strategies of Crime Control in Contemporary Society', *British Journal of Criminology*, **36** (4): 445–72.

Genders, E. and E. Player (1986) 'Women's Imprisonment: The Effects of Youth Custody', *British Journal of Criminology*, **26** (4): 357–70.

Genders, E. and E. Player (1989) *Race Relations in Prison* (Oxford: Clarendon Press).

Genders, E. and E. Player (1995a) *Grendon: A Study of a Therapeutic Prison* (Oxford: Clarendon Press).

Genders, T. and E. Player (1995b) 'Women Lifers: Assessing the Experience', in T. Flanagan (ed.), *Long-Term Imprisonment* (California: Sage).

Giddens, A. (1981) *Contemporary Critique of Historical Materialism: Power, Poverty and the State* (London: Macmillan).

Giddens, A. (1984) *The Constitution of Society* (Cambridge: Polity Press).

Giddens, A. (1987) 'Time and Social Organisation', in *Social Theory in Modern Society* (Cambridge: Polity Press).

Giddens, A. (1990) *The Consequences of Modernity* (Cambridge: Polity Press).

Gilligan, C. (1982) *In a Different Voice* (Cambridge, Mass.: Harvard University Press).

Gillis, J. (1974) *Youth and History* (London: Academic Press).

Gilroy, P. (1987) *There Ain't No Black in the Union Jack* (London: Routledge).

Goffman, E. (1968) *Asylums: Essays on the Social Situation of Mental Patients* (Harmondsworth: Pelican).

Gormally, B., K. McEvoy and D. Wall (1993) 'Criminal Justice in a Divided Society: Northern Ireland Prisons', in M. Tonry (ed.), *Crime and Justice: A Review of Research*, vol. 17 (University of Chicago Press).

Gottfredson, S. and R. Taylor (1987) 'Attitudes of Correctional Policy Makers and the Public', in S. Gottfreson and S. McConville (eds), *America's Correctional Crisis* (New York: Greenwood Press).

Gouldner, A. (1954) *Patterns of Industrial Bureaucracy* (Glencoe, Ill.: Free Press).

Gouldner, A. (1968) 'The Sociologist as Partisan: Sociology and the Welfare State', *American Sociologist* (May): 103–16.

Graham, J. (1990) 'Decarceration in the Federal Republic of West Germany', *British Journal of Criminology* **30** (2): 150–70.

Graham, J. and B. Bowling (1995) *Young People and Crime*, Home Office Research Study no. 145 (London: HMSO).

Green, P. (1991) *Drug Couriers* (London: Howard League).

Hacker, A. (1992) *Two Nations* (New York: Scribner).

Hagel, A. and T. Newburn (1994) *Persistent Young Offenders* (London: Policy Studies Institute).

Halevy, T. (1995) 'Racial Discrimination in Sentencing? A Study with Dubious Conclusions', *Criminal Law Review*, 267–71.

Hall, S. (1979) 'Drifting Into a Law and Order Society', *The Cobden Lecture* (London: The Cobden Trust).

Hall, S. Critcher, C. Jeffersson, T. Clarke, J. and Roberts, B. (1978) *Policing The Crisis: Mugging, The State, Law and Order* (London: Macmillan).

Hannah-Moffat, K. (1995) 'Feminine Fortresses: Woman-Centred Prisons', *Prison Journal*, **75** (2): 135–65.

Harding, R. (1997) *Private Prisons and Public Accountability* (Buckingham: Open University Press).

Harer, M. and D. Steffensmeier (1996) 'Race and Prison Violence', *Criminology*, **34** (3): 323–50.

Harris, K. (1987) 'Moving Into The New Millennium: Toward a Feminist Vision of Justice', *Prison Journal*, **10**, 27–38.

Harris, R. (1985) 'Towards Just Welfare', *British Journal of Criminology*, **25** (1): 31–45.

Harris, R. and D. Webb (1987) *Welfare, Power and Juvenile Justice* (London: Tavistock).

Hartsock, N. (1987) 'Rethinking Modernism: Minority vs Majority Theories', *Cultural Critique* 7: 187–206.

Harvey, D. (1989) *The Condition of Postmodernity* (Oxford: Basil Blackwell).

Harvey, D. (1994) 'Flexible Accumulation Through Urbanisation: Reflections on Post-Modernism in the American City', in A. Amim (ed.), *Post-Fordism: A Reader* (Oxford: Blackwell).

Hawkins, G. (1983) 'Prison Labour and Prison Industries', in M. Tonry and N. Morris (eds), *Crime and Social Justice: A Review of Research*, vol. 5 (University of Chicago Press).

Hayman, S. (1996) *Community Prisons for Women* (London: Prison Reform Trust).

Hedderman, C. and L. Gelsthorpe (1997) 'Understanding the Sentencing of Women', Home Office Research Study no. 170 (London: HMSO).

Hedderman, C. and M. Hough (1994) *Does the Criminal Justice System Treat Men and Women Differently?*, Research Findings no. 10, Home Office Research and Statistics Department (London: HMSO).

Hebdidge, D. (1979) *Subculture: The Meaning of Style* (Andover: Methuen & Co.).

Heidensohn, F. (1975) 'The Imprisonment of Females', in S. McConville (ed.), *The Use of Imprisonment* (London: Routledge).

Heidensohn, F. (1986) 'Models of Justice: Portia or Persephone? Some Thoughts on Equality, Fairness and Gender in the Field of Criminal Justice', **13** (3/4): 287–98.

Herrnstein, R. and C. Murray (1994) *The Bell Curve* (New York: Free Press).

Hesse, B. (1993) 'Black to Front and Black Again: Racialising Through Contested Times and Spaces', in M. Keith and S. Pile (eds), *Place and the Politics of Identity* (London: Routledge).

Hirschfield, A. and K. Bowers (1977) 'The Development of a Social Demographic and Land Use Profile for Areas of High Crime', *British Journal of Criminology*, **37** (1): 103–20.

Hirst, J. (1995) 'The Australian Experience: The Convict Colony', in N. Morris and D. Rothman (eds), *The Oxford History of the Prison* (New York: Oxford University Press).

Hirst, P. and G. Thompson (1992) 'The Problem of Globalisation', *Economy and Society*, **21** (4): 360–95.

HM Inspectorate of Prisons (1997a) *Young Prisoners: A Thematic Review* (London: HMSO).

HM Inspectorate of Prisons (1997b) *Women in Prison: A Thematic Review* (London: HMSO).

Holdaway, S. (1996) *The Racialisation of British Policing* (London: Macmillan).

Home Office (1933) *Children and Young Persons Act* (London: HMSO).

Home Office (1945) *Prisons and Borstals* (London: HMSO).

Home Office (1968) *Children in Trouble* (London: HMSO).

Home Office (1969) *People in Prison*, Cmnd. 4214 (London: HMSO).

Home Office (1970) *Detention Centres: Report of the Advisory Council on the Penal System* (London: HMSO).

Home Office (1978) *A Survey of the South East Prison Population*, Home Office Research Unit, Research Bulletin no. 5 (London: HMSO).

Home Office (1984) *Suicide in Prison: A Report by HM Inspector of Prisons* (London: HMSO).

Home Office (1985) *New Directions in Prison Design: Report of a Home Office Working Party on American New Generation Prisons* (London: HMSO).

Home Office (1986) *The Report of the Working Party on Suicide in Prison* (London: HMSO).

Home Office (1988) *Punishment, Custody and The Community*, Cmnd. 424 (London: HMSO).

Home Office (1990a) *Crime, Justice and Protecting the Public*, Cmnd. 965 (London: HMSO).

Home Office (1990b) *Report of a Review by Her Majesty's Chief Inspector of Prisons for England and Wales of Suicide and Self-harm in Prison Service Establishments* (London: HMSO).

Home Office (1994) *Race and the Criminal Justice System* (London: HMSO).

Home Office (1995) *Review of the Prison Service Security in England and Wales* (The Learmont Report), Cmnd. 3020 (London: HMSO).

Home Office (1996a) *Criminal Statistics England and Wales 1995* (London: HMSO).

Home Office (1996b) *Prison Statistics England and Wales 1995* (London: HMSO).

Home Office (1996c) *Probation Statistics, England and Wales 1995* (London: HMSO).

Home Office (1996d) *Report on the Work of the Prison Department* (London: HMSO).

Home Office (1998) *Summary Probation Statistics England and Wales 1997*, Statistical Bulletin Issue 12/98 (London: Home Office).

Home Office (1999) *Projections of Long-Term Trends in the Prison Population to 2006*, *Statistical Bulletin*, January (London: HMSO).

Hood, R. (1965) *Borstal Re-Assessed* (London: Heinemann).

Hood, R. (1992) *Race and Sentencing* (Oxford: Clarendon Press).

Hood, R. (1995) 'Race and Sentencing: A Reply', *Criminal Law Review*: 272–9.

Hood, R. and S. Sparks (1969) *Community Homes and the Approved School System* (Institute for Criminology, University of Cambridge).

Hough, M. (1996) 'People Thinking About Punishment', *Howard Journal*, **35** (3): 191–214.

Hough, M. and P. Mayhew (1984) *Taking Account of Crime: Findings from the British Crime Survey* (London: HMSO).

Howard, J. (1777) *The State of Our Prisons* (Warrington; republished: Montclair, NJ, 1973).

Howard, L. (1994) 'Where Do Prisoners Come From? Some Information About the Home Areas of Prisoners in England and Wales', *Research Bulletin* (36), Research and Statistics Department, Home Office (London: HMSO).

Howard League (1997) *Lost Inside – The Imprisonment of Teenage Girls* (London).

Howe, A. (1994) *Punish and Critique: Towards a Feminist Analysis of Penalty* (London: Routledge).

Hudson, B. (1987) *Justice Through Punishment* (London: Macmillan).

Hughes, R. (1987) *The Fatal Shore: A History of Transportation of Convicts to Australia 1787–1858* (London: Collins Harvill).

Ignatieff, M. (1978) *A Just Measure of Pain: The Penitentiary in the Industrial Revolution 1750–1850* (London: Macmillan).

Ignatieff, M. (1981) 'State, Civil Society, and Total Institutions: A Critique of Recent Social Histories of Punishment', in M. Tonry and N. Morris (eds), *Crime and Justice*, vol. 3 (University of Chicago Press).

Innes, J. (1987) 'Prisons for the Poor: English Bridewells 1555–1800', in F. Snyder and D. Hay (eds), *Labour, Law and Crime* (London: Tavistock).

Irwin, J. (1970) *The Felon* (Englewood Cliffs, NJ: Prentice Hall).

Irwin, J. and J. Austin (1994) *It's About Time: America's Imprisonment Binge* (Belmont, CA: Wadsworth).

Jackson, G. (1970) *Soledad Brother: The Prison Letters of George Jackson* (New York: Coward & McCann).

Jacobs, J. (1977) *Stateville: The Penitentiary in Mass Society* (University of Chicago Press).

Jacobs, J. (1979) 'Race Relations and the Prisoner Subculture', in N. Morris and M. Tonry (eds), *Crime and Justice: A Review of Research*, vol. 1 (University of Chicago Press).

Jancovic, I. (1977) 'Labour Market and Imprisonment', *Crime and Social Justice*, (Fall/Winter): 17–31.

Jay, M. (1973) *The Dialectical Imagination: A History of the Frankfurt School and the Institute of Social Research 1923–1950* (London: Heinemann).

Jessop, B. (1988) 'Authoritarian Populism: Two Nations and Thatcherism', in B. Jessop *et al.*, (eds), *Thatcherism: A Tale of Two Nations* (Cambridge: Polity Press).

Jessop, B. (1994) 'Post-Fordism and the State', in A. Amim (ed.), *Post-Fordism: A Reader* (Oxford: Blackwell).

Jones, P. (1996) 'Risk Prediction in Criminal Justice', in A. Harland (ed.), *Choosing Correctional Options That Work* (California: Sage).

Jones, S. (1993) *The Language of Genes* (London: Flamingo).

Jupp, V. (1989) *Methods of Criminological Research* (London: Unwin Hyman).

Keith, M. (1993) 'From Punishment to Discipline: Racism, Racialism and the Policing of Social Control', in M. Cross and M. Keith (eds), *Racism, The City and the State* (London: Routledge).

Kelling, G. and C. Coles (1996) *Fixing Broken Windows: Restoring Order and Reducing Crime in Our Communities* (New York: Free Press).

Kilbrandon Committee (1964) *Report of the Committee on Children and Young Persons (Scotland)*, Cmnd. 2306 (Edinburgh: HMSO).

King, M. and C. Piper (1990) *How the Law Thinks About Children* (Aldershot: Gower).

King. R. (1987) 'New Generation Prisons, The Prison Building Programme and the Future of the Dispersal System', in A. Bottoms and R. Light (eds), *Problems of Long-Term Imprisonment* (Aldershot: Gower).

King, R. (1991) 'Maximum Security Custody in Britain and The USA: A Study of Gartree and Oak Park Heights', *British Journal of Criminology*, **31** (2): 125–93.

King, R. and K. Elliott (1978) *Albany: Birth of a Prison – End of an Era* (London: Routledge & Kegan Paul).

King, R. and K. McDermott (1989) 'British Prisons 1970–1987: The Ever-Deepening Crisis', *British Journal of Criminology*, **29** (2): 107–28.

King, R. and R. Morgan (1980) *The Future of the Prison System* (Farnborough: Gower).

Landau, S. and G. Nathan (1983) 'Selecting Delinquents For Cautioning in the London Metropolitan Area', *British Journal of Criminology*, **23** (2): 128–49.

Langan, P. (1985) 'Racism on Trial: New Evidence to Explain the Racial Composition of Prisons in the United States', *Criminology*, **76** (3) 666–83.

Langan, P. (1991) 'America's Soaring Prison Population', *Science*, **251** (29 March): 1568–73.

Langan, P. and D. Farrington (1998) *Crime and Justice in the United States and in England and Wales 1981–96*, Bureau of Justice Statistics (Washington, DC: US Department of Justice).

Lasch, S. and J. Urry (1994) *Economics of Signs and Space* (London: Sage).

Lawson, D. (1970) *City Lads in Borstal* (Liverpool University Press).

Lea, J. (1979) 'Discipline and Capitalist Development', in B. Fine *et al.* (eds), *Capitalism and the Rule of Law* (London: Hutchinson).

Lea, J. (1986) 'Police Racism: Some Theories and Their Policy Implications', in R. Matthews and J. Young (eds), *Confronting Crime* (London: Sage).

Lea, J. (1997) 'Post-Fordism and Criminality' in N. Jewson and S. MacGregor (eds), *Transforming Cities: Contested Governance and New Spatial Divisions* (London: Routledge).

Lea, J. (1998) 'Criminology and Postmodernity', in P. Walton and J. Young (eds), *The New Criminology Revisited* (London: Macmillan).

Lea, J. and J. Young (1984) *What Is To Be Done About Law and Order?* (Harmondsworth: Penguin).

Leander, K. (1995) 'The Normalisation of Swedish Prisons', in V. Ruggiero, M. Ryan and J. Sim (eds), *Western European Prison Systems* (London: Sage).

Lefebvre, H. (1991) *The Production of Space* (Oxford: Blackwell).

Lemert, E. (1970) 'Juvenile Justice Italian Style', *Law and Society Review*, **20** (4): 509–44.

Leonard, E. (1982) *Women, Crime and Society: A Critique of Criminological Theory* (London: Longman).

Lerman, P. (1982) *Deinstitutionalisation and the Welfare State* (New Brunswick, NJ: Rutgers University Press).

Lévi-Strauss, C. (1992) *Tristes Tropiques* (Harmondsworth: Penguin).

Levitas, R. (1996) 'Fiddling While Britain Burns? The Measurement of Unemployment', in R. Levitas and W. Guy (eds), *Interpreting Social Statistics* (London: Routledge).

Levitas, R. and W. Guy (1996) *Interpreting Official Statistics* (London: Routledge).

Liebling, A. (1992) *Suicides in Prison* (London: Routledge).

Liebling, A. and T. Ward (1994) *Deaths in Custody: International Perspectives* (London: Whiting & Birch).

Linebaugh, P. (1977) 'The Tyburn Riot Against the Surgeons', in D. Hay *et al.*, *Albion's Fatal Tree* (Harmondsworth: Penguin).

Lloyd, C. (1990) *Suicide and Self Injury in Prison: A Literature Review*, Home Office Research Study no. 115 (London: HMSO).

Lloyd, C., G. Mair and M. Hough (1994) *Explaining Reconviction Rates: A Critical Analysis*, Home Office Research Study no. 136 (London: HMSO).

Longford Committee (1964) *Crime – A Challenge To Us All* (London: Labour Party).

Lowman, J., R. Menzies and T. Palys (1987) *Transcarceration: Essays in the study of Social Control* (Aldershot: Gower).

Lynch, J. (1988) 'A Comparison of Prison Use in England, Canada, West Germany and the United States', *Journal of Criminal Law and Criminology*, **79**: 108–217.

Lynch, J. *et al.* (1994) *Profile of Inmates in the United States and in England and Wales, 1991*, US Department of Justice, Bureau of Justice Statistics. NCJ-145863.

Lyotard, J. (1986) *The Postmodern Condition* (Manchester University Press).

MacKinnon, C. (1987) *Feminism Unmodified: Discourses on Life and Law* (Cambridge, Mass.: Harvard University Press).

Maden, A., M. Swinton and J. Gunn (1992) 'The Ethnic Origin of Women Serving a Prison Sentence', *British Journal of Criminology*, **32** (2): 218–22.

Maguire, M., J. Vagg and R. Morgan (1985) *Accountability and Prisons* (London: Tavistock).

Mair, G. (1986) 'Ethnic Minorities, Probation and the Magistrates Courts', *British Journal of Criminology*, **26** (2): 147–55.

Mair, G. and C. Nee (1990) *Electronic Monitoring: The Trials and Their Results*, Home Office Research Study no. 120 (London: HMSO).

Maltz, M. (1984) *Recidivism* (Orlando: Academic Press).

Marsh, A., J. Dobbs, J. Monk and A. White (1985) *Staff Attitudes in the Prison Service*, Home Office Research Study no. 84 (London: HMSO).

Martinson, R. (1979) 'Symposium on Sentencing', *Hofra Law Review*, **7** (2): 243–58.

Marx, K. (1970) *A Contribution to the Critique of Political Economy* (London: Lawrence & Wishart).

Marx, K. (1984) *Capital*, vol. 1 (London: Lawrence & Wishart).

Marx, K. and F. Engels (1975) 'Debates on the Law of the Thefts of Wood', in K. Marx and F. Engels, *Collected Works*, vol. 1 (London: Lawrence & Wishart).

Massey, D. (1997) 'Space/Power, Identity/Difference: Tensions in the City', in A. Merrifield and E. Swyngedouw (eds), *The Urbanisation of Injustice* (New York University Press).

Mathieson, T. (1974) *The Politics of Abolition* (Oxford: Martin Robertson).

Mathieson, T. (1983) 'The Future of Control Systems: The Case of Norway', in D. Garland and P. Young (eds), *The Power to Punish* (London: Heinemann).

Mathieson, T. (1990) *Prison on Trial* (London: Sage).

Mathieson, T. (1991) 'The Argument Against Building More Prisons', in J. Muncie and R. Sparks (eds), *Imprisonment: European Perspectives* (London: Harvester/Wheatsheaf).

Matthews, R. (1979) 'Decarceration and the Fiscal Crisis', in B. Fine (ed.), *Capitalism and the Rule of Law* (London: Hutchinson).

Matthews, R. (1987) 'Decarceration and Social Control: Fantasies and Realities', in J. Lowman *et al.* (eds), *Transcarceration: Essays in the Study of Social Control* (Aldershot: Gower).

Matthews, R. (1992) 'Replacing Broken Windows: Crime, Incivilities and Urban Change', in R. Matthews and J. Young (eds), *Issues in Realist Criminology* (London: Sage).

Matthews, R. (1994) *Prisoners Abroad* (Centre for Criminology, Middlesex University).

Matthews, R. (1995a) 'Crime and Its Consequences in England and Wales', *The Annals of the American Academy of Political and Social Science*, **539** (May): 169–83.

Matthews, R. (1995b) 'The Diversion of Juveniles from Custody: The Experience of England and Wales 1980–1990', in G. Albrecht and W. Ludwig-Mayerhofer (eds), *Diversion and Informal Social Control* (Berlin: Walter de Gruyter).

Matthews, R. (1996) *Armed Robbery: Two Police Responses*, Crime Detection and Prevention Series no. 78 (London: Home Office).

Matthews, R. (ed.) (1988) *Informal Justice?* (London: Sage).

Matthews, R. (ed.) (1989) *Privatising Criminal Justice* (London: Sage).

Matthews, R. and J. Young (1992) 'Reflections on Realism', in J. Young and R. Matthews (eds), *Rethinking Criminology: The Realist Debate* (London: Sage).

Mauer, M. (1994) *Americans Behind Bars: The Sentencing Project* (Washington).

May, M. (1973) 'Innocence and Experience: The Evolution of the Concept of Juvenile Delinquency in the Mid-Nineteenth Century', *Victorian Studies*, **18**: 17–29.

Mayhew, H. and J. Binny (1971) *Criminal Prisons of London* (London: Frank Cass & Co.).

McCleary, R. (1961) 'The Governmental Process and Informal Social Control', in D. Cressey (ed.), *The Prison: Studies in Institutionalisation, Organisation and Change* (New York: Holt, Rinehart & Winston).

McConville, S. (1995) 'The Victorian Prison: England, 1865–1965', in N. Morris and D. Rothman (eds), *The Oxford History of the Prison* (Oxford University Press).

McConville, S. and S. Hall-Williams (1987) 'The English Response to the Penal Crisis', in S. Gottfredson and S. McConville (eds), *America's Correctional Crisis: Prison Populations and Public Policy* (New York: Greenwood Press).

McGowan, R. (1995) 'The Well Ordered Prison in England 1780–1865', in N. Morris and D. Rothman (eds), *The Oxford History of the Prison* (Oxford University Press).

McMahon, M. (1990) 'Net-Widening: Vagaries and the Use of a Concept', *British Journal of Criminology*, **30** (2): 121–50.

McNay, L. (1992) *Foucault and Feminism* (Cambridge: Polity Press).

Melossi, D. (1978) 'Georg Rusche and Otto Kirchheimer: Punishment and Social Structure', *Crime and Social Justice*, (9).

Melossi, D. (1979) 'Institutions of Social Control and Capitalist Organisation of Work', in B. Fine *et al.* (eds), *Capitalism and the Rule of Law* (London: Hutchinson).

Melossi, D. (1994) *The Effect of Economic Circumstances on the Criminal Justice System*, Report Presented to the 11th Criminological Colloquium (Strasbourg: Council of Europe).

Melossi, D. and M. Pavarini (1981) *The Prison and the Factory: The Origins of the Penitentiary System* (London: Macmillan).

Merton, R. (1957) *Social Theory and Social Structure* (New York: Free Press).

Messerschmidt, J. (1993) *Masculinities and Crime* (Boston: Rowman & Littlefield).

Miles, R. (1993) *Racism After 'Race Relations'* (London: Routledge).

Millham, S., R. Bullock and P. Cherrett (1975) *After Grace-Teeth: A Comparative Study of the Residential Experiences of Boys in Approved Schools* (London: Human Context Books).

Millham, S., R. Bullock and K. Hosie (1978) *Locking Up Children* (Farnborough: Saxon House).

Milne, S. (1997) 'Facts that Fail to Fit the Figures', *Guardian*, 16 April.

Mingione, E. (1996) 'Urban Poverty in the Advanced Industrial World: Concepts Analyses and Debates', in E. Mingione (ed.), *Urban Poverty and the Underclass* (Oxford: Blackwell).

Morgan, R. (1991) 'Woolf: In Retrospect and Prospect', *Modern Law Review*, **54** (5): 713–25.

Morgan, R. (1994) 'An Awkward Anomolie: Remand Prisoners', in E. Player and M. Jenkins (eds), *Prisons After Woolf* (London: Routledge).

Morgan, R. (1995) 'Prison', in R. Walker, *Interpreting Crime Statistics* (Oxford: Oxford Science Publications).

Morgan, R. (1997) 'The Aims of Imprisonment Revisited', in A. Liebling and T. Ward (eds), *Deaths in Custody: International Perspectives* (London: Whiting & Birch).

Morgan, R. and M. Evans (1994) 'Inspecting Prisons: The View from Strasbourg', in R. King and M. Maguire (eds), *Prisons in Context* (Oxford: Clarendon Press).

Morris, A. and H. Giller (1987) *Understanding Juvenile Justice* (London: Croom Helm).

Morris, A., H. Giller, E. Szwed and H. Geach (1980) *Justice for Children* (London: Macmillan).

Morris, A. and M. Tonry (1990) *Between Prison and Probation* (New York: Oxford University Press).

Morris, A. and C. Wilkinson (1995) 'Responding to Female Prisoners' Needs', *Prison Journal*, **75** (3): 295–306.

Morris, L. (1996) 'Dangerous Classes: Neglected Aspects of the Underclass Debate', in E. Mingione (ed.), *Urban Poverty and the Underclass* (Oxford: Blackwell).

Morris, N. (1974) *The Future of Imprisonment* (University of Chicago Press).

Morris, T. and P. Morris (1963) *Pentonville: A Sociological Study of an English Prison* (London: Routledge & Kegan Paul).

Morrison, W. (1996) 'Modernity, Imprisonment and Social Solidarity', in R. Matthews and P. Francis (eds), *Prisons 2000* (London: Macmillan).

Mott, J. (1985) 'Prisons and Prisoners in England and Wales, 1970–1982', Home Office Research Study no. 84 (London: HMSO).

Moxon, D. (1988) *Sentencing Practice in the Crown Court*, Home Office Research Study no. 102 (London: HMSO).

Moxon, D. and C. Whittaker (1996) *Imprisonment For Fine Default*, Research Findings no. 35, Home Office Research and Statistics Directorate (London: HMSO).

Mountbatten, Lord (1966) *Report of the Inquiry into Prison Escapes and Security* (London: HMSO).

Murray, C. (1996) *The Emerging British Underclass* (London: Institute for Economic Affairs).

Murray, C. (1997) *Does Prison Work?* (London: Institute of Economic Affairs).

NACRO (1991) *Seizing the Initiative: Final Report on the DHSS Intermediate Treatment Initiative to Divert Juvenile Offenders from Care and Custody, 1983–1989* (London: NACRO).

Naffine, N. (1997) *Feminism and Criminology* (Cambridge: Polity Press).

Nagel, W. (1977) 'On Behalf of a Moratorium on Prison Construction', *Crime and Delinquency*, **23**: 154–72.

National Audit Office (1985) *Home Office and Property Services Agency: Programme for the Provision of Prison Places* (London: HMSO).

Neale, K. (1991) 'European Prison Rules: Contextual, Philosophical and Practical Aspects', in J. Muncie and R. Sparks (eds), *Imprisonment: European Perspectives* (London: Harvester/Wheatsheaf).

Newburn, T. (1997) 'Youth, Crime and Justice', in M. Maguire, R. Morgan and R. Reiner (eds), *The Oxford Handbook of Criminology*, 2nd edn (Oxford: Clarendon Press).

Nottingham Juvenile Liaison Bureau (1985) *The Limits of Diversion*, Second Annual Report (Nottingham: NJLB).

Nuttall, C. and K. Pease (1994) 'Changes in the Use of Imprisonment in England and Wales 1950–1991', *Criminal Law Review*, 316–21.

O'Brien, P. (1982) *The Promise of Punishment: Prisons in Nineteenth Century France* (Princeton University Press).

Offe, C. (1984) *Contradictions of the Welfare State* (London: Hutchinson).

Offe, C. (1985) 'Work: The Key Sociological Category?', in C. Offe, *Disorganised Captalism* (Cambridge: Polity Press).

Orsagh, T. and A. Witte (1981) 'Economic Status and Crime: Implications for Offender Rehabilitation', *Journal of Criminal Law and Criminology*, **72** (3): 1055–71.

Owen, B. and B. Bloom (1995) 'Profiling Women Prisoners', *The Prison Journal*, **75** (2): 165–86.

Page, S. (1993) 'Suicide and the Total Institution', in A. Liebling and T. Ward (eds), *Deaths in Custody: International Perspectives* (London: Whiting & Birch).

Painter, K. (1992) 'Different Worlds: The Spatial, Temporal and Social Dimensions of Female Victimisation', in D. Evans *et al.* (eds), *Essays in Environmental Criminology* (London: Routledge).

Palmer, T. (1992) *The Re-Emergence of Correctional Intervention* (California: Sage).

Parker, H. and R. Newcombe (1987) 'Heroin Use and Acquisitive Crime in an English Community', *British Journal of Sociology*, **38** (3): 321–50.

Parker, H., K. Bakx and R. Newcombe (1988) *Living with Heroin* (Milton Keynes: Open University Press).

Pashukanis, E. (1978) *Law and Marxism: A General Theory* (original Russian edition 1924) (London: C. Arthur).

Pawson, R. and N. Tilley (1994) 'What Works in Evaluation Research', *British Journal of Criminology*, **34** (3): 291–306.

Pawson, R. and N. Tilley (1997) *Realistic Evaluation* (London: Sage).

Pearson, G. (1975) *The Deviant Imagination* (London: Macmillan).

Pearson, G. (1983) *Hooligan: A History of Respectable Fears* (London: Macmillan).

Pease, K. (1985) 'Community Service Orders', in M. Tonry and N. Morris (eds), *Crime and Justice: An Annual Review of Research* (University of Chicago Press).

Pease, K. (1992) 'Punitiveness and Prison Populations: An International Comparison', *Justice of the Peace*, **27** (June): 407–8.

Pease, K. (1995) 'Cross National Imprisonment Rates: Limitations of Method and Possible Conclusions', in R. King and M. Maguire (eds), *Prisons in Context* (Oxford: Clarendon Press).

Phillips, A. (1993) *The Trouble with Boys* (London: Pandora).

Pitts, J. (1988) *The Politics of Juvenile Crime* (London: Sage).

Pitts, J. (1993) 'Thereotyping: Anti-Racism, Criminology and Black Young People', in D. Cook and B. Hudson (eds), *Racism and Criminology* (London: Sage).

Pitts, J. (1996) 'The Politics and Practice of Youth Justice', in J. Muncie and E. McLaughlin (eds), *Controlling Crime* (London: Sage).

Platek, M. (1996) 'We Never Promised Them a Rose Garden', in R. Matthews and P. Francis (eds), *Prisons 2000* (London: Macmillan).

Platt, T. (1969) *The Child Savers* (Chicago University Press).

Pollock-Byrne, J. (1992) 'Women in Prison: Why are Their Numbers Increasing?', in J. Benekos and A. Merlo (eds), *Corrections: Dilemmas and Directions* (Cincinnati: Anderson Publishing).

Poulantzas, N. (1978) *State Power and Socialism* (London: Verso).

Pratt, J. (1985) 'Delinquency as a Scarce Resource', *Howard Journal*, 24; 93–107.

Pratt, J. (1989) 'Corporatism: The Third Model of Juvenile Justice', *British Journal of Criminology*, **29** (3): 236–55.

Pratt, J. (1990) 'Crime, Time, Youth and Punishment', *Contemporary Crisis*, **14**: 219–42.

Prison Reform Trust (1993) *Women Prisoners on Remand* (London: Prison Reform Trust).

Prison Reform Trust (1997) *The Rising Toll of Prison Suicide* (London: Prison Reform Trust).

Radzinowicz, L. and J. King (1977) *The Growth of Crime* (London: Hamish Hamilton).

Rafter, N. (1983) 'Prisons for Women 1970–1980', in M. Tonry and N. Morris (eds), *Crime and Justice: An Annual Review of Research, vol. 5* (University of Chicago).

Rafter, N. (1985a) 'Gender Prisons and Prison History, *Social Science History*, **9** (3): 233–47.

Rafter, N. (1985b) *Partial Justice: Women in State Prisons 1800–1935* (Boston: Northeastern University Press).

Reiss, A. (1986) 'Why are Communities Important in Understanding Crime?', in A. Reiss and M. Tonry (eds), *Communities and Crime* (University of Chicago Press).

Rock, P. (1996) *Restructuring a Women's Prison* (Oxford: Clarendon Press).

Rose, N. (1987) 'Beyond the Public/Private Division: Law, Power and the Family', *Journal of Law and Society*, **14** (1): 61–77.

Rose, N. and P. Miller (1992) 'Political Power Beyond the State; Problematics of Government', *British Journal of Sociology*, **43** (2): 173–205.

Roshier, B. (1989) *Controlling Crime: The Classical Perspective in Criminology* (Milton Keynes: Open University Press).

Rothman, D. (1971) *The Discovery of the Asylum: Social Order and Disorder in the New Republic* (Boston: Little, Brown & Co.).

Rothman, D. (1973) 'Decarcerating Prisoners and Patients', *Civil Liberties Review*, **1**: 8–30.

Rothman, D. (1980) *Conscience and Convenience: The Asylum and Its Alternatives in Progressive America* (Boston: Little, Brown & Co.).

Rothman, D. (1981) 'Doing Time: Days, Months and Years in the Criminal Justice System', in H. Gross and A. von Hirsch (eds), *Sentencing* (New York: Oxford University Press).

Rotman, E. (1990) *Beyond Punishment: A New View on the Rehabilitation of Criminal Offenders* (Connecticut: Greenwood Press).

Ruggles-Brise, E. (1921) *The English Prison System* (London: Macmillan).

Rusche, G. (1978) 'Labour Market and Penal Sanctions: Thoughts on the Sociology of Criminal Justice', *Crime and Social Justice* (Fall/Winter): 2–8.

Rusche, G. and O. Kirchheimer (1968 [1939]) *Punishment and Social Structure* (New York: Russell & Russell).

Rutherford, A. (1983) 'A Statute Backfires: The Escalation of Youth Incarceration in England in the 1970s', in J. Doig (ed.), *Criminal Corrections: Ideals and Realities* (Lexington, Mass.: D. C. Heath & Co.).

Rutherford, A. (1984) *Prisons and the Process of Justice* (London: Heinemann).

Rutherford, A. (1986) *Growing Out of Crime* (Harmondsworth: Penguin).

Rutherford, A. and R. Morgan (1981) *No More Prison Building* (Howard League, June).

Said, E. (1993) *Culture and Imperialism* (London: Chatto & Windus).

Sampson, R. and J. Lauritsen (1997) 'Racial and Ethnic Disparities in Crime and Criminal Justice in the United States', in M. Tonry (ed.), *Ethnicity, Crime and Immigration* (University of Chicago Press).

Sanders, A. (1997) 'From Suspect to Trial', in M. Maguire, R. Morgan and R. Reiner (eds), *The Oxford Handbook of Criminology*, 2nd edn (Oxford: Clarendon).

Santos, B. (1987) 'Law: A Map of Misreading. Towards a Postmodern Conception of Law', *Journal of Law and Society*, **14** (3).

Sayer, A. (1992) *Method in Social Science: A Realist Approach*, 2nd edn (London: Routledge).

Scarman, Lord (1982) *The Scarman Report: The Brixton Disorders 10–12 April 1991* (Harmondsworth: Penguin).

Schur, E. (1973) *Radical Non-Intervention: Rethinking the Delinquency Problem* (Englewood Cliffs, NJ: Prentice-Hall).

Scottish Office (1993) *Report on HM Special Unit, Barlinnie* (Edinburgh: HMSO).

Scull, A. (1977) *Decarceration: Community Treatment and the Deviant* (reprinted 2nd edn 1984) (New Jersey: Prentice Hall).

Seear, B. and E. Player (1986) *Women in the Penal System* (London: The Howard League).

Sennett, R. (1991) *The Conscience of the Eye: The Design and Social Life of Cities* (New York: Knopf).

Shaw, M. (1992) 'Issues in Power and Control: Women in Prison and Their Defenders', *British Journal of Criminology*, **32** (4): 438–53.

Shaw, M. (1996) 'Is There a Feminist Future for Women's Prisons?', in R. Matthews and P. Francis (eds), *Prisons 2000* (London: Macmillan).

Shaw, R. (1992) *Prisoners' Children: What are the Issues?* (London: Routledge).

Shaw, S. (1985) 'Reflections on "Short Sharp Shock"', *Youth and Policy*, **13** (Summer):1–5.

Shearing, C. and P. Stenning (1985) 'From the Panopticon to the Disneyworld: The Development of Discipline', in A. Doob and V. Greenspan (eds), *Perspectives in Criminal Law* (Ontario: Canada Law Books Inc.).

Sherman, L., P. Gartin and M. Buerger (1989) 'Hot Spots of Predatory Crime: Routine Activities and the Criminology of Place', *Criminology*, **37** (1): 27–55.

Sim, J. (1994) 'Reforming the Penal Wasteland: A Critical Review of the Woolf Report', in E. Player and M. Jenkins (eds), *Prisons After Woolf: Reform Through Riot* (London: Routledge).

Simon, J. (1993) *Poor Discipline: Parole and the Social Control of the Underclass 1890–1990* (University of Chicago Press).

Skogan, W. (1990) *Disorder and Decline: Crime and the Spiral of Decay in American Neighbourhoods* (New York: Free Press).

Skogan, W. (1995) 'Crime and the Racial Fears of White Americans', *The Annals*, **539**: 59–72.

Smart, B. (1983) 'On Discipline and Social Regulation: A Review of Foucault's Geneological Analysis', in D. Garland and P. Young (eds), *The Power to Punish* (London: Heinemann).

Smart, C. (1979) 'The New Female Criminal: Reality or Myth?', *British Journal of Criminology*, **19** (1): 50–9.

Smart, C. (1992) 'Feminist Approaches to Criminology or Postmodern Women Meets Atavistic Man', in L. Gelsthorpe and A. Morris (eds), *Feminist Perspectives in Criminology* (Buckingham: Open University Press).

Smith, D. (1983) *Police and People in London* (London: Policy Studies Institute).

Smith, D. (1997a) 'Ethnic Origins, Crime and Criminal Justice', in M. Maguire, R. Morgan and R. Reiner (eds), *The Oxford Handbook of Criminology*, 2nd edn (Oxford University Press).

Smith, D. (1997b) 'Ethnic Origins, Crime and Criminal Justice in England and Wales', in M. Tonry (ed.), *Ethnicity, Crime and Immigration* (University of Chicago Press).

Soja, E. (1989) *Postmodern Geographies: The Reassertion of Space in Critical Social Theory* (London: Verso).

Solomos, J. and L. Back (1996) *Racism and Society* (London: Macmillan).

Sparks, R. (1981) 'Multiple Victimisation: Evidence Theory and Future Research', *Journal of Criminal Law and Criminology*, **72** (2): 762–78.

Sparks, R. (1994) 'Can Prisons be Legitimate? Penal Politics, Brutalisation and the Timeliness of an Old Idea', in R. King and M. Maguire (eds), *Prisons in Context* (Oxford: Clarendon Press).

Sparks, R. (1996) 'Penal Austerity: The Doctrine of Less Eligibility Reform', in R. Matthews and P. Francis (eds), *Prisons 2000* (London: Macmillan).

Sparks, R. and A. Bottoms (1995) 'Legitimacy and Order in Prisons', *British Journal of Sociology*, **46** (1): 45–62.

Sparks, R., A. Bottoms and W. Hay (1996) *Prisons and the Problem of Order* (Oxford: Clarendon Press).

Spierenburg, P. (1984) *The Spectacle of Suffering: Executions and the Evolution of Repression* (Cambridge University Press).

Spinellis, C., K. Angelopoulou and N. Koulouris (1996) 'Foreign Detainees in Greek Prisons: A New Challenge to the Guardians of Human Rights', in R. Matthews and P. Francis (eds), *Prisons 2000* (London: Macmillan).

Steenhuis, D., L. Tigges and J. Essers (1983) 'Penal Climate in the Netherlands', *British Journal of Criminology*, **23** (1): 1–16.

Stevens, P. and C. Willis (1979) *Race, Crime and Arrests*, Home Office Research Study no. 58 (London: HMSO).

Sumner, M. and H. Parker (1995) *Low in Alcohol: A Review of International Research into Alcohol's Role in Crime Causation* (London: Portman Group).

Swaaningen, R. and de Jonge, G. (1995) 'The Dutch Prison System and Penal Policy in the 1990s: From Humanitarian Paternalism to Penal Business Management' in V. Ruggiero *et al.* (eds), *Western European Penal Systems* (London: Sage)

Swyngedouw, E. (1992) 'The Mammon Quest: Globalisation, Interspatial Competition and the Monetary Order', in M. Dunford and G. Kafkalas (eds), *Cities and Regions in the New Europe: The Global–Local Interplay and Spatial Development Strategies* (London: Belhaven).

Sykes, G. (1958) *The Society of Captives* (Princeton, NJ: Princeton University Press).

Sykes, G. and D. Matza (1957) 'Techniques of Neutralisation: A Theory of Delinquency', *American Sociological Review*, **22** (December): 664–70.

Tarling, R. (1993) *Analysing Offending: Data Models and Interpretations* (London: HMSO).

Tchaikovsky, C. (1991) 'Mixed Prisons: Misogynistic and Misguided', *Prison Report* (London: Prison Reform Trust), **16** (Autumn): 12–13.

Thomas, C. (1977) 'Theoretical Perspectives on Prisonisation: A Comparison of the Importation Model and Deprivation Models', *Journal of Criminal Law and Criminology*, **68** (1): 135–45.

Thompson, E. P. (1967) 'Time and Work Discipline in Industrial Capitalism', *Past and Present*, **36**: 57–79.

Thompson, E. P. (1975) *Whigs and Hunters: The Origin of the Black Act* (London: Allen Lane).

Thornberry, T. and R. Christianson (1984) 'Unemployment and Criminal Involvement', *American Sociology Review*, **49**: 398–411.

Thorpe, D. Smith, D. Green, C. and Poley, J. (1980) *Out of Care* (London: George Allen & Unwin).

Tomasevski, K. (1994) *Foreigners in Prison* (Helsinki: European Institute for Crime Prevention and Control).

Tonry, M. (1995) *Malign Neglect: Race Crime and Punishment in America* (New York: Oxford University Press).

Tonry, M. (1997) 'Ethnicity Crime and Immigration Comparative and Cross National Perspectives', *Crime and Justice*, **21** (Chicago: University of Chicago Press).

Trickett, A., D. Ellingworth, T. Hope and K. Pease (1995) 'Crime Victimisation in the Eighties: Changes in Area and Regional Inequality', *British Journal of Criminology*, **35** (3): 343–59.

Trickett, A., D. Osborn, J. Seymour and K. Pease (1992) 'What is Different About High Crime Areas?', *British Journal of Criminology*, **32** (1): 81–9.

Tumim, S. (1996) 'The State of the Prisons', in R. Matthews and P. Francis (eds), *Prisons 2000* (London: Macmillan).

Vass, A. (1990) *Alternatives to Prison: Punishment Custody and the Community* (London: Sage).

van Swaaningen, R. and G. de Jonge (1995) 'The Dutch Prison System and Penal Policy in the 1990s', in V. Ruggiero, M. Ryan and J. Sim (eds), *Western European Penal Systems* (London: Sage).

von Hirsch, A. (1992) 'Proportionality in the Philosophy of Punishment', in M. Tonry (ed.), *Crime and Justice: A Review of Research*, **16** (Chicago: University of Chicago Press).

von Hirsch, A. (1993) *Censure and Sanctions* (Oxford: Clarendon Press).

von Hirsch, A. and J. Roberts (1997) 'Racial Disparity in Sentencing: Reflections on the Hood Study', *The Howard Journal*, **36** (3): 227–36.

Wacquant, L. and W. Wilson (1993) 'The Cost of Racial and Class Exclusion in the Inner City', in W. Wilson (ed.), *The Ghetto Underclass* (London: Sage).

Walker, J., P. Collier and R. Tarling (1990) 'Why are Prison Rates in England and Wales Higher than Australia?', *British Journal of Criminology*, **30** (1): 24–36.

Walker, M. (1995) *Interpreting Crime Statistics* (Oxford: Oxford Science Publications).

Walker, N. (1981) 'Feminist Extravaganzas', *Criminal Law Review*, 378–86.

Walker, N. and M. Hough (1988) *Public Attitudes to Sentencing: Surveys from Five Countries* (Aldershot: Gower).

Walklate, S. (1995) *Gender and Crime: An Introduction* (London: Prentice Hall/Harvester-Wheatsheaf).

Wallace, D. (1980) 'The Political Economy of Incarceration in Late US Capitalism 1971–77', *Insurgent Sociologist*, **9**: 59–65.

Ward, D. and G. Kassebaum (1965) *Women's Prison: Sex and Social Structure* (London: Weidenfeld & Nicolson).

Waters, R. (1990) *Ethnic Minorities and the Criminal Justice System* (Aldershot: Avebury).

Webb, S. and B. Webb (1963) *English Prisons Under Local Government* (London: Frank Cass & Co.).

Weber, M. (1948) *From Max Weber: Essays in Sociology*, ed. H. Gerth and C. W. Mills (London: Routledge & Kegan Paul).

Webster, C. (1996) 'Local Heroes: Violent Racism, Localism and Spacism Among Asian and White Young People', *Youth and Policy*, **53**: 15–27.

Weiss, R. (1986) 'The Reappearance of the Ideal Factory: The Entrepreneur and Social Control in the Contemporary Prison', in J. Lowman *et al.* (eds), *Transcarceration: Essays in the Sociology of Social Control* (Aldershot: Gower).

Weiss, R. (1987) 'Humanitarianism, Labour, Exploitation and Control: A Critical Survey of Theory and Research on the Origin and Development of the Prison', *Social History*, **12** (3): 331–50.

White, P. (1995) 'Homicides', in M. Walker (ed.), *Interpreting Crime Statistics* (Oxford: Oxford Science Publications).

Whatmore, P. (1987) 'Barlinnie Special Unit: An Insider's View', in A. Bottoms and R. Light (eds), *Problems of Long Term Imprisonment* (Aldershot: Gower).

Williams, R. (1980) *Problems in Materialism and Culture* (London: Verso).

Wilson, J. and G. Kelling (1982) 'Broken Windows: The Police and Neighbourhood Safety', *Atlantic Monthly*, 29–38.

Wilson, W. J. (1987) *The Truly Disadvantaged* (Chicago: University of Chicago Press).

Wilson, W. J. (1996) *When Work Disappears: The World of the New Urban Poor* (New York: Knopf).

Windlesham, Lord (1993) *Responses to Crime: Penal Policy in the Making* (Oxford: Clarendon Press).

Woolf, Lord Justice (1991) *Prison Disturbances April 1990* (London: HMSO).

Worrall, A. (1990) *Offending Women: Female Law Breakers and the Criminal Justice System* (London: Routledge).

Worrall, A. (1997) *Punishment in the Community: The Future of Criminal Justice* (Harlow: Longman).

Worrall, A. and K. Pease (1986) 'The Prison Population in 1995', *British Journal of Criminology*, **26** (2): 184–8.

Wright, K. (1989) 'Race and Economic Marginality in Explaining Prison Adjustment', *Journal of Research in Crime and Delinquency*, **26**: 67–89.

Wrong, D. (1994) *The Problem of Order* (Harvard University Press).

Young, I. (1990) 'The Ideal Community and the Politics of Difference', in L. Nicholson (ed.), *Feminism/Postmodernism* (New York: Routledge).

Young, I. (1997) *Intersecting Voices: Dilemmas of Gender, Political Philosophy and Policy* (New Jersey: Princeton University Press).

Young, J. (1970) 'The Zookeepers of Deviancy', *Catalyst* **5**: 38–46.

Young, J. (1992) 'Ten Points of Realism', in J. Young and R. Matthews (eds), *Rethinking Criminology: The Realist Debate* (London: Sage)

Young, J. (1998a) 'Writing on the Cusp of Change: A New Criminology for an Age of Late Modernity', in P. Walton and J. Young (eds), *The New Criminology Revisited* (London: Macmillan).

Young, J. (1998b) 'From Inclusive to Exclusive Society: Nightmares of the European Dream', in V. Ruggiero, N. South and I. Taylor (eds), *The New European Criminology: Crime and Social Order in Europe* (London: Routledge).

Young, P. (1989) 'Punishment, Money and a Sense of Justice', in P. Carlen and D. Cook (eds), *Paying For Crime* (Milton Keyness: Open University Press).

Young, P. (1992) 'The Importance of Utopias in Criminology Thinking', *British Journal of Criminology*, **32** (4): 423–37.

Young, W. and M. Brown (1993) 'Cross National Comparisons of Imprisonment', in M. Tonry (ed.), *Crime and Justice: A Review of Research*, **7** (Chicago: University of Chicago Press).

Zatz, M. (1984) 'Race Ethnicity and Determinate Sentencing', *Criminology*, **22** (2): 147–71.

Zedner, L. (1991) *Women, Crime and Custody in Victorian England* (Oxford: Clarendon Press).

Zedner, L. (1995) 'Wayward Sisters: The Prison for Women', in N. Morris and D. Rothman (eds), *The Oxford History of the Prison* (New York: Oxford University Press).

Zimring, T. and G. Hawkins (1991) *The Scale of Imprisonment* (Chicago: University of Chicago Press).

Index